VERTICAL MAN

VERTICAL MAN

The human being in the Catholic novels of Graham Greene, Sigrid Undset, and Georges Bernanos

by
J. C. Whitehouse

The Saint Austin Press
1999

THE SAINT AUSTIN PRESS
296 Brockley Road
London   SE4 2RA
Tel   +44 (0) 181 692 6009
Fax +44 (0) 181 469 3609

Email: books@saintaustin.org
http://www.saintaustin.org

A catalogue record for this book is available from the British
Library.

ISBN 1 901157 01 6

Designed and printed by NEWTON Design & Print

For Nan, with thanks and love

CONTENTS

FOREWORD

This book is written both for those who wish to see a religious humanism worthy of the name and those for whom the expression is self-contradictory. I think I understand enough of Wittgenstein to appreciate his observation in his *Philosophical Remarks* that he would have liked to dedicate it to the glory of God, but that to do so nowadays would be chicanery, since the action would not be rightly understood. I simply ask the reader to treat what I have written as an honest attempt to understand some aspects of our experience of ourselves and others.

PREFACE

As a religious and philosophical system, Catholicism has traditionally proposed both belief in God and a specific view of human nature. A number of Catholic theologians and philosophers, writing in the decades up to and including that of the Second Vatican Council, expressed a degree of discontent with such ways of reflecting on human beings and formulating ideas about them and urged the need for a more dynamic and existential concept of man. Recently, the emphasis in Catholic thinking has shifted even more radically. The old view of a creature in an individual relationship with his creator ('vertical man') has largely given way to a representation of the human being as a nexus of social relationships ('horizontal man').

Although easy to exaggerate and parody, this tendency is real and striking. It is the chief characteristic of what can be seen and described as a change of emphasis within a Church seeming to tone down its traditional eschatological mission and become increasingly another socially benevolent institution, and of a move from a Catholic to a post-Catholic (or at best a neo-Catholic) literature. Like all institutions and literatures, both are and have always been deeply influenced by the societies in which they are embedded and the ideologies which surround them. They are not, or not yet, totally identifiable with them, however. In both cases, there has been a two-way stimulus and irritation. Even in the most completely pluralist, relativist and pragmatic society, human beings, religion and literature are still what they are, and we shall always return to the fundamental data of our situation. That means that we shall never be quite without a more or less conscious perception of ourselves as creatures hungry for truth, meaning, happiness and - whatever we take the word to mean - salvation.

The objective possibility of achieving salvation through religious faith and a right understanding of our nature and destiny is not the issue here. My aim is simpler and less controversial. It is merely to suggest, through a reflection on the ways of seeing and depicting human beings in the work of three major twentieth-century Catholic novelists, that the danger of religious, philosophical, imaginative and existential impoverishment is real but not inescapable. There are other and deeper ways of seeing ourselves and the central choices of our lives and, since there is nothing new but only what has been momentarily forgotten, they will surface again sometime and somewhere. One day, new Catholic writers will appear. Until then, we should be thankful for those we have.

ACKNOWLEDGMENTS

I wish to express my gratitude to all those whose writings have made me think, and in particular to those mentioned in this book. My debt to Jill Wheeldon, Sally Newbery and Anne Croasdell for their intelligence, patience and good humour in what must have seemed the interminable and thankless task of preparing my manuscript is enormous.

The following persons and organisations gave me permission to quote from the work of the writers to whom this study is chiefly devoted: for Graham Greene, Viking Penguin Inc. (Penguin USA); for Sigrid Undset, the Estate of Sigrid Undset and Mrs Christianne Undset Svarstad, to whom I am particularly grateful; for Georges Bernanos, Henry Holt and Company, The Bodley Head, Editions Plon and Editions Gallimard. In the case of quotations from critical works on these authors and from all other related writings, whether in book or periodical form, I acknowledge the permission of the publishers or editors cited in the appropriate references.

Finally, I thank the editors of the following publications for allowing me to incorporate in an amended form material of my own which originally appeared in them: *Journal of European Studies* (xvi (1986) 1-27); *Modern Language Review* (73 (1978) 241-249 and 80 (1985) 571-585); *Renascence* (38, 1 (1985) 2-12); *Research in English and American Literature* (2 (1984) 387443); *Romance Studies* (10 (1987) 95-106); *Historical and Cultural Contents of Linguistic and Literary Phenomena* (XVII FILLM (1989) 290-299).

It is with literature as with religion. It shows another world, but one to which we feel the tie.

Herman Melville, *The Confidence Man*

Chapter 1

CHANGING CATHOLIC WAYS OF SEEING HUMAN BEINGS

But the Church also looks forward beyond the humane society and 'beyond' politics. This 'beyond' should not be understood, however, in any sense which implies a gap, or a separation between two realities. The Church does not give its attention to humane values in passing, as it were, and then turn its back on these, focussing attention on something else. The Church's concern, which goes beyond them, also includes them. One might best describe it by saying that it takes up the vital human concern and projects it beyond itself, thus giving to human society - the whole world, if you like a further 'dimension', the eschatological dimension.
Giles Hibbert, Man, *Culture and Christianity*.

LETTING MAN BE

There is a developed and well documented (although often, and sometimes wilfully, misunderstood) tradition of Catholic thought about human nature. For theologians, attempting to understand the nature of human beings has been almost as basic a concern as reflecting on the mysteries of the Godhead. From St Augustine onwards, they have treated the problem at length and in depth and a consistent doctrine of human nature has been apparent. It is no accident that the entry on Man in the *New Catholic Encyclopaedia* is one of the longest and most complex in that extremely orthodox work.

Nevertheless, Catholic thinking on this question has at very least undergone a change of emphasis over the last fifty years, and

1

the ordinary Catholic today sees himself differently from the way in which his father or grandfather saw themselves. There have been changes which may be seen either as radical transformations or as minor adjustments, but which are certainly real and striking. They were prefigured in the writings of certain European Catholic philosophers and theologians in the decades preceding and encompassing the Second Vatican Council (1962-1965), and in the work of important and serious clerical commentators on Catholic (and other) literature like Charles Moëller and Hans Urs von Balthasar there is some evidence of a direct connection with images present in the Catholic imaginative literature of the time. The aim of this essay is to present these philosophical ideas and their literary equivalents.

A striking feature of European culture in much of the twentieth century has been the existence of a large body of Catholic fiction, often of a high quality and attracting a wide readership. In common with all literature, it is an imaginative study of human situations. Like much of the best writing, it has a great deal to say, explicitly or implicitly, about the nature of 'man, the heart of man and human life', and possibly says it more strikingly and immediately than writing of a more abstract or more purely intellectual kind. Traditionally, however, Catholic views of man have been largely non-literary, at least in their official formulations, and have taken the form of propositions rather than pictures. Since there has been evidence in the work of recent Catholic thinkers that such formulations are seen as restricting and inhibiting, that there is a desire for more dynamic and less static ways of thinking about human beings, and that we should now see ourselves horizontally rather than vertically, it seems useful to attempt to draw the two perspectives, the literary and the philosophical, together.

Until the nineteen-sixties, the Church had apparently changed little since the Counter-Reformation. Areas of investigation and methods of enquiry were traditional and almost unchanging, and the whole enterprise was virtually an exclusively clerical undertaking. For several centuries, official Catholic thought on human nature had been deeply influenced by the work of St Thomas Aquinas and his successors, and a received and perpetuated body of analytical and abstractly-formulated reflection had become dominant at the expense of other and perhaps equally valid ways of thinking about human beings. A need for less restrictive and more open-ended ways of considering such matters was felt, including a desire both to examine the implications of non-Catholic thought and to concentrate on existential experience, although this was not to reach its peak or find its full, open and even official expressions until the upheavals of the nineteen-sixties.

Thomism, the core of Catholic ontological thinking, was until very recently the inspiration of the teaching in seminaries, colleges and universities run under ecclesiastical auspices. This meant that directly or indirectly it influenced the patterns of thought of most educated Catholics who took their faith seriously and devoted some intellectual energy to exploring its implications. It proposed the rational soul, which included the sensitive and vegetative principles, as the form of the body, constituting with it the unity of human nature. The soul was thus our life principle. Human beings were seen as independent persons or selves and not merely as attributes or adjectives. Man was seen as the image of God, standing in a special relationship to Him and the rest of creation, vitiated by the Fall, the result of his own misuse of his freedom and will, redeemed by Christ and given the opportunity to become whole and holy again through the sacraments and the Holy Spirit as vehicles of divine grace. Capable of great good and great evil, a creature of enormous potentialities subject to the attractions of both sanctity and evil, he was fundamentally a unity of body and soul, a unity which would finally and eternally be achieved at the resurrection of the body. As a moral creature able to distinguish between right and wrong, both rationally and spiritually, he was, within the limits set by his fallen nature as a result of sin, free and autonomous.

Within the Catholic tradition, *psychology* as such remained very largely a branch of philosophy, and was most frequently investigated and expressed in impersonal and general terms. There has, however, been a strand of that tradition which has sought to put forward psychological insights in other ways and notably in the language of introspection. For some centuries, that element remained parallel and rather subordinate to more formal and more apparently objective enquiry and speculation and, as part of the official body of received and transmitted wisdom, has only surfaced intermittently. It has, however, always shown a certain tenacious presence. St. Augustine's *Confessions*, propounding the view that our knowledge of the nature of the soul can only be based on the immediate data of self-consciousness, and that our awareness of our own being, willing and thinking is dark and imperfectly perceived, is an early example of such an approach, and even in the feudal Europe of the late eleventh and twelfth centuries there were strong signs of that specifically Western (and arguably Catholic in origin) phenomenon, the attempt to express perceptions of the human being not simply as a social, economic or military unit, but as an *individual*. It has been convincingly shown by Colin Morris in his *The Discovery of the Individual 1050-1200* (Morris, 1972) that this period increasingly both perceived and gave open recognition to the importance of the individual person. The idea of *incommunicabilitas*, of being specifically an individual self, became a major concept, and Augustine's notion of man as an 'abyss', an unknowable mystery, survived in the later atmosphere of scholastic rationalism. The writings of Richard of St Victor, of St John of the Cross, of St Teresa of Avila and, more recently, of St Thérèse of Lisieux can, in their various ways, be seen as examples of the same kind of introspective and experientially-determined genre.

The partial dethronement of Thomism in the last few decades is probably to some extent attributable to a desire for a return to and a recognition of the validity of such alternative ways of experiencing and reflecting on human nature. Indeed, there have been several attempts to explore modern non-Catholic psychology and Catholic thought on man as complementary rather than contrasting conceptual systems. The Dominican, Victor White, in his aptly-named book *Soul and Psyche* (White, 1960) maintains that such a view is justified for many reasons. Citing, for example, his own personal and pastoral experience and the Biblical connotations, observable especially in the Psalms, of the soul as the centre of all manner of emotions, he explores the implications of this in the work of Aquinas, of many modern theologians, psychologists and psychiatrists, and of novelists such as D.H. Lawrence. Stressing Aquinas's dynamic concept of human nature, he highlights the fact that for St Thomas the soul was the very principle of life and the source of everything in the individual which was alive. Such ideas, White maintains, are echoed in Lawrence's novels and essays. The sad fact is, he suggests, that both Catholic theologians and Catholic psychologists have made untenable and impoverishing distinctions between their respective provinces.

Given insights of this kind, a meaningful similarity between Jung's thought and the ideas expressed by White can be perceived. The reader can see that the latter could, in a sense, 'catholicise' Jung, whose interest in medieval thought, mystic visions, the processes of individuation and the whole question of the fundamental nature of man made him a natural choice of subject of enquiry for White. Jung's refusal of Freud's reduction of the human unconscious to a schematic sexuality and his view of the vital importance of a proper self-knowledge are clear indications of a remarkable identity of interest. Arguing his case for an acceptance of the synonymity of soul and psyche as a fact of orthodox Catholic doctrine, White illustrates what he sees as some quite serious and fundamental misconceptions of that doctrine, using the catechism of his day to provide examples. To illustrate the construction of unmeaningful boundaries, he mentions the Catholic psychiatrist E.B. Strauss, the author *of Reason and Unreason in Psychological Medicine* (Strauss, 1953), but might have referred, equally appropriately, to another Catholic, the neo-Adlerian Rudolf Allers, in whose *The Psychology of Character* (Allers, 1929) such distinctions as those which White criticises are at least implicit. Again and again White stresses both the notion of the wide range of meanings of the word 'soul' and the plain fact of their synonymity or near-synonymity with all those words used to describe the interiorness of man. Expressed in its simplest terms, his argument is basically that, as human and secular insights into our nature grow, so must the corresponding Catholic theological concepts. This in itself is neither a very new nor a very strange idea, although a theologian choosing the technique of exploring Godless psychology as a means of expanding an awareness of personhood is a fairly unusual phenomenon.

VERTICAL MAN

As well as depth psychology, the twentieth-century stream of existential, subjectivist and evolutionist philosophies has added to the Catholic tradition of thought in this area, and the historical emphasis on the analytical and objective approach has, in the case of certain Catholic thinkers, been limited in favour of an exploration of experience and intuition. Many such writers have seemed preoccupied with existence and direct apprehension rather than with the rational approach in the old formal sense. To a large extent, many of them have both kept something of their inherited Catholic idea of man and added a new note to it. Thus Teilhard de Chardin can, following tradition, see human beings both as self-contained, reasoning creatures capable of forming a concept of themselves and at the same time as part of a *hierarchy*, albeit an evolutionary one, of something resembling the Great Chain of Being of the medieval tradition. Evolution has produced in man a creature with a new nature, a new and unique phenomenon different in kind from the creatures which surround him. The growth of consciousness and self-consciousless implies, for Teilhard de Chardin, not only a change in degree but a change in kind, arising from a change in state.

Here, there is an aspect rarely stressed in the theological tradition except in the moral sense, that of *becoming*, and of self-creation. In the way in which Teilhard de Chardin presents it, this notion can be seen as a neglected or half-forgotten one in Catholic thought. The new element which it introduces into the Catholic tradition arises, and this is very important, from the fact that throughout that tradition man has been seen as having a fixed nature, however difficult of definition it might be, which was capable of extension and perfection, whereas Teilhard de Chardin implies that to some extent man *creates* that primary nature itself and can enlarge, develop and enrich it. He is saying, it seems, that rather than the possession of a fixed and constant humanity our characteristic and uniquely human feature is an ability to grow and to become more human.

This trend became disturbingly and powerfully evident in Catholic thought. Charles Davis, the English theologian who left the Church in the nineteen-sixties writes, in a key chapter ('The Change in Man's Self-Understanding') of his book *A Question of*

6

Conscience (Davis, 1967) of a changing idea of human nature which was to influence deeply his thought and his future life. He speaks of a shift from a view of a fixed human nature to one in which a person becomes himself in freedom. For him, the question is not whether the concept of the existence of a human nature is valid, but whether man should see himself either as a static reality, already complete, with limits definitely established, with human nature always the same and change occurring only as an incidental (and minor) modification arising from the need to meet incidental (and minor) differences in specific local and temporal human situations, or as someone who can grow into personhood. *Becoming* is seen as the mode of being proper to man as a conscious, intelligent, free subject. Intelligence grows; freedom can only be attained through a slow maturation, but as it comes the human being slowly realises that he must take charge of his own becoming and decide what sort of a person he wants to be.

Other Catholic theologians have felt the need to re-establish the existential freedom and mystery of the human person. A Dominican, Giles Hibbert, a member of the Order which produced St Thomas Aquinas and has been the repository of Thomist philosophy, writes in his *.Man, Culture and Christianity* (Hibbert, 1967) of the need to think again about human nature and to 'let man be'. In his book, there is evidently a movement towards an enlarged view of the person, deeply influenced in some cases by a reading of modern imaginative literature and a more direct contemplation of lived historical and existential experience. There is a sense of the need for seeing the truth without the intervention of a system of thought, although the system may come later. For such writers, the recognition of a human being as a *mystery* implies the recognition of him as a *person*. This recognition is fundamentally a perception involving mutual communion and, Hibbert implies, this is almost all one can say about the concept of the person. The difficulty, he says, is to reconcile the person seen analytically, as the scholastics saw him, and the person seen in his living, mysterious reality, and he goes on to suggest that the adoption of the analytical views as dogma has led to an impoverished concept of the person in Catholic thought and understanding. But the application of Aristotelian thought, he maintains, has on the other hand brought great advantages. It prevents an excess of idealistic speculation and, if taken as a *point of departure*, using imagination and psychological insight, it opens the way to a true appreciation of human nature. This true appreciation is not reducible to a *concept*, but must be seen as an understanding of our own relationship with him as another person.

What we should perhaps see in such ideas is a more imaginative and subjective interpretation of the scholastic schema than had been usual, illuminated by reflection on the complexities of man seen in a philosophical and everyday world coloured by existential thought. In Hibbert's case, all these are seen through literature, that study which, according to Iris Murdoch, is our best school, for it is 'an education in how to picture and understand human situations' (Murdoch, 1970, 65). They are very perceptively illustrated in his comments on the Birkin/Ursula relationship in *Women in Love*.

Further examples of a growing concern with self-consciousness and freedom as dominant aspects of the human person can be seen in several other major Catholic thinkers of recent years. In particular the theme of self-creation and of the 'winning' of personhood or selfhood, as summarised by Davis, has been a recurring one. Gabriel Marcel, for example, sees the human being in modern life as often reduced to an economic and social function and stresses the obvious oversimplification of such a reductionist view. As an antidote, he emphasises the mystery of being. His concern has been to show, in his philosophical writings and in his plays, his own concept of man as an entity defining himself in a community of selves, gowing and becoming more richly and deeply himself in this situation of intersubjective awareness. For Marcel, man creates himself by shedding *having* (to which wishes, fears, desires belong) and by collaborating with other selves, helping them to achieve their own freedom without using them as a means to his own ends. This stress on growth, becoming and self-creation has with some justification caused him to be labelled a Christian existentialist. However, it is important to remember that his philosophy is, in at least one sense, opposed to that of atheistic existentialism, in that his freedom is not ultimately pointless and doomed to absurdity, for it is that of aspiring to a higher order of being, a purer mode of living. Man lives in relation to a transcendent order, is a meaningful rather than a pointless passion, and moves from a primary to a higher condition in terms of that order. Jacques Maritain too has stressed the autonomy of the person and pointed out the dangers of reducing man to a function, as is the case with all societies which do not recognise personhood as the true state of human beings, whether these societies be bourgeois, communist or totalitarian. In this respect, Maritain has much in common with Marcel and Mounier and the existentialists, given his view of human freedom as creative and involving an orientation towards other persons. Much of Mounier's work is a plea for the importance of the person, whom he sees as a spiritual being constituted by a manner of subsistence and independence of being, maintaining those qualities by his free adherence to a freely-accepted hierarchy of values which he assimilates and lives out in responsible commitment, acting and unifying himself in freedom and developing his unique personhood by creative action. For him, there is a similar mystery at the heart of human life, and a stress on the ineffable quality of personhood, which is more than any attempt at definition can suggest or any static intellectual concept exhaust.

The consensus was perhaps that there is a human nature but that traditional concepts, with their varying degrees of inaccuracy, abstraction and impersonal generalisation, have in some sense and to some degree erected barriers between human beings and the direct and intimate perception of other persons. In such a situation, the best course was, it seems, to accept the mystery, in all its banality and profundity. One can properly speak of evolution rather than revolution here, since this kind of reflection has not only been apparent amongst the more radically minded theologians and philosophers. The same orientation is also clear, although in a more 'spiritual' and less 'secular' presentation, in the works of such extremely orthodox writers as Gerald Vann, the author of *The Heart of Man* (Vann, 1946) and *Moral Dilemmas* (Vann, 1945) amongst other books. Like Mounier, he stresses the mystery at the heart of man, suggesting that traditional formulations of a view of the human being must be considered both in their own light and in that of lived experience, and maintains that one cannot *know* a man by *knowing about* human nature. He also suggests that although that nature has limits it is not static. There is a difference of emphasis, however, in that he pays rather more attention to the traditional moral aspect of the question, echoing Mounier and Maritain in his view of individualism and egocentricity as potentially disruptive factors, since they are likely to empty rather than fulfil the personality. A clear distinction is made between the *individual* and the *person*, using the former word to symbolise the destructive aspects of selfhood (i.e. selfishness) and the latter to epitomise its constructive and unifying ones, which can only be fostered by a recognition of other selves, a rootedness in the human community and a dependence on God.

We have thus some evidence of a fairly sustained and interesting debate on human nature on the part of a wide range of reflective and speculative Catholic writers and of a variety of responses to the confrontation of experience of life and the analytical formulation of concepts of human nature. From what we have seen so far, two potentially useful points emerge. The first is that it would be easy and dangerous to take a simplistic view of both what the Catholic concept of man might be and of the shift of emphasis in that concept. The second is that the concept was not quite as static and definitive as one might assume. It was not - or not simply - a case of *Rome locuta, causa finita* (Rome having spoken and the matter being closed). It is possible to detect both a tradition and a parallel, if rather unofficial, dialectical relationship to it. Certain intelligent Catholics of this period seemed to feel that the ways in which Man was often defined and depicted within their system of thought were unsatisfactory because they were at best incomplete and at worst potentially misleading, and that other ways of reflecting on human nature were necessary.

One such way, urged a century earlier by Newman (Newman, 1960) and implicitly proposed in the work of Hibbert and Mounier, was the study of imaginative literature. The remedy to an aridly academic approach suggested by many of them - the immersion in specific human situations and predicaments - is the very matter of that particular undertaking. Indeed, at the time when they were writing, there was already an existing body of Catholic literature which might have been expected to provide an accessible and acceptable starting-point for this kind of reflection. The end of the nineteenth century had seen the Catholic revival in French literature, and the first five or six decades of the twentieth produced a parallel phenomenon in most Western European countries. Writers of the international status of Mauriac, Bernanos, Undset, Chesterton, Belloc, Greene, Waugh and their contemporaries elsewhere either enjoyed established reputations or were actively acquiring them. It is in their work that we can see the fullest and richest expression of the view of human beings their more specifically philosophical counterparts were trying to suggest. Unfortunately, there is a further complicating factor. The developments culminating in the Second Vatican Countil, which stressed openness to the outside world, brought a radically new emphasis to Catholic ways of picturing human beings. The innovation was a heightened perception of the importance of the social dimension in human life and an often rather curt dismissal of the primacy of the movement of the individual towards or away from God. Martha sometimes seemed to have ousted Mary.

FROM ESCHATOLOGY TO SOCIOLOGY?

Around forty years ago, Evelyn Waugh could write as follows in his review of Graham Greene's then recently published *The Heart of the Matter* (1948):

> In the last twenty-five years, the artist's interest has moved from sociology to eschatology. Out of hearing, out of sight, politicians and journalists and popular preachers exhort him to sing the splendours of high wages and sanitation. His eyes are on the Four Last Things, and so mountainous are the disappointments of recent history that there are already signs of a popular breakaway to join him, of a stampede to the heights (Waugh, 1977, 161).

In making such assertions, he put his finger on a distinguishing feature of the Catholic novel of his time: a concern with the deep nature of human beings seen in the light of their relationship with the postulated or real entity called God. Albert Sonnenfeld probably had something like this in mind when he offered his own brief definition of the Catholic novel:

> There is something called the Catholic Novel: it is a novel written by a Catholic, using Catholicism as his informing mythopoeic structure or generative symbolic system, and where the principal and decisive issue is the salvation or damnation of the hero or heroine (Sonnenfeld, 1992, vii).

With a few reservations (and many Catholic would reject the final clause) we could accept that sentence as a fertile and illuminating statement about the Catholic literature of a generation or so ago. It is less relevant to any of the later literature written by Catholics. There is a gap between the religious consciousness of writers like Waugh himself, or Bernanos, Greene or Undset and that of many present-day Catholics. To put matters simply, but perhaps not too crudely, many younger Catholics now see their religion less as a system of preparing the individual for the Four Last Things that Waugh talks about (namely Death, Judgement, Heaven and Hell) and more as a philosophy of socially benevolent collective action. 'Sin', 'holiness', 'salvation' and 'damnation' are no longer frequent lexical items or dominant concepts. What we might tentatively call the classical Catholic novel flourished in an era in which both the institutional Church and individual Catholics were distinct from the society surrounding them. Clearly formulated dogmas requiring full and unconditional assent, teaching on matters of morality that required obedience under pain of sin, a liturgy and an international administration conducted in Latin, practices of piety familiar throughout the Catholic world and strange elsewhere, all helped to make the Church a separate, ubiquitous and clearly recognisable institution wherever one went. The way that individual Catholics ordered (or failed to order) their lives, the things they saw as right or wrong, their habits of religious practice or the way in which they rejected or temporised with their religion, all were characteristic of a particular kind of religious or spiritual sensibility. From that kind of pre-Vatican II Catholicism, we have moved on to a situation in which there are wide local and individual variations in ecclesiastical patterns, a world-wide use of vernaculars, a new emphasis on the human being as a social unit and a massive increase, if we are to accept the findings of the surveys, in individual judgement and *selective* belief and practice (Hornsby-Smith, 1987). Philip Stratford's brief but lucid and helpful vignettes of Catholic attitudes in the England and France of the earlier days of Greene and Mauriac are no longer fully relevant (Stratford, 1963, 4-7, 20-22). Catholics now see themselves in a different way and live different lives. They are no longer readily distinguishable from their non-Catholic neighbours, their Church is not so very unlike other socially active institutions, and their literature, as Newman said it would, 'resembles the literature of the day' (Newman, 1960, 246). Prophetic voices were never absent. Over half a century ago that arch-Catholic writer, Bernanos, had already provided in his *Le Crépuscule des vieux* his own idiosyncratic picture of the convergent, integrated, tamed and secularised Church of the future (Bernanos, 1956, 88).

There seems to be some measure of agreement that the Catholic novel is now either disappearing or at least is rather well hidden. Albert Sonnenfeld talks about it as 'an apparently dying form' (Sonnenfeld, 1983, vii), and Gene Kellogg says that this 'flowering of major literary achievement... tapered off - perhaps ended - when Roman Catholicism ... "joined the modern world" after the Second Vatican Council' (Kellogg, 1970, I).

Indeed, anyone trying to write on a Catholic literature of the seventies or eighties has a very hard job. There are Catholics who write novels, Catholics who even mention Catholicism in their work, and writers who, as we say nowadays, come from a Catholic background. None of them, it seems to me, has written anything that could be called a Catholic novel in the sense in which *The Power and the Glory* or *Kristin Lavransdatter* or *Brideshead Revisited* are indubitably powerful, and specifically powerfully *Catholic* novels. Works informed by that older Catholic view of man as a creature of enormous individual worth, living in a special and dynamic relationship with his Creator, taught by the Church Christ founded and moving gradually towards salvation or damnation no longer seem quite relevant to the newer, post-Council and conciliatory Catholic world of community and communications.

There are of course many aspects of current Catholic thinking which might offer some explanation of the disappearance of a noticeable Catholic literature in the old sense. The most important is a new view of human beings, and if we look at non-literary Catholic reflections in this area, we may understand better what has happened to the Catholic novel.

A consideration of the essential differences between two ecclesiastically-approved and much-used Catholic doctrinal manuals offers a readily perceivable epitome of the direction taken by 'official' Catholic thinking about human beings. In the first, Charles Hart's *The Student's Catholic Doctrine* (1916, many subsequent reprintings) the subject is dealt with in eschatological terms. Significantly, the first entry under 'Man' is 'The End for which Man was created', and the subject is dealt with from the point of view of the Fall, the Incarnation, the Redemption and the other usual aspects of the older view. The reader is assumed to have a rational and analytical mind. The second, the Dutch *New Catechism* (1967) introduces the same section in terms of social life, describing the elements of our existence (sic) as being (in this order) 1. We live together with others; 2. We live on this earth; 3. We are part of this world; 4. But (are) endowed with a certain freedom and spiritual quality. In short, it ultimately reaches Hart's starting-point. Here, a kind of basic existential consciousness rather than a rational mind is assumed.

The consequences of this change are apparent in an article by a Catholic priest, Peter Verity. If the Church is to survive, he says, the Christian must be a *Weltchrist*, a 'Christian-in-the-world:

> 'Once again, after sixteen centuries, Christians are being forced to look outwards rather than at each other. The alternative for the Church is at best irrelevance and at worst annihilation' (Verity, 1987, 57).

For him, dialogue with the world means not the expounding of dogma (however obliquely performed) but 'A journey together to a place where neither had been before' (Verity, 1987, 56), and he refers to a Church which is 'urged to listen and receive as much as it offers and speaks... dialogue is today pre-eminently the style best suited to modern times' (Verity, 1987, 59). In other words, in a world of social action, the old certainties have gone and some relativism seems inevitable.

What can be fairly clearly seen in developments of this kind is a movement away from a picture of man as an individual in a unique relationship with his Creator through a new appreciation of existential freedom and ultimately to *an image of the human being as a nexus of social relationships.*

The shift in the Catholic understanding of human nature and the human situation that emerged during the late sixties and early seventies was, however, more radical than might have been expected. A debate centred on ways of understanding the individual in himself and in his relations with other individuals, a debate conducted by individual Catholics writing as individuals with no reference to their official status or ministerial functions (where they in fact had any) no doubt influenced some of the collective and authoritative documents and declarations issued by the Second Vatican Council itself. Both the individual debate and the official documents had a common feature. Social action tended to replace the struggle for personal salvation as the criterion of a rightly ordered human life. To return to Waugh's terms, sociology ousted eschatology. That shift of emphasis can be detected over a whole range of symptomatic writings of the nineteen-sixties and seventies. Brian Wicker's *Culture and Theology* (Wicker, 1966), for example, is deeply indebted to the work of philosophers and writers who see human beings as individuals only because they are part of a community and as fulfilling themselves only in terms of a web of social relationships. The Jesuit A.H.J. Kloosterman's selective and simplistic *Contemporary Catholicism* (1972) which relies heavily, amongst other sources, on the documents of Vatican II, and particularly on *The Church in the Modern World* (1965), dismisses the negative, 'individualistic', 'abstract', 'objective' 'verticalization' of the older way of seeing the relationship of man with his Creator (Kloosterman, 1972, 48) and condemns the 'essentialism' of neo-scholasticism, which he dismisses as a 'one-sided view of man (which) neglected the differences that make men unique. It made men robots who were all the same' (Kloosterman, 1972, 49). Fortunately, Kloosterman goes on to say, the insights of existential have opened Catholic eyes, and we now see that the 'verticalism, concerned only with the relation between this individual and his God, must be replaced by a new morality that stresses the importance of socialisation' (Kloosterman,. 1972, 63). What we have here is not simply a case of an individual writer expressing a strongly felt personal opinion at odds with official teaching. His reading of *The Church in the Modern World* provides much of his vocabulary and many of his ideas, and Paul V's encyclical *Populorum Progressio* (1967) is not dissimilar in tone or content. The significance of such writing, individual or official, is not so much that it proposes a 'new' outward-looking morality (for the Church, following Christ, has always enjoined a concern for others) but that it proposes a new perspective in which to see human beings. In the older view, that concern for others (charity) was a necessary element of the means of achieving individual salvation. In the new vision, the motivation behind it seems to be to produce a decent, humane and fraternal world: 'our goal must be a world where liberty is real; a world where Lazarus can sit at Dives' table' (*Populorum Progressio*, 47). Such a world is not, presumably, seen or proposed as an end in itself, but as the means of creating an environment in which man could be himself, fully and harmoniously. As a goal, however, it does seem to represent a considerable shift from 'faith fruitful in good works' to good works hopefully fruitful in faith. The transformation of a vertical to a horizontal orientation indicates a major change in the conceptual understanding of human life and destiny.

The pendulum certainly swung, in some cases seemingly far enough to jam at an extreme point. The same period saw the growth of (to use Terence Eagleton's title as a blanket term) the *New Left Church* (Eagleton, 1966). Its preoccupation with the ideas and world-view of Marxism produced, in those circles in which such concerns were dominant rather than merely evident, a major transformation of the Catholic concept of man.

Human beings were increasingly and indeed almost exclusively discussed in terms of those particular aspects of their existence which its proponents saw as ignored, misunderstood or largely rejected in Catholic thought: namely, those of the social, political and economic dimensions of their lives.

Adrian Cunningham's *Adam* (1968) is of considerable symptomatic interest from this point of view, since it offers at once a radical critique of established Catholic thought concerning human nature and a picture of human beings as deeply social and historical creatures. In this sense, it is a useful guide to currents of thought that, once articulated, directly and indirectly helped to shape and guide the minds of a whole generation of Catholics. Man and the world, Cunningham maintains, are inseparable, because the only way we can know man is as a 'being-in-the-world'. The true interpretation of man as seen in Biblical or Christian terms is not 'that of the isolated individual, but of man seen from within the life of the people of God; it is the point of view of a group-historical existentialism' (Cunningham, 1968, 79) in which 'the individual spirit lives solely by virtue of sociality and the "social spirit" becomes real only in individual embodiment. Thus general sociality leads to personal unity. One cannot speak a *priori* of either personal or social being' (Cunningham, 1968, 43).

Man, says Cunningham, does not equal the individual, although many Catholics have often assumed this to be the case (Cunningham, 1968, 35). For him as for Brian Wicker, the human being does not stand apart from the world in isolated mental consciousness, and we are individuals only because we already share in a community. He is unhappy with traditional formulations stressing 'transendance' (Cunningham, 1968, 70), and proposes a concept of the human person in which the individual can only become important, can only become himself, in his relationships with other individuals and with society. And yet Cunningham realises that Man is not simply the world or society, that as well as a partial synonymity there is an inevitable distance: for him 'the inseparability and the gap are an irreducible presupposition of being human' (Cunningham, 1968, 71).

Catholic thought in this area, he continues, has been too individualistic, too concerned with establishing that man's relationship with God is on a one-to-one basis. Emphasis on the individual is totally unjustified, says Cunningham, and can lead to seeing the world and history as no more than an interruption to the more important business of saving one's own immortal soul:

> In passing we might note that a centring of fallenness on the individual complements our emphasis on 'fallen nature' to produce a profoundly pessimistic and conservative view of social relations... It is then an easy move to see the world as at best a distraction from the

essential task of individual supernatural salvation. (Cunningham, 1968, 26).

Indeed, for Cunningham it is only in terms of the group that man can *be* an individual. He writes of 'the relevant sense of the existentiality of the group within the terms of which the individual is precisely individual' (Cunningham, 1968, 34). The almost unavoidable conclusion of the particular line of thought he follows is that ultimately the correct concept of man as a social being, the correct perception of the world (the 'reality which is always to be overcome') (Cunningham, 1968, 31) must take the form of a total commitment to Marxism and to the quite possible redundancy of remaining a Catholic: 'While believing that a total socialist humanism may finally make membership of the Church redundant, there is here and now a sufficient reason for remaining in it'. (Cunningham, 1968, 194)

If man's deep nature is such that his potentialities are to be fully realised in corporate human life as it is capable of being lived at some future time on earth, then Christianity is bound to become no more than an adjunct to a 'total socialist humanism'. Such a view is of course wildly incompatible with the ancient Christian concept of man more or less out of place in the world, where he has no lasting abode.

To argue that Marxism as a philosophy (as distinct from political systems claiming to be Marxist) may have valid and valuable insights into the human condition to offer to Catholic thought is reasonable. To suggest that Marxist thought may one day replace Catholic thought may be a plausible, although highly debatable, philosophical or historical hypothesis. To see the two systems as more than tangentially connected (even though both may have their roots in the same divine discontent, as Greene's *Monsignor Quixote* suggested) (Greene, 1982, 106-107) is erroneous. As the closing pages of his book indicate, Cunningham is at least half-aware of this, and feels obliged to acknowledge, rather grudgingly, what is lacking in the 'social' view of man:

> What is lacking to Christianity in Marxist terms is the theme of this book; what is lacking to Marxism in Christian terms is most importantly that substantial and subtle concept of personality, of its uniqueness and

inexhaustible richness which flows from the Christian tradition. This criticism has been made so often that the Christian Marxist or socialist has an understandable temptation to dismiss it as the woolly mystifying liberal humanism that it so often is. But in substance we must hold it to be accurate (though obviously this does not mean that one ceases to be a Marxist) (Cunningham, 1968,193).

Oddly enough, the missing dimension he speaks of has been described perceptively and graphically by the agnostic philosopher Patrick Corbett in his short but illuminating analysis of the Catholic position in his comparative study of ideologies:

> However much it may be true that man is made for life in society and cannot exist outside society, it is also true that he is not exclusively, not even primarily, made for social life: he is made by God for God; he is therefore, as an individual, prior to society. That fact alone explains the moral order; and the recognition of it alone endows the moral order with its proper strength. For the moral order simply prescribes the conditions that men must observe in their conduct with each other for each to be to God as God requires. Thus the moral order has no existence except in God, and no strength except though faith in God. As applied to the particular problem of war: there can be no peace between men unless there is peace within each one of them: unless, that is, each one builds up within himself the order God requires. Only in our common position as the children of God can we find and accept that absolute and universal equality on which the moral order rests only so can man find peace. (Corbett, 1965, 35).

My suspicion is that Catholic thought, at least in its more superficial forms, has done what Edward Schillebeeckx pointed out long ago that it might do. In the preface to his *God and Man* (1969) he suggests that 'there is a more and more clearly growing conviction that man's salvation comes about within his daily life in the world', in his relationship with the 'strictly secular', that it is possible to see growing resistance to any "unworldly" faith; for example a Christianity which exists beside and above ordinary, everyday life'. This produces, he maintains, 'a tendency towards a form of Christianity with a "Church" and a threat that it will be replaced by the idea of human solidarity'. Later in the same work he proposes the mystery of God as the centre of man's essence, in which the human being 'becomes himself only in moving outwards from his own centre of life towards God... in a deeper introversion, so as to press on in grace through the most profound depths of his subjectivity to God; more accurately, to experience God's presence within him.' Christian tradition, he tells us, 'has summed up this theological conception of man in the expression *imago Dei*: man is the image of God' (Schillebeeckx, 1969, 210-214). His own 'theological definition of man' posits the human person as primarily orientated towards the divine (i.e. vertically) and in a relationship with God who is a mystery as man is a mystery: 'the whole crux of my definition is precisely the mystery of God. The essence of man can only be defined in correlation with God' (Schillebeeckx, 1969, 215). The idea of that kind of relationship - parallel to but not excluding the necessity of being and working in the world - is what is missing from much recent Catholic thought on man. Coupled with a reflection on certain kinds of Catholic literature, it could have provided the basis for a meaningful Catholic anthropology.

That unwillingness to accept the by now at least commonly welcomed and extolled simplicities of a 'relevant' Catholicism is maintained right down to *New Elucidations* (Schillebeeckx 1986), where the chapter 'Flight into Community' is of particular interest. It has also been apparent in the work of Hans Küng, whose well known *On Being a Christian* (1977) both presents the opening out to the world after the Second Vatican Countil in a far from completely enthusiastic light and insists on the absolute primacy of the orientation of man's life towards God.

All these represent the old 'vertical' view, the perspective that makes Catholic literature of the recent past so difficult of access to today's Catholic and non-Catholic readers. The horizontalism of the recent decades rejected that upward movement in favour of an emphasis on the lateral. My hope as a reader is that somewhere there is or will be a dimension that can incorporate both in a meaningful aesthetic, imaginative and intellectual pattern. Where it may be, I do not know, although from the purely theological and philosophical point the new *Catechism of the Catholic Church* (1994) and the writings of John Paul II certainly seems to offer a basic for it.

The foregoing brief and purely indicative survey of certain changes in the view of Catholic man produced and disseminated over decades by a variety of writers - collective and individual, lay and clerical, all of varying degrees of orthodoxy - suggests that there have been two major modifications. The first was a new stress on the dynamic and experiential dimension of our humanity. The second was a growing conviction that it can only find its true fulfilment in terms of social interrelation. The former, a variant on the older verticalism, comes close to the picture of man provided by traditional twentieth-century Catholic literature. I can only see the latter - a form of horizontalism - as the matter of literature, which is concerned with individuals in specific situations, in a limited sense. The social and political dimension of the novels of Böll and Greene perhaps illustrate this in that they show the desire to create an 'inhabitable land' in which the human being is an end in himself, over whom no social or economic system, no empire, commune or collective has any prescriptive rights, and in which he is not exhaustively described by a potential for correct socialisation. Even there, however, that dimension is an element of a whole, and not the whole itself.

Albert Sonnenfeld talks of the 'ironic prophecy' of the Catholic novelists of the mid-twentieth century. In protesting that they were novelists who also happened to be Catholics, and not Catholic novelists, they were, he says, quite right. In his view, Vatican II 'marked the legitimisation and consecration of a host of modernist longings that were both a reflection and a cause of the "decline and fall" of that possibly perverse and reactionary nostalgia which made the Catholic novel possible' (Sonnenfeld, 1982, viii). Whether or not one agrees with his analysis of individual Catholic novels or his judgements on their authors, he is offering there a fairly accurate description of the overall trend in the later works of the writers he uses to make his point, those of Greene (with the exception of *Monsignor Quixote* (1982)) and Heinrich Böll in particular. This may or may not be part of their general refusal to be seen as mouthpieces for an ideology. They (or at least many of them) rejected the label of 'Catholic writer' in order to remain free (Greene, 1948, 38, 42 and Böll, 1961, 402-403).

I am not suggesting a direct and simple relationship of cause and effect between the newer Catholic ways of thinking about human beings and the disappearance of the Catholic novel. As far as I know, there is no compelling evidence to make us picture contemporary 'Catholics who write', to use Greene's phrase, poring over the writings of a Kloostermann or a Cunningham, or consciously and conscientiously adopting a choice of matter and form of expression suitable for the ideas they contain. What I am suggesting is the obvious fact that literature is not produced in a vacuum, and that the air that Catholic writers and their readers have breathed over the last few decades is very different from that breathed by their counterparts of forty or fifty years ago. Those readers may find the new atmosphere rich and heady or thin and impoverished, but it seems to be all that is currently available. Perhaps one day a newer kind of 'dissident' Catholic will produce a newer vertical novel. For the moment, however, a way of picturing human beings is to some extent in abeyance, and Auden's *Epitaph* takes on a new meaning:

> Let us honour if we can
> The vertical man
> Though we value none
> But the horizontal one.

Chapter 2

THREE WRITERS AND THEIR BACKGROUND

There was once a kind of imaginative writing that provided us with a rich and illuminating image of ourselves. Before it disappears into literary history, we need to reflect on it, and encouraging such reflection is the purpose of this chapter. Catholic literature was an international and multicultural phenomenon, and to write about it inevitably means selections and omission and hence simplification. The reasons for choosing the three writers in question certainly include personal preference, but are also wider and perhaps more objective. Importance has certainly been one of them. By this I mean, in this context, the ability of a given body of work to attract a wide - even a world-wide - readership, to stimulate serious and intelligent critical attention both within and outside specialist or academic circles, and to establish itself indubitably as literature. This the novels of Greene, Undset and Bernanos have clearly done, even on the narrowly externalist view of literature as simply that which we decide to call literature. Their writings can fairly safely be assumed to have had some influence on the ways in which twentieth-century Catholic (and perhaps even non-Catholic) man has seen himself, even if, at the very least, such influence has been ill-defined, sometimes misunderstood and in any case impossible to quantify. All were widely translated. Several of Greene's and Bernanos's novels have been filmed, and both Undset and Bernanos also attracted great attention as writers of non-fictional works, particularly as moralists, political and philosophical essayists and as figures active in the ideological struggles of their time. Greene's popularity as an 'entertainer' and to a lesser extent as a playwright has been considerable. In short, all three were major literary and cultural figures of their age, and their work part of that world literature Goethe envisaged, in which each of the nations would have its voice.

They were also Catholic writers in the strict sense, that is, authors whose faith had personal meaning and value, informed their minds, imagination and work, and made its presence felt. Given differences of culture, domestic and family background, education, way of life and temperament and the fact that two of them were converts and the third a born Catholic, they might be expected to illustrate rather individual views of, and insights into, the question of what man is. To find no major differences might lead some to suppose that a specific ideology replaced personal and individual perceptions, others to assume that such perceptions cohere to give an overall concept or image which naturally coincides with that of speculative moral and pastoral theology. To put it more simply, one may wonder whether they saw man in a certain way because they were or became Catholics, or whether they remained or became Catholics because they saw man in a certain way. Those simple questions are perhaps too simple and the truth of the matter may be that, as men and women of creative imagination and perception, they found that their understanding of man and theology enriched and illuminated each other and that the relationship between the two was coalescent rather than antithetical.

Since they are losing or have lost their status as contemporaries (who are often assumed to have some 'special' and 'immediate' significance for us) and are becoming figures from the past (which need to be 'examined', or 'interpreted'), a study of what they have to say becomes especially important. The images of the human person they offer to Catholic and non-Catholic alike are those of an earlier generation. Each of them is directly concerned with the *nature* of his or her major figures, anxious to see and show what kind of people they are. This preoccupation goes beyond the analysis or presentation of character. Indeed, from that point of view most of their heroes and heroines could be summed up quite simply. Their *humanity*, however, is a different matter. It is simultaneously complex and simple, difficult to define, mysterious yet clear. Given this, it is perhaps inevitable that their creators should all feel the need from time to time to make *general* statements about human beings. Even the most superficial reading of the texts in question makes it clear that their authors are often given to asides, interpretations and comment, presented either authorially or through the words or thoughts of their characters, and that these observations and reflections constitute a distinct element in the novels. They may be brief (as is usually the case with Greene), longer and more complex (as with Undset) or almost short essays in themselves (as on occasion with Bernanos). Their importance is however qualitative rather than quantitative, for they help form the intellectual and imaginative world which the reader must temporarily inhabit. They also offer a series of steps towards a fuller and deeper *understanding* of that world, which must in some way and to some extent be an image of the real world which their creators have known.

The twentieth century has been marked by scepticism, relativism and a heightened sense of the shapelessness and randomness of human life. Yet we still want there to be some point to it. The tension inherent in the basic and permanent oscillation of the human mind between an awareness of absurdity and a need for a sense of purpose has been particularly evident in our age, and indeed a perception of existential absurdity has often been matched by a teleological backlash. It is possible to see totalitarian politics of both the right and the left, the search for commitment in literature and even its opposite, the view of literature as an autonomous object separate from life and investigated for its own sake, and of the whole idea of art for art's sake, as attempts to create or justify at various levels and in various ways, a number of aims and purposes. All causes which demand the acceptance of a system of beliefs and a mode of action and conduct are particularly attractive in a situation where a sense of pointlessness and aimlessness is the norm for persons of intelligence and sensitivity. For those who see in it no more and no less than a particular variety of such a deliberately sought and accepted cause, Catholicism is simply one manifestation of a general tendency. A given individual may prefer it on aesthetic or other grounds to Marxism, or secular humanism, or the cult of the Superman, but it can quite easily be seen as merely one of a wide range of types of explanation and commitment which can be chosen as antidotes to contingency and meaninglessness. Any point, even the point of learning to live with pointlessness, seems better to the twentieth-century mind than pure and simple absurdity. The sense of despair so characteristic of much modern thought and intelligently evaluated experience can only, it seems, be cured or alleviated by the discovery or creation of aims and significance and scales of value. Humankind cannot, as Eliot told us, bear too much reality, and if undifferentiated and meaningless existence is seen, as the twentieth century has tended to see it, as reality, we seek to escape it in our philosophies, our arts, our politics and our religions. The dreadful suspicion that such systems are the creations of our bad faith is the other major characteristic of our thought, and has two possible consequences. These seem to be either the total rejection of anything which might be seen as giving any significance to human life, or the submission of the critical intelligence to the explanatory possibilities of the particular ideology we want to accept. The rise and fall of such ideologies in the twentieth century is perhaps an indication both of the strength of desire for justificatory and explanatory philosophies and of the irrepressible nature of the European tradition of critical analysis. In a situation in which all beliefs are tolerated and none is sacrosanct, oscillation and flux are counterbalanced by commitment and explicit or implicit apologetics. Consequently, either a sceptical relativism or a dogmatic tone of justificatory rhetoric have been a characteristic of much twentieth-century European culture.

In that permanent choice between absurdity and significance, the attractions of Catholicism are evident. Essentially, faith is an act of the will (made possible, in the Catholic scheme of things, by grace) like any other. As an explanatory and moral system, it has much to offer, and it is not by chance that the number of twentieth-century European writers who were Catholic by upbringing, later conscious choice, or a combination of both, is high. What is more significant, however, is that many such writers were also 'Catholic writers', or writers whose work was influenced by their faith and who were seen in that light by their readers and critics. The Catholic novel, difficult to define but plain to see, became a feature of the literature of Europe during the last decades of the nineteenth century and the first decades of the twentieth, a recognisable and not inconsiderable literary phenomenon.

It made its appearance rather earlier in France than elsewhere, and the general Catholic literary movement has continued there well into the twentieth century. It is visibly perpetuated in the novels of Bernanos, Mauriac, Julien Green and Daniel-Rops, and subsists in later writers such as Cayrol, Sulivan and Maurice Clavel. Outside France, it can be seen as a rather later phenomenon, but affirmations of belief, conversions or a recovery of faith were frequent among literary people in, for example, both England and Scandinavia during the late nineteenth and early twentieth centuries. By the time of G.K. Chesterton (1874-1936), Hilaire Belloc (1870-1953) and Maurice Baring (1874-1945) Catholic fiction, in a different and perhaps more accessible form than that taken by its French sibling, was of rather more than embryonic proportions. Its growth in the works of Greene and Waugh can be easily traced. In the reaction against naturalism in the same period, Scandinavia too saw the upsurge of a less marked but nonetheless noticeable alliance of fiction and Catholicism. By the nineteen-twenties and thirties, there was an evident and well-established tradition of Catholic fiction in western Europe that had reached maturity both qualitatively and quantitatively. It was in this context that the writers we shall examine were working, and before we go on to a detailed analysis of their work it would be useful to make a few brief general observations on their individual backgrounds.

ENGLAND MADE ME: GRAHAM GREENE (1904 - 1991)

Greene probably stands out as the English writer coming closest to what many readers and critics see as the typical, and possibly the only, kind of Catholic novelist. Unlike Waugh's literary Catholicism, his is full (or, some would insist, over-full) of sympathy, compassion and suffering, and has none of the cold, satirical, intellectual and emotional distance which his co-religionist made into such a powerful component of some of his work. Unlike Chesterton's, it has little rational and intellectual basis, and seems to be a result of an emotional need, or of the memory of such a need, rather than the foundation for a reasonable and harmonious way of living. Although it may ultimately entail, frequently in a rather mystical way, a notion of human solidarity and fraternity, it is also to some extent a marker, a badge which separates one human being from another.

Philip Stratford's brief but interesting analysis of the general shape and texture of Greene's Catholicism (Stratford, 1964) raises some interesting points. The first is connected with the nature of English Catholicism at the time when Greene was most productive: isolated, united, proselytising, orthodox in attitudes and practice and needing to explain itself because it was not understood by the outsider. This is contrasted to French Catholicism of the same period, which is seen as characterised by passive endurance, variety of observance and practice, and by being firmly embedded in the national tradition and forming an important stratum of it. If we accept such a view as reasonably valid, then Greene can be seen as noticeable both as a member of a minority and as a highly individual member of it, one who refused much of the surrounding culture and also took a rather idiosyncratic attitude towards that section of it which he did accept. Any twentieth-century Englishman who is a Catholic is *ipso facto* an exception, a member of a minority group. Of any given random group of ten Englishmen, only one is likely to be a Catholic. Of any given random group of ten English Catholics, perhaps only one (and particularly in the days before the Second Vatican Council, when Greene was producing most of his more markedly Catholic fiction) would have expressed more than a slight sympathy with his views. It is perhaps only gradually that the English reading public has been able to begin to form a balanced and comprehensive view of his Catholicism, as distinct from appreciating it as a literary device. It has not, over the last hundred years or so, been unusual to have Catholic writers in England, but it has been rather more unusual to have Catholic writers of the kind which Greene represents. The history of post-Reformation English Catholic literature has yet to be written, but one can imagine that when it is, the chapter on Greene's precursors will perhaps be rather slim.

What can be suggested as a way of focussing Greene is a reflection on his literary antecedents at another level, that of literary techniques and influences. Stratford points out that very early in his career as a novelist, Greene had read a great deal of Mauriac (*Thérèse Desqueyroux* in 1930, *Le Noeud de vipères* in 1933, *Dieu et Mammon* in 1936 and the *Vie de Jésus* in 1937) but points out that although these might be seen as a seminal influence, Greene did to some extent deny that they were a conscious one (Stratford, 1964, x). He was also responsible, just after the second World War, for initiating the Collected Edition of Mauriac's novels for Eyre and Spottiswoode and saw the first six titles through the press. What many critics have suggested as more fruitful fields of investigation in this regard, however, are the adventure novel (Conrad and Stevenson), thrillers (Rider Haggard, Anthony Hope, John Buchan) and Jacobean tragedy (Ford, Tourneur and Webster). To this already quite impressive list one might add, since the publication of *Lord Rochester's Monkey* in 1974, the licentiousness and poetry of the Restoration. Such a varied literary ancestry might well explain the mixture of the strong and gripping narrative line of many of his novels *(Brighton Rock)*; their occasionally rather melodramatic qualities *(The End of the Affair)*; their occasional bloodiness and cruelty *(The Quiet American)*; and the preoccupation with sexuality and 'the sins of the flesh' (of which any might serve as an example). A simpler explanation might, however, equally well be provided by Greene's own note on the subject, in which he describes the influence on him of Marjorie Bowen's *The Viper of Milan* (1906), which he read at the age of fourteen. After finishing it, he found that he had to write, and that his writing was stamped, perhaps permanently, with certain characteristics:

> I began to write. All the other possible futures slid away: the potential civil servant, the don, the clerk had to look for other incarnations. Imitation after imitation of Miss Bowen's magnificent novel went into exercise books - stories... marked with enormous brutality and despairing romanticism. It was as if I had been supplied once and for all with a subject (Greene, 1951, 15-16).

More important than influences, however, in Greene's case, are antipathies - the banality and boredom of the world without God, facile optimism, conventional piety, pharisaism and something which is more important than these, the pathetic inadequacy of human attempts to explain our nature and our life.

With Greene, a dissatisfaction with the world does not lead to a wholehearted commitment to schematic political or social causes, as a reading of *Monsignor Quixote* makes abundantly clear. Solutions come from a relationship with God or not at all. Understanding is the first essential in the movement towards a better way of living, and it comes from reflection, not action. Even a character such as Leon Rivas, who might be seen as an exception to this, is important in *The Honorary Consul* (1973) for his understanding and sharing of the sub-human lot of the local poor rather than for his revolutionary activities. In a certain sense, Greene has always stood aside, refused commitment. Rather than incorporate plans for action, his novels propose a constant tension between what might be good and what might be humanly useful or desirable. In this, he is a writer for whom the individual human person is of supreme importance, is indeed the most important fact of human fife. This seems to be a major theme of Greene's from *The Man Within* to *The Human Factor*, *Doctor Fischer of Geneva* and *Monsignor Quixote*. It has been the abiding element In his work against the background of a world in which, both in reality and in fiction, fascism, communism, American and European imperialism, oligarchy, conventional piety, rationalism and secular humanism have had their day. All that remains for Greene is faith, hope and charity, and, however diluted these may become, they are the only way to salvation in either human or theological terms. There is in his novels a displacement of relative importance from the question of personal salvation in *Brighton Rock* and *The Heart of the Matter* (which can be seen as involving principally faith and hope) to that of an increased awareness of inter-relatedness and interdependence in *The Honorary Consul* (which can be seen as involving chiefly charity), but it is a change of emphasis rather than a radical transformation. What has not changed is the perception that reality is the ordinary, the everyday, the human being in all his misery and his occasional happiness, with his crying need for a life that is a true life. Beyond the restatement in his novels of Rimbaud's declaration that 'la vraie vie est absente' there is an occasional sense of what real life could conceivably be, of how we occasionally glimpse it and often miss it. Nothing will foster it except a proper understanding of the theological virtues. In this sense, what shapes Greene's work more profoundly than anything else is a hazy, imperfect, dim and often clouded perception of what real life might be, and an acute sense of its absence.

NOBODY IS SIMPLY NORWEGIAN: SIGRID UNDSET (1891-1949)

Since Undset as a Norwegian Catholic novelist is a rather more isolated literary phenomenon than either Greene or Bernanos, it is perhaps useful to attempt to relate her work to the general movement of Scandinavian literature of her time.

A major feature of literature in Norway in the twentieth century has been the development of the novel as a genre which has both remained realistic and yet found itself opposed to the mechanistic or deterministic view of man dominating much intellectual scientific and artistic endeavour in the late nineteenth and early twentieth centuries. The major interest of Undset's fiction probably arises from the fact that it remains embedded in an established tradition of realism without being limited by it. In the sense that it is in its own way authentic and assumes that there is both an inner and an external reality of which literature can provide an expression, it belongs to the major tradition of developed European fiction and at the same time renews it by reinforcing concepts of human freedom and dignity. Individual and racial memory, sexual impulses and drives, the movements of the subconscious are important in her work, but so are also the conscious, cognitive and conative aspects of the life of the mature human being. What A.H Winsnes calls her Christian realism (Winsnes, 1953) is that dimension in her novels which separates her to some extent from other Scandinavian writers who sought religious faith, but whose spirituality remained intensely individualistic and deeply subjective. The Hound of Heaven did not seek her out remorselessly; she found and kept her faith because of her perception and acceptance of reality rather than as a result of a flight from it. The realism of Christianity found as deep a response in her as the realism of the honest observation, assessment and depiction of the external natural world. There is no flight from that world in her novels, but a reflection on it in terms of a tough and realistic faith.

Scandinavia's major contact with, and influence on, the main movements in European literature had occurred in the late nineteenth century, when the literatures of that region, with Norwegian literature taking an honourable part, had filled a very important place. It is against the background of these times, and most importantly against that of the 'New Awakening' in Scandinavian literature, that both the modern Norwegian novel and Undset's own fiction should be seen. The chief theorist of this movement, and its most influential apologist, was the Danish academic and critic Georg Brandes (1862-1927). In 1871, after long periods of residence in Paris, Rome and London and an important meeting with Ibsen in Dresden, Brandes returned to Copenhagen determined, with the Norwegian dramatist's blessing and approval, to break what he saw as the defunct northern literary tradition and to awaken the Scandinavian soul. Ibsen was to provoke the Norwegians, Brandes the Danes. The latter's important series of lectures on *Main Currents in Nineteenth-Century European Literature*, given between 1872 and 1890 and published between 1901 and 1905, proposed as its major thesis the notion that literature should contain ideas, and that those ideas should reform and revitalise society, and has obvious affinities with certain of Ibsen's plays.

Brandes's influence was powerful, and the younger Scandinavian writers and critics followed his call wholeheartedly, providing a focus for the more liberal elements in Scandinavian society. His literary doctrines advocated realism, naturalism, positivism and utilitarianism, and it is as a result of a sharing of such views that Ibsen produced his series of 'social plays' in the eighteen-eighties (of which *Ghosts* (1881) and *Rosmersholm* (1886) might be taken as examples) and that novelists like Alexander Kielland (1869-1906) and Biornsterne Bjornson (1832-1910), the latter over a very long period indeed, devoted so much of their creative energy to writing novels with the same kind of social and philosophical themes.

Although Brandes himself was later much influenced by Nietzsche and rejected his own earlier liberal ideas as 'a little

Darwinism, a little emancipation of women, a little morality of happiness, a little free thought, a little cult of the people, etc.' (Gustafson, 1966, 18) their influence was nevertheless long-standing and determined the general direction of Scandinavian literature for many years. This persistence is seen quite clearly in much of Bjornson's work, where the novels consist largely of an exposé of those very themes which Brandes had by then rejected.

It was against literature of the type advocated by the earlier Brandes and produced by Bjornson and Kielland, that Undset reacted to some extent, fairly visibly at least by *Jenny*. She found it bookish and didactic; it aroused opposition in her and seemed on balance thin and unconvincing. With her compatriot Knut Hamsun (1859-1952) she represents, despite the profound differences, part of that strand in the modern Norwegian novel which complements rather than destroys such a tradition, for she knew it, understood it, and partly sympathised with the ideas inherent in it, although she found them insipid, half-true, and indeed dangerous and vitiating if accepted uncritically, and portrayed them as such in much of her work. Many of her novels of contemporary life consist to some extent of an examination of some of the ideas influencing her contemporaries and of a critique of them, by both characters and author, in the light of new perceptions of reality.

It must be said, however, that in some ways the Norway of the nineteen-twenties and thirties, the most productive period of Undset's life as a writer, remained rather outside the mainstream of European culture. Unmarked by the cataclysmic effects of the First World War, it remained essentially a hard-working, thrifty, self-regarding country, centrist and democratic in politics, stable, and with an increasing number of social welfare projects, a perhaps rather dull society in which a number of 'advanced' ideas such as birth control, the emancipation of women, a certain tolerable degree of self-determination, were allowed to circulate. It was nevertheless a literate culture, with a very high *per capita* production of books, and within it the writer was something of a public figure, who usually had and propounded, and was expected to have and propound, views on matters of public concern. From this point of view, both Undset's fiction on the one hand, and her essays and biographies on the other are interesting. The former is attractive largely in connection with her portrayal of the role of women and family life in that culture. The latter deal with religion, philosophy, psychology, morality and politics from both a national and world-wide point of view.

With her own interest in European culture and her passionate concern for truth and justice, Undset was perhaps the Norwegian writer of her time most open to the outside world, despite the extremely localised setting of her novels. But what has separated her from the spirit of the times in her native land and from the general secular spirit of the modern world was that element which many of her readers have found most attractive (and occasionally most dangerous) in her work: her sense of the tragic dignity of the individual and of the depth and dimension which his relationship with God gives him. That element was largely absent from the literature of her time, both at home and abroad, and it is its presence in her work which more than any other explains the widespread appeal of her novels. It must be remembered that although she is now rather in eclipse outside Norway, she was, during her lifetime, and immediately after her death in 1949, a writer whose work had been translated into many of the major languages of the world and who had been awarded the Nobel prize for literature as early as 1928. Her sense of human dignity also explains the need she felt to profess and explain her views of the human being in essays written in German and published in Germany in the nineteen-thirties, *Begegnungen und Trennungen (Meetings and Partings)* (1931) and *Fortschritt, Rasse, Religion (Progress, Race and Religion)* (1935). Such works are an epitome of the views which shape her novels and, expressed in forthright terms and addressed to a particular nation at a particular time, explain the hatred she aroused in those who saw her books as dangerous, subversive and powerful. It is clear why the Nazis eliminated them from libraries and bookshops in Germany in 1936 and in occupied Norway in 1940.

Although Norway is a highly literate and indeed a highly literary country, it is one of the smallest language communities in the world, and the fate of the Norwegian writer outside his own country is always to be read almost exclusively in another language. It is very likely that during her lifetime Undset was read more widely in translation, and particularly in English translation, than in Norwegian. There is also the fact of her world literary status as a Nobel prize-winner, the rather particular nature of her role as one of the leaders of the Norwegian resistance in exile in the USA during the Second World War, and, between the two wars, of her long acquaintance with and love of England. All this has meant that her readership in those countries and in other English-speaking parts of the world, in Catholic and non-Catholic circles alike, was very wide indeed.

A CERTAIN IDEA OF FRANCE: GEORGES BERNANOS (1988-1948)

Bernanos the novelist is easy to caricature and difficult to understand. This is because he is to some extent, as has been suggested (Griffiths, 1966, 358) the heir to many of the fixed ideas and passions of the Catholic literary revival in France at the end of the nineteenth century, the polemical and missionary movement which was to continue in a striking and idiosyncratic form up to the Great War. The ways in which his ideas and attitudes are expressed in his novels and polemical writings reflect the whole ethos of that age, and he is often seen as belonging simply to an easily-identifiable, monolithic and unchanging tradition which could be called that of the nationalistic, anti-democratic and anti-republican, deeply conservative, chauvinistic and xenophobic French Catholic Right. The presence of such traits in his work is undeniable, but to see it exclusively in that way is simplistic and distorting. There are other aspects of Catholic literature in general, and of Bernanos's fiction in particular, which are rather different and equally worthy of note, even if they are perhaps less striking and less polemically clear-cut.

If we are to understand Bernanos, whose first novel, *Star of Satan*, was not published until 1926, when he was in his late thirties, we must consider the fiction of his productive years as a novelist both against the general background of the development of Catholic idea and attitudes which was taking place during his youth and early manhood and in contradistinction to it. The earlier stages of the French Catholic Revival in literature can with some justice be seen as a period of anti-rationalism marked by a deep sense of the primacy of enthusiasm and fervour and a direct and intuitive response to the demands of Catholic belief, which found its expression in mysticism and a sense of direct personal religious revelation. In the eyes of others as well as in its own, the whole movement was an isolated, visionary and missionary minority. Totally opposed to what it saw as the crass and deluded society of its time, it was tinged with anti-intellectualism, violence and exaggeration and occasionally, in its most extreme manifestations, with unconscious near-heresy or false emphasis in doctrinal matters. The vigour and enthusiasm of many of its proponents were often those of the recent convert, whose reaction (and it is important to note that they were, in the literal sense of the word, reactionaries) was manifold - a revulsion against the banality and meaninglessness of the purely secular world, against the vulgar conformist pieties of much nineteenth-century Catholicism, and (perhaps feeling that they were more Catholic than the Pope) against the whole of the relatively liberal policies of Leo XIII, including his advocacy of the rigorously intellectual approach to theology contained in Thomist philosophy. A concern with an intense (and intensely personal) religious experience was apparent. The literary Catholicism of this time was, in short, an uncomfortable, highly idiosyncratic and essentially emotional experience, the product of a certain time, a certain place, a certain nexus of circumstances and situations, a certain perhaps rather exacerbated sensibility sharpened by surrounding opposition and dislike.

Against such qualities, however, must be set some rather different ones, which although perhaps less readily discernible were equally important. Sudden and emotional conversions were not quite universal. One notable exception, Paul Bourget (1852-1934), refused to talk about such an event in his own case, maintaining that he had entered the Church as a result of a gradual process of reasoning and reflection, and the general pattern of his concerns and methods as a novelist gives credence to such a statement. It is also possible to see indications that there was rather more subtlety and variety in the general corpus of shared ideas within the movement than might at first be supposed. The differing ways of seeing the Jews propounded, for example, in Bloy and Péguy do lead to the suspicion that not everything in the general pattern of the thought of the Catholic Revival was as clear-cut and polemically simple as might be imagined. Bourgeois capitalism was as much anathema to the Catholic writers of the late nineteenth and early twentieth centuries as it was to a Marxist. Many of the Catholic novels of the earlier twentieth century castigated (as Bernanos's were to do later) Catholic society and the Church for their neglect of the poor and for their indifference towards the oppression to which the poor were subjected. Baumann's ideas on social reform, anti-democratic and anti-socialist as they were, seem genuine, if uninspiring and paternalistic. There was also a certain amount of sympathy for such Catholic social movements as *Le Sillon*, even if there was also a counterbalancing suspicion and reserve. Although the recommendations of the papal encyclical *Rerum Novarum* (1891) were viewed with some reservations, there is constant evidence of a concern for the material and moral squalor of the exploited classes, and it is perhaps possible that this anti-capitalist, anti-bourgeois bias created, or perhaps more accurately reinforced, the strain of anti-semitism sometimes apparent in the literature of the period.

Nor should it be forgotten that many of the novelists who espoused Catholic ideas and ideals were rather different in personality and attitudes from the more 'typical' flamboyantly militant of its leaders. Writers such as Bourget, already mentioned, and François Mauriac (1895-1970) were of a more reflective and less aggressively dogmatic turn of mind than some of their contemporaries. Perhaps it is sufficient here to say that literary Catholicism up to the First World War was not a seamless or homogeneous artistic and philosophical phenomenon.

The background to Bernanos's fiction is therefore not entirely a simple one, although the ideas which helped to form his outlook can be traced back to those of a slightly earlier period. A fervent Catholic, reaching young manhood and maturity in a secular, republican France which seemed totally opposed, philosophically and politically, to all that he felt and believed, he could not but be attracted by the rather heady Catholic 'thought' of his time. Some of the ideas which formed the background to his development may be obscure and to an unsympathetic outsider muddled and obscurantist, but whatever criticism one may make of Bernanos one cannot condemn him for superficiality. He can be seen as a writer with two obsessions: France and human society on the one hand, and the nature of the human being and his destiny on the other. Even within the first obsession, which is largely that of his polemical writings, there is a whole range of ideas, responses and preoccupations which in both depth and scope goes far beyond the concerns of his predecessors. The enormous horrors of the years in the trenches, the deep and bitter sense of the betrayal of a whole generation of Frenchmen, his anguish at the cowardice, selfishness and mediocrity of the France of the inter-war years, the struggle against all philosophies which destroyed the dignity of man by debasing the true concept of him and making him into no more than a cog in a mechanism, his acute sense of the lack of any true leadership in France in particular and Europe in general, his opposition to the totalitarian movements of the nineteen-thirties, all meant that his polemical writings, although often bitter and sweepingly destructive, could sometimes achieve the passionate and searing lyricism of *A Diary of my Times* (1938).

Bernanos can then with certain reservations be seen as the inheritor of a tradition of polemical writing. He can perhaps also be seen as representing in some ways the continuation of a certain tradition of the French Catholic novel. In a certain sense, some of the mystical and social concerns, which marked the work of his predecessors, are apparent in his own fiction. Here, the force which produced his polemical works seems to have gone underground and brought to the surface all the deep obsessions which lay behind whatever he wrote. In the world of the novels, from *Star of Satan* (1926) to the publication of *The Open Mind* in 1943 and the posthumous appearance of *Night is Darkest* in 1950, the reader is faced with the most profound reflections of a man at the limits of his experience and with characters whose actions lead them to a confrontation with the transcendent, where either the crucial choices of their lives have to be made or the inevitable consequences of those choices faced. In these limit situations, the possibility of liberation, of full humanity, is of a rather different kind from that suggested sometimes with nobility and sometimes evoked by a bitter picture of its absence, in the polemical essays. In the latter, it is fundamentally the liberty and dignity of man amongst his fellow men which is the issue. In the novels, it is the liberty of a person to be more fully and more intensely himself. The two are linked but not identical, for although a social recognition of human freedom and dignity is a precondition of the fullness of being, it is simply a framework for that fullness and not the fullness itself. A single insight might give rise to both kinds of writing, as the fate of Republican prisoners in the Spanish Civil War gave rise to both *Diary of my Times* and *Mouchette*, but both the way in which that insight is eventually expressed and the implications which are drawn from it are rather different. That difference between one of Bernanos's most moving polemical works and one of the most haunting of his novels illustrates very graphically the two paths his reflection often took, and the difference between his ideas about men in society and about man both influenced by that society and yet beyond it in his ultimate importance is implicit in it. The novels demand much reflective and imaginative sympathy on the part of the reader, and the simple certitudes that one might previously have felt about his work are easily shaken by an attentive reading of it. The concerns so strikingly expressed in his fiction are those which must be taken fully into account when assessing Bernanos either as a Catholic novelist or simply as a novelist, and this is the aim of the chapter of this study which is devoted to his work.

In some ways, Bernanos sometimes comes close to the image of the Catholic novelist as exemplified by a writer like Bloy. In certain novels, his concern with the private, the interior and even occasionally with the overtly mystical and the apparently miraculous (as in *Star of Satan*) his attack on modernism and on a Catholicism which seeks an accommodation with the world (as in the untranslated *L'Imposture*), and to a lesser extent in the *Diary of Country Priest* (1936) lack nothing of the intransigence of those of his predecessors. In others, however, he is far away from that image. Indeed, many of his novels are in fact not 'religious' with regard to external matters and contain little obviously 'Catholic' subject matter. Catholicism is barely mentioned in, for example, *Mouchette* and *Night is Darkest*. They deal with matters that are of fundamental human concern, even if they do so in ways that only a Catholic could deal with them. In approaching in such a manner the ontological mystery at the heart of human life Bernanos perhaps comes closest to the good if not the archetypal Catholic novelist. His novels are not 'about' modernism, or social Catholicism, or psychological and moral problems à la Bourget, but about the fundamental difficulties of being human and of consciously or unconsciously orientating our lives.

Chapter 3

GRAHAM GREENE

I would not claim to be a Catholic writer, but a writer who in four or five books took characters with Catholic ideas for his material.   Graham Greene, *In Search of a Character.*

Many readers have discerned and reacted in various ways to the theological dimensions in Greene's novels. There may be some justification for the point of view put forward by John Atkins that this element has been wrongly seized upon and examined to the detriment or neglect of others, and doubly so because it is 'on the surface, planted there rather weightily in many cases by Greene himself, but it is a surface growth' (Atkins, 1966, xi). Fewer readers and critics have concerned themselves seriously with the more fundamental question of how Greene sees human beings and of the image of the human person which he presents to the reader. The sanctity or sinfulness of his characters, their possible salvation or damnation, the nature of their view of human society have been discussed, but not the basic data of humanity implicitly (and sometimes explicitly) suggested in the novels. It is possible to believe that certain critics have in fact seen Greene's work almost as a series of illustrations of problematic examples in moral theology (e.g. Moëller, 1953). It is less easy to find any evidence that they have been read analytically in the light of the general way of understanding and picturing the human person which they incorporate. Even Terry Eagleton's intelligent (if ultimately unsatisfying) study of them in *Exiles and Emigres* (Eagleton, 1970) does not in this respect go beyond pointing out the general contrast between the portrayed or presented unworthiness of human nature and the need which Greene's characters feel to find a way of accepting this, of relating in some meaningful way to it, and of transforming the existential mess they live in (Eagleton, 1970, 108-137).

THE UNEDIFYING BUT UNIQUE INDIVIDUAL

It is clear, however, that even at the most obvious and striking level, that of the seediness so often detected in his characters by such critics, there is a great deal of perhaps unsystematic but nevertheless quite wide-ranging reflection on human nature in all Greene's work. Observations are often made through the words of a particular character who voices some weary and disillusioned truism about human weakness or the sameness of our basic nature. This is usually exemplified by reference to unedifying, and by implication more or less universal, patterns of behaviour or predictable series of reactions. Our common humanity, stripped of pretence and protection, is, we learn, evident in the brothel where all our superficial differences disappear. Human faults are simple, predictable, universal: 'a glass too much, a girl now and then (...) it's human nature. I am human'. In the squalor of the tropics, human nature is at its least-disguised, its shabbiest and seediest. We all love and need our comforting and encouraging little illusions, and their very simplicity makes them all the more attractive, as is the case with the pencilled political slogans which the Mexican priest notices on the girlie calendar in *The Power and the Glory*. Seen at this immediately accessible level, human beings are not impressive or endearing creatures, and Greene's fiction is liberally sprinkled with adulterers, weaklings, renegades, traitors, whores, cowards and failures of one kind or another. Even the benign and tolerant Monsignor Quixote finds it hard to trust his parishioners, and the girls in the mixed party visiting the Trappist monastery where he has just died, who are attracted by the celibacy and silence and the notice 'Clausura', 'as though beyond it there might be secrets more interesting and perverse than anything the young men could offer' are late examples of the persistent Greenean touch.

What is more important than this easily-recognisable and readily-assimilable comment, however, is the series of reflections on the basic questions which life makes human beings ask, and which are forced on one or more of the major characters in a given novel. Scobie in *The Heart of the Matter*, the Mexican priest in *The Power and the Glory*, Sarah, Bendrix and Henry in *The End of the Affair*, Fowler in *The Quiet American* are all obliged, as a result of disturbing experiences in their lives, to wonder what men and women are, what their importance is, and how they do, or can, or should relate to each other. Bendrix, for example, in the face of the apparent pointlessness of Sarah's death and his loss of her, ironically expresses in his talk with Fr Crompton one of the basic premises of the latter's faith, the importance of the individual.

The fact that he is ostensibly attacking and mocking such a view (although he has in fact moved some way towards accepting it) is not particularly important. It is the statement of it that matters, for it indicates a possible view of human beings which Greene, however obliquely, introduces into the novel at a point when Bendrix sees life at its bleakest and most desolate and all meaning seems totally absent. Despite the bitterness of his remark, he knows that in his relationship with Sarah, in her diary, in his memories of her and his love for her, he has had glimpses of another person in her complexity and simplicity as a human being, and that this perception, heightened by his loss, will remain with him. And Sarah herself, in her diary, has reflected on just such odd and apparently remote matters. What, she wonders is the essential nature of a human being? If one can rid a personality of its accidents, its external, visible characteristics, what is left? No doubt she would never express the question in those terms to herself or to anyone, Bendrix included, with whom she might want to discuss it or feel able to do so. Nevertheless, that is clearly what she means and what she wants to know when she asks herself in her own simple and direct language in her diary, 'What happens if you drop all the things that make you I?' The answer is concerned with what, in *Brighton Rock*, Greene calls 'the deepest mind, the plane of memories, instincts, hopes', and it is not surprising that Sarah's conclusion is that eventually it is God. There can ultimately perhaps only be two possible answers: nothing, or everything. The convinced Catholic must necessarily be presumed to find, as these have found, the second mysterious and indescribable alternative, even if like the not unsympathetic Bishop of Mopoto in *Monsignor Quixote*, he expresses himself in riddles, suggesting that perhaps we are all fictions in the mind of God. Just as Bendrix's love for Sarah grows as he finds out more about her as a human being (which means in effect, finding out more about that part of her which lies deeper than accidents and externals) so does his affection for and understanding of the pathetic and cuckolded Henry. The same sort of process is also evident in *The Quiet American*, when Fowler, asking the kind of question which for Greene's characters often begins to lead to knowledge, both of a particular and of a general kind, of their fellow men and women, says of his relationship with Pyle that it was while wondering what a man is that he felt his first affection for him.

APPROACHES TO THE PUZZLE

In Greene's novels, love of a human being and thought about his nature and that of the multitude of persons around us whose surface we never penetrate are always very closely interlinked. Man is devious, mysterious, complicated, full of hidden thoughts and ulterior motives even when apparently and superficially comprehensible, describable and predictable. Beyond a certain stage of insight, the first immediately recognisable and apparently valid series of general observations about a rather unsatisfactory humanity appear misleading and distorting, clouding real knowledge by their specious credibility and apparent wisdom. It is impossible to decide whether this clash of perceptions is an element of a conscious technique. It is, however, there for those who care to reflect on it. Every man woman and child has regions of his being which are infinitely more extensive and less amenable to notice and description than we can assume, and cannot be exhausted by any statement we make about human beings in general or about him as an individual in particular. In the words of Leon Rivas, the revolutionary priest of *The Honorary Consul*:

> I have never met a simple man. Not even in the confessional, though I used to sit there for hours on end. Man was not created simple. When I was a young priest I used to try and unravel what motives a man or woman

had, what temptations and self-delusions. But I soon learned to give all that up, because there was never a straight answer. No-one was simple enough for me to understand. In the end I would just say "Three Our Fathers, three Hail Marys. Go in peace" (Greene, *The Honorary Consul*, 1973, 228-229).

It is only the love and, in many senses of the word, the understanding, of a Bendrix, a Fowler, a Sarah, a Scobie and even, despite his disclaimer, of a Leon Rivas, that can make any sense, however incomplete or tentative, out of such ignorance and confusion. What strikes the reader very forcibly is that such characters, like Querry in *A Burnt-Out Case*, can only begin to see what in the novels seems to lie at the heart of every human being when they have both perceived their own selfhood and that of others and have also in some way and to some degree gone beyond selfishness. The break in the egocentricity of their own physical and psychic life, which is clear in all the novels and which for Greene seems to be a precondition of human growth, brings with it a deeper love of others and a fuller understanding of their fellows. Human self-centredness, what Querry calls 'self-expression', is seen as corrosive and finally destructive of even the self which it seeks to express:

> Self-expression is a hard and selfish thing. It eats everything, even the self. At the end you find that you haven't got a self to express. I have no interest in anything any more, doctor. I don't want to sleep with a woman nor design a building (Greene, *A Burnt-Out Case*, 1961, 52).

At the basis of this understanding of other selves, or at least of that perception of their elusiveness and irreducibility which is a preliminary to even the most superficial knowledge of them, lies a complex of emotions and attitudes which might be given any one of a number of possible names. Prominent amongst these are compassion and pity. The individual reader may react to their presence in a number of ways. The reflections of the author on his characters may be seen as tired, shabby, mawkish little aphorisms, as expressions of acute perception and insight, as drab, tired and superficially worldly-wise observations or as exemplary wisdom expressed with lapidary economy. In the first place, it is their existence rather than their validity which should be noted. The novels can be seen to some extent as a conscious and continuous exploration of the idea that awareness of another as a person inevitably and always brings with it a sense of the complexity of his being and a feeling of sympathy and shared humanity. The simple schematic view produced by convention, prejudice, social, political, religious and psychological differences disappears. Received ideas crumble and are replaced by a sense of another complex, different and yet not alien reality, and the suffering and pain of a different subjectivity become apparent and can be shared. In *The Power and the Glory*, for example, the priest, while in prison, both feels pity for the other inmates and can understand why the pious middle-class woman who speaks to him is appalled by her incarceration with the unlovely dregs of Mexican society, perceiving that both her upbringing and the shock of her experience prevent her from seeing them as her fellow human beings:

> When you visualised a man or woman carefully, you could always begin to feel pity... that was a quality God's image carried with it... Hate was a just a failure of the imagination (Greene, *The Power and the Glory*, 1959, 169-170).

Once the other is seen as a person, understanding and pity follow in Greene's novels. Without that necessary view of him, he is to a greater or lesser extent an object, and what is worse, frequently an awkward, embarrassing, squalid, inconvenient and possibly dangerous one. The 'failure of the imagination' entails in fact precisely an inability to see the reality and detail in another human being, whom Greene sees as the image of God. *The Heart of the Matter* is perhaps the novel in which he tries hardest to make this point and to drive it home at every development of the story. Scobie's pity for both Louise, his wife, and Helen, the girl with whom he commits adultery, is constantly made obvious to the reader. It comes into being because he sees their pain, their suffering, and, to some extent, the aridity of their individual lives. In his relationship with Louise, Scobie sees that he is 'bound by the pathos of her unattractiveness', is 'aware of the enormous breach pity had blasted through his integrity', and feels Helen's ugliness 'like a handcuff on his wrists'. He is forced to reflect on the compelling and, paradoxically, potentially unhelpful nature of such sentiments, and to wonder what the limits to them could be. Perhaps, he reflects, even the planets would claim our pity if we got to the heart of the matter. Indeed, it is because in this particular novel the emotion is so suffocatingly pervasive, permeating all Scobie's thought and feelings, that the reader senses, even if only vaguely, a kind of distortion, a falsification or weakness in his insights. If this is so, it is ultimately because he sees feeling as more important than truth:

> The truth, he thought, had never been of any real value to any human being - it is a symbol for mathematicians to pursue. In human relations, kindness and lies are worth a thousand truths (Greene, *The Heart of the Matter*, 1951, 141).

Here, as elsewhere, it seems that Greene differentiates between love and pity, and this distinction is of importance when reflecting on the novels. Scobie's pity, for all its worth, lacks the astringency which is sometimes the only thing which can, however slowly and painfully, eventually bring healing. There are indications that he is occasionally and imperfectly aware of this, and in them it is possible to sence the implication that Greene cannot see pity as a totally adequate response in human relationships. As well as seeing another person's weakness and vulnerability, we can often sense, perhaps in spite of that pity, his autonomy, his otherness and his separateness from ourselves. Thus when Scobie returns, exhausted and worried, from a trip up-country, and Louise stays up after he has gone to bed, attending to her own duties, he suddenly, briefly and unexpectedly sees her in a new light as 'someone of human stature with her own sense of responsibility, not simply the object of his care and kindness' (Greene, *The Heart of the Matter*, 1951, 100).

HUMAN STATURE

This perception illustrates the difference between love and pity and makes the latter seem in some sense and to some extent an egocentric and lesser response. It strengthens, momentarily at least, a certain suspicion on the part of the reader that there is something not entirely commendable about Scobie's concern for others and suggests the possibility that it can be seen as the product or manifestation of an exacerbated and slightly morbid sensitivity. What Scobie finds ultimately impossible to bear is perhaps not so much the suffering of others as the effect of that suffering on himself, and this is why his pity expresses itself in passivity and sadness. The truth - that element in human relationships which he sees as having no real value and which consequently to some extent eludes him here - is that the unhappiness of both Louise and Helen has its origin not so much in a lack of the kindness and comforting lies which he considers much more important, as in the inadequacy of their inner lives and their relationship with other people, notably himself. Louise's formal and rather sterile suburban piety and her acceptance of the protectiveness which ruins her marriage, Helen's ignorance and despair and her use of her affair with Scobie as a palliative for them are the causes of their dejection and bitterness. If Scobie had seen both women more as 'of human stature (...) not simply as the object of his care and pity', their situation and his would perhaps have developed differently. It is a failure to recognise truthfully, to see their human stature, which helps to prolong and confirm the wretchedness of the lives of the victims of his pity. After his death, one must presume, Louise will be as much the object of Webster's idealisation as she had been of Scobie's solicitude, and Helen's despair will continue into and beyond her affair with Bagster.

One cannot help but wonder whether Greene was fully aware of the implications of giving Scobie even such a brief insight of this kind. Although it is a fleeting one and uncharacteristic of the general pattern of his attitudes towards the two women, or indeed towards anyone else, from Yusef and Wilson to the dying child, it has, while it lasts, much in common with those of other characters in other novels. The autonomy and independent importance of others are seen by Bendrix, for example, in *The End of the Affair*, in his observation that 'we are possessed by nobody, not even by ourselves'. The implication is that people are, like Sarah, persons whose being cannot simply be seen as equivalent to the ideas which others have about them, and whose inner life escapes the full knowledge of their fellows. What human beings think and feel has dimensions outside the perceptions of such activities that they themselves and others may achieve. What is striking is that the recognition of the full humanity of others, their importance in themselves, and the beginnings of any knowledge of them is closely linked to some kind of awareness of God. In Bendrix's case, for example, there is a suggestion that a view of the kind expressed above arises as a result both of his reflections after his loss of Sarah and of what can be seen as his incipient and reluctant belief, expressed in a surface hostility which slowly gives way to a tired resignation, in some sort of remote and yet very personal power which has fundamentally affected his own life and that of Sarah and Henry. These ideas, which are major ones in Greene's fiction, are suggested very clearly (although not untypically in the form of a question) by Querry, in *A Burnt-out Case*, when he suggests that the love of God and the love of one's fellow human being are in some sense inseparable: 'Perhaps it's true that you can't believe in a God without loving a human being, or love a human being without believing in God' (Greene, *A Burnt-out Case*, 1961, 52).

Although this statement is an explanation of his own disbelief, detachment and lack of feeling, concern or desire, it illustrates the conceptual possibility of an opposite situation, one in which those negatives would be positives, even if imperfectly, confusedly and messily. In this sense, it calls to mind incidents in the novels which can be seen as moments of perception of the importance of each individual human being, those for example in *The Power and the Glory* in which the Mexican priest offers his own salvation for that of his child, or in *The Heart of the Matter* in which Scobie asks for peace for the dying six-year-old survivor of the SS43 and offers his own in return. They are illustrations of the great importance the religious view of man gives to even the most apparently insignificant of individuals, an importance which goes beyond the temporal and secular and includes a sense of the eternal value of each and every human person. The tiny speck of life for whom the Mexican priest prays, a child ancient before her time, doomed to a life of physical and moral squalor, violence and perhaps despair is, in his words, 'more important than a whole continent' and is seen in quite a different way by him from that in which the politicians, the police, the anti-clericals, who are all concerned with larger things, could ever see her.

THE MYSTERY OF RELIGION AND THE MYSTERY OF THE HUMAN PERSON: GOD'S IMAGE IN MAN

Given the importance of the religious dimension in certain of Greene's novels, it might be tempting to assume that the criticisms made by, for example, Atkins of their theological content could be extended to cover the religious view of human beings portrayed in them. If it is possible to argue that Greene can be seen as having been able to 'plant a surface growth' of theological concepts in them, it is also possible to suggest that he might also be able to impose on them an equally extrinsic view of man. In this connection, it is worth noting that there is at least some indication that Greene was perhaps aware of this possible way of both seeing life and of reading his work. Criticisms which are actually or potentially made in real life can readily be transposed to the plane of fiction, and it would not be surprising to find a response of some kind in the novels. In *A Burnt-out Case*, where Catholicism is criticised by an ex-Catholic hero, or at least by one whose Catholicism is in a state of temporary or permanent suspension, there is to some extent an answer to those who would claim that Greene simply sets out to christianize or catholicize feelings and reactions which are not necessarily specifically Christian or Catholic, but merely attributes of human beings in general, whether they have a given religion or none. Just such a charge is in fact made by Quarry to the Superior of the missions where he has sought escape and anonymity:

> You always try to draw everything into the net of your faith, Father. Gentleness isn't Christian, self-sacrifice isn't Christian, charity isn't, remorse isn't. Haven't you ever seen a dog weep? In the last cooling of the world, when the emptiness of your belief is finally exposed, there'll always be some bemused fool who'll cover another's body with his own to give it warmth for an hour more of life (Greene, *A Burnt-out Case*, 1961, 83-84).

It is not surprising to find that the Superior (or Greene through him?) attempts to make some kind of answer to this charge. He does so indirectly in his sermon preached in *petit-nègre* in the heat of the morning sun. The preaching is of the simplest kind, the examples chosen are banal and linked closely to the experience of his illiterate congregation, and yet the implications of what he has to say indicate a way of looking at the question which Querry has raised, of attempting to answer it, and of driving that answer home. The basis of his argument is that all the good that is in men (Christian or otherwise) is Yezu in them, the bad when Yezu is not in them. This not only implies that grace perfects rather than changes human nature, but also that Christ can be present in all men at all times, and that He is a God who exists through all eternity. It urges those hearing it (including both Querry, who gives a ghost of a smile as he recognises the response to his criticism, and Colin, the atheist doctor in the leper colony) to see human nature in terms of eternity and in relation to an eternal God and eternal values. In this simplest of homilies, the whole nature of the general Catholic view of man is raised by implication and example. It is interesting to note that this reply is given by a priest who is characterised by great practical intelligence and a robust common-sense, and not by one of the more subtle or theologically-minded members of the community such as Fr Thomas. Real knowledge of men and of human activities lies behind the answer, and its effects are probably twofold, in that the reader assumes both that it is an honest statement of a way of seeing man and that it is the one which coincides most closely with Greene's own. It is the answer which Catholic faith must give, and although faith is not knowledge, it is a willingness to accept the truth of a particular possible interpretation of human life and nature. The argument is expressed in simple terms, but it is about complex things. Greene does not deny (and indeed tends to stress) the complexity of the human personality and of human relationships, but he does suggest, in the example given above and elsewhere, that we need a belief in God (although we may deny His existence) if we are ever to begin really to understand our fellow men and women.

The unavoidable link between the difficulty of understanding other persons and religious concepts is stressed in many of his novels. One unfathomable mystery suggests another, and the feeling that understanding escapes us suggests the need to posit the possibility of a perfect comprehension. Both Thomas Hardy's view that the tragedy of the universe is that there is no intelligence anywhere capable of understanding it fully and its possible alternative, belief in God, lie at the heart of the matter here. Those parts of the universe with which our daily lives are primarily concerned, human personality and human situations, need to be understood more fully than we can ever understand them. In this situation, we can either assume, with Hardy, that they are ultimately incomprehensible, or that there is a God who himself understands, and can perhaps help our own understanding. For the Catholic, Anselm's summary of Augustine's work, '*credo ut intellegam*', is relevant here: faith can illuminate this area as well as others. For the unbeliever, it implies an attempt to evade the absurdity of human life, an inability to live with what we know and with that only, a leap into the irrational of the kind condemned by Camus in the *Myth of Sisyphus*. Whatever their underlying view, Greene's characters are often aware of the difficulty of knowing other people fully and of the ways in which this perception is linked with the need and the possibility or impossibility of considering the idea of God. Thus Fowler, in *The Quiet American*, suggests that it is precisely because we cannot understand each other that we have invented a Being capable of knowing and comprehending what eludes and mystifies us:

> .... accepting the fact that no human being will ever understand another, not a wife, a lover, a husband, a mistress, nor a parent a child? Perhaps that's why men have invented God - a being capable of understanding (Greene, *The Quiet American*, 1956, 72).

Bendrix's statement of the same general notion in *The End of the Affair* is similar. He talks of 'getting to the end of human beings', meaning presumably abandoning the attempt to understand them in simplistic terms or tiring of their general unsatisfactoriness and untidiness, and then moving on to a self-induced belief in God as the next tactical move in a strategy for coping with life:

> When we get to the end of human beings we have to delude ourselves into a belief in God, like a gourmet

who demands more complex sauces with his food (Greene, *The End of the Affair*, 1959, 176). It is ironical of course that when he thinks this he is by no means 'at the end' of Sarah and does not want God, and that a more complete understanding of a human being and the first tentative movement towards perceiving God are later to be closely linked when he receives Sarah's letter and finally reads her diary. The implications are that, even in his own terms, his rather sophisticated bit of human wisdom becomes meaningless as he sees more clearly that God and His image, man, are equally mysterious and indissolubly linked.

This point is made again and again in the novels. The priest in *The Power and the Glory* can see, and tries to express in the terminology of his own theological training, what binds totally disparate people together. The unity, which is there because all men are alike in the sense that they are in some way like God, can be seen, but not fully explained by reason. Given his premises, it is not irrational in itself:

> But at the centre of his own faith there always stood the convincing mystery - that we are made in God's image. God was the parent, but he was also the policeman, the criminal, the priest, the maniac and the judge (Greene, *The Power and the Glory*, 1959, 129).

Human beings are alike and can see each other as persons because they are all 'made in God's image'. It is important to understand some of the implications of this expression. What it means is that man is like God and that there is a reflection of God in him. It does not mean that God is man, or that man is God, or that man is simply a passive vehicle through whom God operates (although man can make the choice of being that). It is the idea of likeness which is of great importance, for from it arises the notion that God can in some way be seen in man, and in some way be affected by what is done to his human creatures. What Greene is saying in the thoughts he gives the priest is in fact that however remote the likeness may seem, however difficult it may be to find a reflection of divinity or to perceive any trace of God's presence, in individual human beings faith tells the believer that this is how he must see his fellow men and women.

The perception may be very vivid in certain crucial human situations, such as the one he depicts in *The Power and the Glory*. One of the problems in this particular case is of course that Greene's language is poetic, in that its meaning lies beyond but not totally separate from the literal denotation of the constituent words. To say that God 'was' any of the people he mentions is to speak figuratively and not literally. No-one could say of himself or anyone else that he was God, but each could say that either was in some sense like Him. This must be the meaning of the priest's thoughts, and it is important to realise this, for the expression 'made in God's image' has been either intentionally or deliberately misinterpreted by certain of Greene's critics. David Pryce-Jones in particular simply and wrongly takes the phrase to mean that each human individual is no more than a puppet carrying out the will of God and that human beings are unfree and simply pawns in a series of moves designed by God to accomplish his purposes. Thus, he maintains, they 'cannot be properly distinguished by the individual moral considerations of their actions, for every action - even sex and killing - is in God's image' (Pryce-Jones, 1963, 58). This deterministic view of human nature and human actions, which are all seen as predestined and morally equivalent because they all work towards God's purpose, is in accordance with neither Catholic theology nor with internal evidence in the novel. In the former, the phrase simply cannot be understood in that way, for there man is seen as free to further or to hinder the working of grace and the movement towards salvation and is capable of knowledge, freedom and autonomous action, the very qualities which in fact make him like God. With regard to the latter, there are indications in the novel that the priest is aware of his own freedom, and indeed of being *abandoned* by God in the sense that he is left to make his own decisions and to act as he sees best. In the general Catholic, and in Greene's own particular, view of man, to be made in God's image means that human beings are to some degree capable of cognition, free will and projective activity and are recognisable as human beings precisely because of these attributes, which can produce a movement towards wholeness perhaps hindered by our selfishness and blindness but which can nevertheless be recognised and fostered. This is the sense of the words of Fr Rivas in *The Honorary Consul* when, in the shantytown in which he and his revolutionary companions are holding their kidnapped victim he describes the Church as being 'the world, this barrio, this room'. It is because as a man, a Catholic and a priest he can see God's image in all men, and consequently their human stature and dignity despite their degradation in the harsh conditions of Latin America, that he has decided, as a free human being (and not as God's puppet), to take extreme action in order to bring about conditions in which those qualities can flourish rather than atrophy. Although the circumstances are very different, the same perception lies behind Sarah's wish to escape from selfishness and her desire to love others for themselves. She knows that if she loves God, she will love His creatures, those other selves who are both not him and yet like him:

> Let me think of the strawberry-mark on Richard's face. Let me see Henry's face with the tears falling. Let me forget me, Dear God, I've tried to love you and have made such a hash of it. If I could love you, I'd know how to love them (Greene, *The End of the Affair*, 1959, 143-144).

She approaches this state, kissing Smythe's birthmark, beginning to understand her separation from Bendrix and asking God to give him her peace. The love of God can also, as Monsignor Quixote knows, lead to that most difficult achievement, the love of oneself. This is the sense of his instinctive reaction when he fears, wrongly and comically, that he is about to be shot by a secret policeman, and wants it to be in the back of the neck, not in the face, 'for the face in its way is the mirror image of God' (Greene, *Monsignor Quixote*, 1982, 113).

Love and knowledge, as has been suggested above, or sometimes love and the desire for knowledge and understanding, are closely related in the novels. There is often a potential or actual link between the perception of another human being as a self and love for that other person. Carlyon, in *The Man Within*, sees this kind of love as being exemplified in a woman's love for a man. Only a woman, he says, can love a real person (as distinct from, presumably, an idealised or romanticised concept of one). It is worth noting, however, that his own relationship with Andrews shows something of the same insights and attitudes. Bendrix too is aware of the link between knowledge and love. He knows that Sarah has known him in many ways, and has loved him for what he is, without illusions and with total honesty, and is humbled and wondering when faced with the realisation:

> It's a strange thing to discover and to believe that you are loved, when you know that there is nothing in you for anybody but a parent or a God to love (Greene, *The End of the Affair*, 1959, 104).

Scobie, watching his wife, feels that love desires knowledge and without it cannot last, cannot in any profound sense, really be:

> When he was young he had thought love had something to do with understanding, but with age he knew that no human being understood another. Love was the wish to understand, and presently with constant failure the wish died, and love died too or perhaps changed into this painful affection, loyalty, pity (Greene, *The Heart of the Matter*, 1951, 308).

This is perhaps not quite the declaration of the impossibility of love he takes it to be. Total love and total understanding are both beyond the powers of human beings to achieve, but imperfect love can subsist, roughly and sporadically reappearing, along with imperfect knowledge and understanding. Only a relationship in which the total truth of another person was perceived and understood would satisfy Scobie, and his love for Louise, if imperfect, is nevertheless real. At times, at least, it goes beyond an agglomeration of the secondary feelings he mentions, although they are components of it. Like all absolutes, absolute love is impossible for human beings in their earthly life. Like all human desires and efforts, the desire and effort to love and understand is doomed to a greater or lesser extent to failure, and to realise this is part of any human experience in such matters. Also like all human efforts, however, it has its partial and temporary successes, and there are moments when, in Scobie's case, these are visible. To feel the absence of a good is to value that good, and this is in effect what happens both here and in other situations in the novels. Even as the circumference of awareness expands, the surrounding area of ignorance becomes more clearly seen.

Knowledge and understanding can never be complete, and the realisation that there are areas - chronological, social, domestic, sexual - of the beloved's life which will always lie outside the lover's knowledge becomes sharper. Bendrix sums up such an awareness:

There are times when a lover longs also to be a father and a brother: he is jealous of the years he hasn't shared (Greene, *The End of the Affair*, 1959, 21 1).

The idea of the link between love and knowledge is even more apparent when a relationship is viewed from the outside. From an external viewpoint, the question is even more confused, the situation even more difficult to understand, particularly when one or both of the partners is apparently unattractive and even unlikeable. In such cases, the love is incomprehensible to outsiders precisely because it is based on a knowledge which they do not share. Fowler, reflecting on Vigot, the *Sûreté* officer who 'so strangely loved his wife, who ignored him, a flashy and false blonde', realizes that it is impossible to love without intuition, that is, without the direct knowledge, understanding and acceptance of the fact and nature of another self. For the onlooker, who does not share these insights, Vigot's love is inexplicable. Such knowledge of the reality of another person is also the essence of the perhaps slightly romantic but not unconvincing relationship between Elizabeth and Andrews in *The Man Within*. From the early pages of the novel, the girl emerges as a person. The young man is with her 'as in the presence of a mystery'. She, in her turn, senses something of his own complexity, which lies behind the misleading simplicity of the concept Andrews has of himself, and sees him as someone who 'forgot his own details (...) believed himself a coward and nothing else'. Both of them are aware of the contrast between random superficial character and the essential and real inner self, and see that the former represents no more than a schematisation, and hence a simplification, of the latter.

LOVE, SEXUALITY AND LUST

Parallel with this reflection on the interrelationship between love and knowledge there runs a constant stream of meditation on the nature of love itself. Here, one of Greene's major themes is an awareness of the exclusive, partial and consequently falsifying nature of almost any observation that can be made about it. Love, it is implied in the novels, may be this, or that or the other, but is not solely and exclusively any one of them. In *The End of the Affair*, Sarah's reaction to Smythe's rationalist explanation of human and divine love can perhaps be taken as the essence of what Greene has to say here. When the proselytising free-thinker has exhausted his catalogue of all the definitions of love (the desire to possess, to surrender, to shrug off responsibility, to be admired, to find a confessor, a father, a mother, to fulfil biological instincts), her response is to feel that all this is true, but that it does not go far enough. She has sensed all that in herself and Bendrix, but there is always something else; the spade has not yet touched rock. Love is more complex and lasting than many people can imagine. Its durability is constantly examined and evaluated by many different characters, and many interpretations of these reflections are possible. Bendrix's statement to Henry epitomises one of the basic desires of the lovers in Greene's novels ('I wanted love to go on, never to get less') is met by the latter's cautious, decent, moderate, commonsense reply, 'it's not in human nature. One has to be satisfied', which is the opposite of what Sarah is later to say (and which may be Greene's final considered view, if we remember the closing paragraph of *Monsignor Quixote*) namely, that 'Love doesn't end'.

Its durability, however, may well be linked to its relationship with other factors, notably with a concept of human beings as in some way aware of God. For Sarah, love can continue, despite separation, in other ways and in other modes than those of the immediate sexual relationship or in the memory of the ghost of that relationship. She feels that if she loves God, she will love others more and not less. Bendrix and Scobie try to exclude an awareness of God from human love, the former towards the end of *The End of the Affair*, the latter at specific moments in *The Heart of the Matter*. Both of them see God as an impediment to love for a human being, an external factor making demands incompatible with those of human love, whilst Sarah finally sees that meeting them is necessary if human love is not to fail. In such cases, what Bendrix has earlier called 'the winning cards - the cards of gentleness, humility and trust' have to be played in a different manner from the one he had envisaged if the end of love, where 'there is never victory: only a few minor tactical successes before the final defeat of death or indifference' and 'insecurity is the worst sense that lovers feel (...) in a beleaguered city, every sentinel is a potential traitor' is to be avoided.

Love is so inextricably mixed up with so many other emotions and relationships in Greene's novels (pity, a sense of responsibility, understanding, belief in God) that it is easy to lose sight of the underlying factor common to all such feelings and ways of seeing things, which is a lived awareness of another person's own and separate humanity. Nowhere is this more clearly expressed than by Scobie, talking to Helen in one of their wearied, wearying encounters, where he sees the implications of their adulterous relationship clearly and she 'uttering phrases read in how many books' does not. There is only one real, very simple and basic reason why he is prepared to make great sacrifices (even that of his work, which means a great deal to him) for her sake: 'I suppose because you are a human being'. By virtue of her perceived selfhood, she has tremendous claims on his time, emotions and attention.

Such relationships, as Sarah sees, are much more complicated than Smythe's account of human love, and infinitely more subtle than any exclusively sexual explanation. This idea is apparent as early as *The Man Within*, when Andrews compares the attraction of Lucy ('no love and no reverence (...) the added spice of reciprocal desire') with the feelings of 'mystery' and 'sanctity' which 'blurred and obscured his desire with love' aroused in him by Elizabeth. Although he himself is not mature, experienced, perceptive or articulate enough to analyse and understand such feelings fully, they are clearly akin to those of later and older lovers such as Bendrix or Scobie who can begin to do so. The former can say that his passion for Sarah had destroyed simple lust forever, and that he would never again be able to enjoy a woman without love; the latter, urged by Helen not to bother about consequences and to abandon caution, recognises in her bitter words ('the hard swearing of the netball team') the dependent, helpless and despairing child that she is. In all three cases, isolated sexuality is insufficient. Once a possible or actual relationship which includes other aspects of personality has been achieved or imagined as a potentiality, the exclusively sexual is relegated to a lesser place. However major a role fornication and adultery may appear to play in Greene's novels, they are no more than stages on the way to other kinds of relationships, which may include them but which in a real sense go beyond them. There is in fact a constant diminishing of the human importance of purely sexual attraction *in isolation*. In some novels, in fact, its insignificance is stressed. In *The Honorary Consul*, for example, a meal shared, it is suggested, is more intimate than the sexual act and sexual attraction is often provoked by the insignificant and trivial. Where it is not merely symptomatic, transient lust can be instantly and tragically destructive, as in *The Power and the Glory*, where once, 'seven years ago, for five minutes' the priest had sinned and 'a whole world had died'. It is the isolation of sexuality from other aspects of the human psyche that created lust, which is dehumanised desire. Because it is not fully human, it is in the novels at best second-rate and at worst repulsive. In Greene's fiction, those who have achieved a certain maturity recognise it for what it is, have an idea of its nature, and can see it objectively and dispassionately. Others, who are more impressionable and vulnerable, are appalled by it. That is what lies, in *Brighton Rock*, behind Pinkie's extreme and destructive puritanism. The 'Saturday night gymnastics' of his parents and his own 'horrified virginity', the prick of sexual desire which disturbed him 'like a sickness', his recollection of Annie Collis, pregnant twice before she was fifteen, his vow to be a priest 'to keep away from all this', and his sudden articulateness when describing, with fascinated horror, sado-masochistic pornography and sentimental love stories, are all produced by a sensitivity which is doing no more than recoil, albeit violently, from incompletely human feelings and the distortion of the natural.

His obsession drives him to destroy both Rose, who is good and human, and himself. What might have been a holy awe or a sense of compassion becomes a hatred - *corruptio optimi pessima* -

and the blighting of natural reticence and modesty produces an impaired and incomplete human being. This partly external and partly internal distortion of a cluster of emotions and desires, in which an adolescent sensitivity to the powerful and apparently overwhelming and dehumanising blindness of immediate physical desire dominates all other aspects of human sexuality, produces a serious imbalance in Pinkie. Its symptoms may be morbid, but the reaction itself, in Greene's eyes, is not basically unhealthy. The wounded psyche takes refuge in flight, and towards the end of the novel there are signs that some kind of healing process might be beginning. At one level, the earlier, simple description of his relationship with Rose ('She was good ... and he was damned. They were made for each other') is still apparently valid, but at another, that of their unity and love, where Rose can see the child in him and he himself has some perception that the world he has wanted to destroy is the world in which and for which God himself suffered, it is no longer accurate.

But the child whose life has been blighted by too early, too close and too limited a view of sexuality is not the only, although he is the most powerful, Greenean archetype. Through the eyes of certain adult characters who, whatever their failings, have a certain sensitivity and intelligence, Greene shows the reader a brief glimpse of limited and limiting sexual relationships. Scobie and Fowler are clearly far from perfect human beings, but at least they have, to varying degrees, some understanding of the complexity of human life. They can see that only the emotionally crippled or psychologically hemitrophied such as Bagster in *The Heart of the Matter* or Granger in *The Quiet American*, (whose deepest sexual experience was copulating with a Chinese woman and Negress together in a Saigon brothel) can really live with lust as an isolated phenomenon. In *The Honorary Consul*, even the smooth and disillusioned Eduardo Plarr, womaniser and connoisseur of whores, can see that, 'in a real love affair ... you are interested in a woman because she is someone distinct from you' and his reflections on the code of etiquette used in the brothel indicate that this distinction between genuine and feigned sexual relationships is generally recognised. Fowler's need for fidelity, Scobie's pity, Bendrix's increase in love for Sarah as he finds out more about her inner life highlight a major theme in Greene's novels: if sexuality is restricted to the satisfaction of simple and immediate physiological excitement, to the epidermal and neural, it is not enough to satisfy a fuller humanity. It is only meaningful as part of a wider relationship in which two human beings learn to know, love and respect each other. This relationship may in particular cases be impossible to achieve, as it is to varying degrees and in different ways with Pinkie, Scobie, and Bendrix, but it is potentially one in which human beings become more rather than less human. Pinkie is horrified by all sexuality because he sees it as inhuman; Scobie and Bendrix reject a restricted sexuality and need a more human kind, that glimpsed in Monsignor Quixote's reaction to the audience at the soft-porn movie he accidentally sees in Valladolid, when he 'longed for one of them to laugh - even you, Sancho - so that I could laugh too' (Greene, *Monsignor Quixote*, 1982, 120).

PAIN AND SUFFERING

In Greene's novels, the situation of the individual is part of the overall human situation, his experience part of that of mankind in general. More often than not, both of these are largely unsatisfactory, vitiated by original and actual sin. The description in *The Power and the Glory* of the prison cell which the priest shares with other outcasts and misfits offers an image, in its starkest form, of the world of Greene:

> This place was like the world: overcrowded with lust and crime and unhappy love: it stank to heaven, but he realised that after all it was possible to find peace there, when you knew that the time was short (Greene, *The Power and the Glory*, 1959, 161).

Even Fellows, who restricts his ambitions to his desire for 'a life of ease, safety, tolerance and complacency', is aware of the dangers which life holds for his daughter and of the anxiety inseparable from love for any other human being: 'You cannot control what you love - you watch it driving recklessly towards the broken bridge, the torn-up track, the horrors of seventy years ahead' (Greene, *The Power and the Glory*, 1959, 51) and knows that her present innocence and happiness are doomed: 'Life hadn't got at her yet; she had a false air of impregnability'. It is a world in which we, whatever our views, must at times accept the dreadful, the unthinkable. The priest in *The Power and the Glory* now no longer feels much as he consumes the body and blood of God in a state of mortal sin ('but life breeds its excuses'). It is also one in which the human environment is so bleak and grey that indifferent or hostile nature, even in the tropics, is less perhaps drearily repellent than what human beings have created for themselves:

> The ATS or the WAAF, the blustering sergeant with the big bust, the cookhouse with the potato peelings, the Lesbian officer with the thin lips and the tidy gold hair, the men waiting on the common outside the camp, among the gorse bushes ... (Greene, *The Heart of the Matter*, 1951, 87).

In it, happiness often seems to be either the result of ignorance and selfishness or is a second best alternative to changelessness, (a theme stated and developed by Greene on many occasions) and apparent safety is no more than an illusion, 'the camouflage of an enemy who works in terms of friendship, trust and pity'. Pain, reflects Scobie, pain inflicted and pain suffered, is inevitable in any human relationship. If one avoids it once, twice, it will be offered again a third time and will be inescapable ('to be human, one had to drink the cup'), in his case, to watch the child die and to be unable to bear her suffering. In the words of the Superior of the mission to Querry, the burnt-out case who maintains that he can no longer feel anything, 'suffering is something which will always be provided when it is required'. It will always be possible for one's features to acquire the lines that make a human being.

INNOCENCE, SIN AND FREEDOM

There are three other aspects of human experience which shape the material of Greene's novels and thus create an image of the human situation: innocence, sin and freedom. These come into play within a framework provided by certain Catholic ideas concerning the human person which are implicit, sometimes only indirectly or perhaps not at all perceived by the reader, and in some cases perhaps only unconsciously or semiconsciously incorporated by the author himself.

The first of these, innocence, is seen, paradoxically enough, as both destructive and fragile, and in some ways dangerous if it persists. The innocence of children, as has been seen with Coral Fowler, with the Mexican priest's child, with Pinkie and with Helen, is transient and doomed to fade or be effaced. The child is after all, human, a 'jungle of complications' and because he or she is an embryonic adult, there is, says Greene, 'always one moment in childhood when the door opens and lets the future in', a moment which marks the journey towards the lostness typified by Sarah's girlhood. The word can be used in two senses in relation to Greene's work. The first is that of a childlike purity of motive and hence of candour, spontaneity and guiltlessness. In this sense, one could see Monsignor Quixote, Coral Fowler *in The Power and the Glory*, Marie Rycker in *A Burnt-out Case* and the young boy who opens the door to the second priest at the end of *The Power and the Glory* and perhaps even the lieutenant of police in the same novel as being, in their varying ways and to varying degrees, unspoilt human beings. The second is that of a childish and immature unawareness of the implications and probable consequences of a given course of action. It may or may not include the gentleness of the dove, but it certainly does not include the wisdom of the serpent, both of which are counselled for the Christian. Pyle, the quiet American, is of course, the prime example here.

There is little that can be profitably said about the first kind of innocence, except that it appears intermittently in the novels, that there is a perception of it and a certain nostalgia for it, and that it resurfaces powerfully in *Monsignor Quixote*. Given the general tone of Greene's writing and his apparent preference for seeing things from the point of view of the black square (Greene, *Why Do I Write?*, 1948, 32) its role is often that of an indicator of what we lose in life. The second kind, however, even when it might have the appearance of evil, is evident to Greene's major characters for what it really is, and attracts a certain amount of comment. The reaction of Scobie, for example, when after an arid discussion with Helen about their affair in relation to his religious beliefs, he is urged by her to go to communion and to assume that one more sin will not make any difference, is characteristic both of the character and of a certain kind of authorial stance adopted by Greene:

He thought: pious people, I suppose, would call this the devil speaking, but he knew that evil never spoke in these crude answerable terms: this was innocence (Greene, *The Heart of the Matter*, 1951, 253).

This protective pity, the result of a confrontation between a certain experience and consequent understanding of the world in one person and lack of sophistication and judgement in the other, is matched in other cases, notably in the attitude which Fowler instinctively adopts towards his new acquaintance, Pyle:

That was my first instinct: to protect him (...) Innocence always calls mutely for protection, when we would be so much wiser to guard ourselves against it: innocence is like a dumb leper who has lost his bell, wandering the world, meaning no harm (Greene, *The Quiet American*, 1956, 40).

No doubt a harder-hearted Scobie would also have echoed the wisdom of Fowler's hindsight.

In the novels, the innocent adult of this kind may be guiltless, but he is not harmless. Pyle, because he is gentle but not wise, destroys those around him. Fowler's later comment on him, at the scene of the explosion in Saigon which Pyle has made possible, amid the mangled bodies of women and children, echoes and amplifies the earlier one:

He looked white and beaten and ready to faint, and I thought, 'What's the good? He'll always be innocent, you can't blame the innocent, they are always guiltless. All you can do is control them or eliminate them. Innocence is a kind of insanity' (Greene, *The Quiet American*, 1956, 213).

This is also the way in which, at a totally different level, Bendrix sees Parkis, the incompetent private detective whom he has hired to spy on Sarah: he is another person who, with the best of intentions, will almost certainly do more harm than good. Proud of his son's natural brightness, he is training him inefficiently but conscientiously in his own rather dubious trade and, even worse, has named him Lance, confusing Galahad's quest for the Grail and Lancelot's adultery with Guinevere. The same pity and exasperation are evident as Bendrix wonders why one has the desire to tease the innocent. Is it perhaps from envy? Innocence may seem enviable, but it is in fact intensely dangerous. Pyle wants to encourage the Third Force and National Democracy, Parkis to encourage his son in the way of Truth and Virtue. One gets the blood of women and children on his shoes, the other sets the wrong example to his boy. The response in both cases is the same: 'I didn't know' and 'I hadn't heard'. Guiltlessness and harmlessness are not synonymous in the novels.

The whole question of sin in Greene's work has been raised and discussed elsewhere, perhaps most interestingly in Philip Stratford's comparative study of Greene and Mauriac, *Faith and Fiction*, and less successfully in many others. Despite the angry puzzlement or indulgent condescension with which many critics approach this question, it must in the first place be accepted as a basic fact, a *datum*, of Greene's fiction. Human beings are quite simply seen as eminently capable of moral blindness, wrong desires and actions, and wrong attitudes towards themselves and others. This need not surprise anyone, but it does seem to surprise many readers to find such things in the work of a Catholic who presumably believes that the moral teachings of his faith are to be given due weight. Like most serious novelists, Greene takes heightened situations which both illustrate and intensify those of ordinary life and so encourage a reflection on both fiction and experience. The isolation of a single thread or a group of threads from the total texture of an individual life for aesthetic purposes (Scobie's and Bendrix's adultery, Sarah's move beyond ordinary human love, Querry's emptiness and final absurd end, Fowler's involvement with Pyle) must necessarily, because isolating one element means neglecting others, simplify and therefore to some extent distort the totality. Even the most realistic fiction is art before it is documentary, and this is an idea which must be kept in mind when reflecting on Greene's work. It is probably failure to do so which has produced so much of the adverse comment on it. If Pinkie's despair and the Mexican priest's moral weakness are primarily and in the widest sense of the word artistic devices, they must be judged as such, and in the framework in which they are relevant (that of Catholic belief) rather than simply as moral problems or as illustrations of what one critic has called 'frustrations that result from local or social personal prejudices' (Weightman, 1973, 275). Sin is ubiquitous in Greene's novels, pervasive, ancient, inevitable, dreary in its sameness, whether it is at the level of the Bagsters, the Parkinsons, the Grangers of this world, the level of surrender to a debased sexuality, or that of the Mexican priest, Scobie, Sarah, the level of a deeper infidelity, or that of Pinkie, Querry or Eduardo Plarr, the level of refusal and despair. The priest in *The Power and the Glory* has something to say about most kinds. In the hut with the *mestizo*, unable to avoid the latter's shambling and repellent confession, the 'awful jumble of the gross, the trivial and the grotesque', he reflects on the sameness of sin, of whatever particular kind it may be, and the need for any love capable of including human sinfulness to be enormous and all-embracing:

> How often the priest had heard the same confession - Man was so limited; he hadn't even the ingenuity to invent a new sin: the animals knew as much (..) it was too easy to die for what was good or beautiful (...) it needed a God to die for the half-hearted and the corrupt (Greene, *The Power and the Glory*, 1959, 123-124).

He also knows that the danger of sin is that it is a dehumanising process which can finally cut off the personality from God, the source of its own full humanity, so that it withers and dies, and we become the unreflecting slaves of random sensation and undirected impulse. Without the supernatural, the natural disintegrates. This is the whole message of the doctrine of original sin and its continuing manifestation in actual sin, and it is implicit in the priest's reflection on the cumulative effects of wrong actions: 'One day they would choke up, he supposed, altogether the source of grace' (Greene, *The Power and the Glory*, 1959, 74). It would be wrong to assume, he sees, that it is only the grosser and more readily-visible sins which can cause this. Faced with the lieutenant of police and his own portrait as a wanted criminal on the wall in the *jefe*'s office, he thinks about his past, his narrowness and self-righteousness as a young (and innocent) man and reflects that, surprisingly perhaps, it might well be the most venial sins which do the most harm:

What an unbearable creature he must have been in those days and yet in those days he had been comparatively innocent.

That was another mystery: it sometimes seemed to him that venial sins - impatience, an unimportant lie, a neglected opportunity - cut you off from grace more completely than the worst sin of all. Then, in his innocence, he had felt no love for anyone: now, in his corruption, he had learnt... (Greene, *The Power and the Glory*, 1959, 179-80).

This is not, as Pryce-Jones, for example, has suggested, simply Greene being personal and paradoxical and superimposing the symbols of Catholicism on a pre-existing vision (Pryce-Jones, 1963, 100). In the Catholic tradition, pharisaism, coldness, a purely formal acquiescence to doctrine, lack of charity and the conviction of one's own rectitude have always been seen as manifestations of one kind of condemnable pride. The pharisee who thanked God that he was not as others is an abiding image in it. But the lost sheep, the tears of Mary Magdalene, the repentant thief on the cross, are also numbered among its powerful symbols. When Greene says that the greater the sin, the greater the scope for grace and forgiveness, he is not simply uttering a personal feeling, however important that feeling may (or may not) have been in both his personal and his artistic life. It is a conviction which is in accordance with age-old Catholic doctrine, and even if his novels are personal and imaginative interpretations of what he believed life had shown him, they are also in a sense reflections of what the Catholic sees as revealed truth. It is legitimate to reject both the personal vision and the doctrine, to find both equally unsatisfactory or illusory, but not to play one off against the other.

The importance of these observations in the present context is that in Greene's novels the perception by a character of his own weakness and sinfulness marks a shift both in his own way of seeing himself and of knowing and relating to others. Here, the almost perverse blindness of the blameless but foolish is in striking contrast to the insights achieved by the guilty but lucid. Foolishness cannot damn, but neither can it enlighten. The gifts of lucidity are achieved at the price of anguish and loss. Suffering is not gratuitous in the novels, for it brings with it some kind of apparent or surmised perception. Bendrix sees and loves Sarah in a new and deeper way, the Mexican priest sees his experience and that of others in a new light, and Querry, despite the emptiness of his life and the apparent absurdity of his death at Rycker's hands, is on the way to a new relationship with other human beings. Pinkie's last thoughts are full of love for Rose, and Scobie's death is marked by charity. Quixote's prayer 'O God, make me human, let me feel temptation, save me from indifference' is the result of a meditation on whether or not he is capable of human love, for if he is not, he must also be incapable of love for God. All have learnt something: that understanding is impossible without charity which, St Paul tell us, is a greater virtue than even hope and faith. It is perhaps not too much to suggest that what they finally see in their own way is their fellow human beings, through those few whom they have come to love fully and to understand better as persons, other selves, as important, as worthy, as of the same weight and dignity, as themselves. Whether they are African lepers, Mexican half-castes, criminals, housewives or cuckolded husbands, their dignity and worth are great not because they are God's puppets but because they are images of Him.

What the Mexican priest learned during the course of *The Power and the Glory*, by seeing others as he saw himself and himself as he saw others, was the mutual responsibility which human beings have for each other, a responsibility 'indistinguishable from love'. This comes from a perception that with his fellow human beings he shared an existential situation in which he would be left to get on with his task alone. For him, there are few of the 'consolations of religion'. God remains a hidden God, abandoning him to the here and now, the world of innocence and guilt, sin and conscious responsibility:

> God had decided. He had to go on with his life, go on making decisions, acting on his own advice, making plans (Greene, *The Power and the Glory*, 1959, 179).

He sees that the existential world will be with him throughout his life, will in a sense be part of him, and that he must be a part of it. Like him, Scobie also perceives the hereness of here and the nowness of now, and knows that he must make what he can of them, relying on his own resources, knowing that they are vitiated and knowing too that he must bear the responsibility for the consequences of his acts:

Was it the butterfly that died in the act of love? But human beings were condemned to consequences. The responsibility as well as the guilt was his (Greene, *The Heart of the Matter*, 1951, 192).

Like both of them, Andrews in *The Man Within*, that early sketch for later Greenean heroes, is left by Elisabeth 'as all the world seemed to leave him, to make his own decisions', abandoned to a world in which all human beings face the same predicaments and the same dilemmas. In this respect, however, Greene's characters are treated with a little more indulgence than those of the existentialist writer as epitomised by Sartre. Acts may count, but human beings will always be too weak to be consistent existentialist heroes. The acts which they commit will be regretted, their will will fail, their determination weaken. As Scobie reflects:

Human beings couldn't be heroic all the time ... (they) must be allowed sometimes in thought to take back their surrender. So many had never committed the heroic act, however rashly. It was the act that counted (Greene, *The Heart of the Matter*, 1951, 279-280).

A GLIMPSE OF ANOTHER DIMENSION

Parallel to this sense of the weakness, obtuseness and existential isolation of humanity, however, there is sometimes the certitude and more often the suspicion that outside our time, perhaps in the glimpses of the possibility of eternity which Sarah awakes in Bendrix, for example, there are forces at work which even in our moments of greatest lucidity we can only dimly sense. It is against this background that Greene's ideas of human nature should be seen. Passages such as that in which Bendrix reflects on the (for him still hypothetical) roles of God and the Devil in human life clearly suggests a second way of seeing things:

I have never understood why people who can swallow the enormous improbability of a personal God boggle at a personal Devil. I have known so intimately the way that demon works in my imagination. No statement that Sarah ever made was proof against his cunning doubts, though he would usually wait till she had gone to utter them. He would prompt our quarrels long before they occurred: he was not Sarah's enemy so much as the enemy of love, and isn't that what the devil is supposed to be? I can imagine that if there existed a God who loved, the devil would be driven to destroy even the weakest, the most faulty imitation of that love. Wouldn't he be afraid that the habit of love might grow, and wouldn't he trap us all into being traitors, into helping him extinguish love? If there is a God who uses us and makes his saints out of such material as we are, the devil may have his ambitions; he may dream of turning even such a person as myself, even poor Parkis, into being his saints, ready with borrowed fanaticism to destroy love wherever we find it (Greene, *The End of the Affair*, 1959, 67-68).

It is perhaps because of this sense of parallel lives, or rather of one life, lived simultaneously both in the here and now and beneath the gaze of eternity, that some critics have seen the theological dimension of the novels as imposed and extrinsic. The truth is perhaps rather that as well as being a teller of tales and a master of cinematic technique, Greene is also, like many novelists of the nineteenth and twentieth centuries, a writer in whose fiction the discursive and reflective dimensions potentially present in the portrayal of contemporary human life play a large part. In some of his work, notably the 'entertainments', reflection, musing, pondering on the ultimate questions of human nature and human destiny is eschewed in favour of direct portrayal, whereas in others, notably the 'four or five books' in which he 'took characters with Catholic ideas for his material', (Greene, *In Search of a Character*, 1961, 26), that reflection is woven inextricably into the thought-processes of the major characters. A stream of consciousness is notable for what it contains rather than for what it excludes, and it seems scarcely surprising that novels which have Catholic or potentially Catholic heroes and heroines of some intelligence and sensibility should be forced by their circumstances to reflect on Catholic ideas, practices and beliefs.

The inclusion of such material may in part be an attempt to heighten dramatic tension or impart a particular colour and flavour to fictional events, but those reflections are in a deeper sense part of the matter of the novels themselves, since they belong to the mental world of the characters who make it up. Scobie without his tortured faith or Louise without her suburban religious conformity would not be themselves. Pinkie without his sexual and religious neuroses, Leon Rivas without his revolutionary extension of Catholic ideas, Bendrix without his waning hesitation, his irony and his imaginative understanding of Sarah's faith, or Monsignor Quixote without his sharp distinction between belief and faith, would be different characters in different novels. Given Greene's Catholicism and the matter of his fiction, religion is an inescapable component of those books in which he reflects on the varieties of response to the problems of whether God exists or cares and how we live or should live. Questions and answers concerning the value of human life, its purposes, needs, ends and nature, and posed in Catholic terms, are in a very real sense part of the fundamental and recurring features of his imaginative landscape.

The cases in which such reflection is overt and more or less fully conscious are easily discernible. There are, however, times when even the seemingly purely visceral reactions of characters who might be seen, perhaps superficially, as rather stupid and by no means reflective also indicate the extent to which Greene's fiction is permeated at all levels by the portrayal of human desires and needs which, if not Catholic in the strictest sense, are precisely those desires and needs which Catholicism would claim to meet. Whether the reader sees Catholic doctrine as comforting illusions arising from a compulsion to seek an explanatory and consoling faith or as sober and objective truth is for critical purposes largely immaterial. What is important is that even in the case of characters who present all the symptoms of a total invincible ignorance, and in contexts in which Catholicism is never apparently considered or even named, there is a situation in which a reading of the text in the light of one's understanding of Catholic doctrine and belief is potentially enlightening. This can be seen by a brief examination of an incident in which an apparently radically different view of life, which both suggests its own incompleteness and, paradoxically its fundamental kinship to the cluster of emotions and ideas incorporated in Catholic belief, is indicated. In it there are desires to have life and have it more abundantly which for the Catholic are doomed to frustration outside Catholicism. Ida Arnold, in *Brighton Rock*, knows what she wants, and knows what is not satisfactory. Lost in thought at Hale's cremation, she suggests at the immediately perceivable level one way, which she sees as clearly incomplete and unsatisfactory, of looking at human existence and human nature, and at the same time, by unconscious implication and by unknowingly stressing their absence, she suggests the more satisfying beliefs of Catholicism. The anodyne sermon comes to an end, the clergyman smiles gently, and Ada reflects as follows:

> It was all over. Ida squeezed out with difficulty a last tear into a handkerchief scented with Californian Poppy. She liked a funeral - but it was with horror - as other people like a ghost story. Death shocked her, life was so important. She wasn't religious. She didn't believe in heaven or hell, only in ghosts, ouija boards, tables which rapped and little inept voices speaking plaintively of flowers. Let Papists treat death with flippancy: life wasn't so important to them as what came after: but to her, death was the end of everything. At one with the One - it didn't mean a thing beside a glass of Guinness on a sunny day. She believed in ghosts, but you couldn't call that thin transparent existence life eternal: the squeak of a board, a piece of ectoplasm in a glass cupboard at the psychical research headquarters, a voice she's heard once at a seance saying, 'Everything is very beautiful on the upper plane. There are flowers everywhere.'
>
> Flowers, Ida thought scornfully; that wasn't life. Life was sunlight on brass bedposts, Ruby port, the leap of the heart when the outsider you have backed passes the post and the colours go bobbing up. Life was poor Fred's mouth pressed down on hers in the taxi, vibrating with the engine along the parade. What was the sense of dying if it made you babble of flowers? Fred didn't want

flowers, he wanted - and the enjoyable distress she had felt in Heneky's returned. She took life with a deadly seriousness: she was prepared to cause any amount of unhappiness to anyone in order to defend the only thing she believed in. To lose your lover – 'broken hearts', she would say, 'always mend', to be maimed or blinded – 'lucky', she would tell you, 'to be alive at all'. There was something dangerous and remorseless in her optimism, whether she was laughing in Heneky's or weeping at a funeral or a marriage.

She came out from the crematorium and there from the twin towers above her head fumed the very last of Fred, a thin streak of grey smoke from the ovens. People passing up the flowery suburban roads looked up and noted the smoke; it had been a busy day at the furnaces. Fred dropped in indistinguishable grey ash on the pink bloss-soms: he became part of the smoke nuisance over London, and Ida wept (Greene, *Brighton Rock*, 1970, 39-40).

Ida wept not because she was a mystic, a seer, a rare soul with special and privileged insights, not because she was a Catholic saint (or even a Catholic sinner), but because she was an ordinary woman, a human being with all the desires and needs of a human being. She needs a view of the importance of human life and of its continuation in a meaningful way, something beyond the temporary resilience and optimism which is all that what she knows can give her, a dimension which she can guess at but which she does not know or understand. In short, she needs all the sense of the importance and status of the human being which only the Incarnation, the Redemption and - at this particular time, in this particular place, in these particular circumstances - the Resurrection of Christ and of the individual human body can give her. Religious aspirations and reflection need not, it would seem, be fully conscious or even moderately systematic in the novels. They are there, and part of the full, if often frustrated, humanity of the characters. They are present in all men and women and occur in all sorts of direct, indirect, or sometimes underground ways. Catholicism is less important as an ideological embellishment to the fiction than as the expression of the only view of man that can make us more fully aware of our humanity and show us how to accept it properly. It was no doubt such an idea, and one set of implications that can be drawn from it, that Martin Green had in mind when, in Yeats's *Blessings on von Hügel,* he attacked Catholic literature so wrathfully (Green, 1967). The suspicion that there is in it a suggestion that Catholicism is a kind of exclusive club for those who know what life is all about and what people are really like is understandable if perhaps not fully justifiable. Opinion here will of course be based on personal reactions and interpretations and it is as difficult to refute such a view as it is to sustain it. To offer Ida Arnold or Bendrix as examples of characters who are not Catholics and who are nevertheless treated with some sympathy and understanding is to invite the observation that it is only to the extent that they begin to perceive, however dimly, the desirability, necessity or rightness of such views that they are presented in that way. One could perhaps more convincingly offer the case of the lieutenant of police in *The Power and the Glory* who, although he is philosophically and ideologically intransigently opposed to all that the hunted priest, and presumably Greene, stand for, is still shown as a man of charity, compassion and intellectual honesty. It is true that certain characters do sometimes recognize their shared Catholicism with a sense of ease and mutual comprehension, as happens, for example during the meeting of Scobie and the Portuguese captain of the *Esperança,* when the latter reacts 'like a man who meets a fellow-countryman in a strange continent'. To share terms of reference with another does not, however, necessarily imply the exclusiveness of those terms. It simply means that they are shared. To recognize that a certain human being understands one's language and shares one's basic ideas does not necessarily imply a view of the inferiority of other human beings, of other languages or of other attitudes, merely a realization that both those concerned understand each other better than others can understand them. For Greene, Catholicism is a club to which anyone can belong - Mexican Indians, British colonial officials, the wives of Whitehall civil servants, Vietnamese housewives, South American revolutionaries. It is for the poor and ignorant, the rich and sophisticated, the worldly and the naive. Men and women of any ideological persuasion can find comfort in the knowledge that their ideas and feelings are shared by others, and whatever part of vanity or superiority there might be in the recognition of a supposed superior truth or rightness in those ideas and feelings may well be a tendency which is attributable to human beings in general. To attribute it solely to Catholics perhaps says as much about the unsympathetic critic as about Greene. To derive comfort from a shared metaphysical or religious view, if it is sincerely and honestly held, is not a very serious offence, but to see others as incapable of understanding or accepting that comfort perhaps is. If one decides that Greene is guilty of suggesting a superior Catholic exclusiveness, one is judging him not on the fact but on the quality of his Catholicism, for if that assessment is valid, it is a judgement primarily on what could be seen as a heretical if hardly rare distortion of Catholicism and the ideas it contains. As a counterbalance, however, there is the whole weight of the all-embracing (catholic?) inclusiveness of *Monsignor Quixote*, in which all men and women are children of God, Marx is a loving, nostalgic and often slightly erroneous prophet, and full humanity is the supreme good.

THE PRIORITIES OF RELIGION

The whole question of the comforting and consoling aspect of religious belief is often touched upon, but no more than touched upon, in Greene's novels. Sarah represents a more conscious version of Ida, and like her reflects on the resurrection of the body. She explores the twin desires to be rid of it and to perpetuate it, and concludes, with an almost certainly unconscious Thomist orthodoxy, that humanity disincarnate is a contradiction in terms. Smythe and Bendrix argue about the last lingering effects of religious belief, with the latter saying that he believes in nothing at all, except now and then in moments of hope. What is more striking and more consistently present in Greene's fiction is an awareness of the difficulty of the implications of faith. It can, for example, easily remain at the level of mere religiosity, or lapse into it. *The Power and the Glory* has many scenes in which the doggedness of the faith of the hunted priest is contrasted with the piety of many of his fellow-countrymen who have still retained habits of practice during the systematic persecution existing around them. These pious practices are treated with some asperity by Greene, even if there is an element of pity in his treatment. For him, Catholicism is essentially a rather tough business. It is not, for example, the decorous little girls piously listening to their mother reading the account of the life of young Juan, sitting 'with beadily intense eyes, drinking in sweet piety,' absorbing the reading 'intently, framing in their minds little pious sentences with which to surprise their parents' who will, the reader is left to assume, greatly further the work of the re-evangelization of their state. It is their brother, rubbing his head impatiently on the whitewashed wall, squashing beetles on the floor and longing for the last chapter in which young Juan will die against a wall shouting '*Vivo el Cristo Rey!*' who at the end of the novel lets into the house the tall, pale, thin man with the rather sour mouth, the priest who will be the next martyr to be hunted down by the lieutenant of police.

In Greene's novels, holiness and faith are of greater importance for human beings than piety. The latter, where it is not grounded in more important virtues, can indeed be counter-productive in the sense that it can thrive to the detriment of charity and understanding. The piety of Rycker in *A Burnt-out Case* or of Louise in *The Heart of the Matter* is in fact to some extent bogus, an affair of externals. Because it does not engage their deepest selves it distorts and destroys rather than enhances their own lives and that of others. Rycker causes Querry's death, and Louise forces Scobie to sacrilege. Rather than a set of external practices and forms of words to be used as a protection against the harshness and complexity of his existence, Greene's human being needs, if he is to make any sense of his life, a way of thinking and imagining which offers him cleansing and restoration to his full and responsible humanity. Existentially, such holiness remains a dimly-perceived notion and is more often discernible by its absence than by its presence. Each individual life is unique, each individual experience intensely personal and incommunicable despite shared circumstances. Birth, childhood, love and death are the lot of all, but all are experienced differently.

The individual, in Greene's view, is both one of many and totally unique. His ways of sensing the potential fullness of his own life are different from those of any other individual. In each case, however, holiness means being himself in the completeness of his being. This is what Bendrix sees when, thinking of those characters in his novels who are unspontaneous and dragging, and who will not come alive, he goes on to reflect on the freedom and initiative of the saints and the dullness of the rest of us:

> Always I find when I begin to write that there is one character who obstinately will not come alive. There is nothing psychologically false about him, but he sticks, he has to be pushed around, words have to be found for him, all the technical skill I have acquired through the laborious years has to be employed in making him appear alive to my readers. Sometimes I get a sour satisfaction when a reviewer praises him as the best drawn character in the story: if he has not been drawn he has certainly been dragged. He lies heavily on my mind whenever I start to work, like an ill-digested meal on the stomach, robbing me of the pleasure of creation in any scene where he is present. He never does the unexpected thing, he never surprises me, he never takes charge. Every other character helps, he only hinders. And yet one cannot do without him. I can imagine a God feeling just that way about some of us. The saints, one would suppose, in a sense create themselves. They come alive. They are capable of the surprising act or word. They stand outside the plot, unconditioned by it. But we have to be pushed around. We have the obstinacy of non-existence. We are inextricably bound to the plot, and wearily God forces us, here and there, according to his intention, characters without poetry, without free will, whose only importance is that somewhere, at some time, we help to furnish the scene in which a living character moves and speaks, providing perhaps the saints with opportunities for their free will (Greene, *The End of the Affair*, 1959, 229).

It is interesting to note that in Bendrix's eyes, sanctity is a positive rather than a negative state, and is characterized by qualities indicative of an increased rather than a diminished humanity. What marks off the saints from the majority of men is the ability to choose freely, to be to a high degree unconditioned by external events and pressures and to have a heightened quality of being. Such people are more fully themselves, more like what we instinctively feel a human being should be, fuller of freedom and poetry. What they feel, think and do may not be very different from what anyone might feel, think or do, but because their lives are lived more consciously and fully, they have in them a dimension which is often lacking in human life in general, a quality of rightness, fittingness and integrity in some way going beyond the probity which it clearly contains. The attraction of their lives lies in something deeper than the exercise of moral virtue in difficult and demanding situations. What might be called their 'poetry' lies in the fact that what they do or try to do is 'something beautiful for God', and in attempting this they begin to penetrate to what is, or what they feel ought to be, the heart of things. This is how Bendrix untimately sees Sarah's actions, and in spite of his own loss and anguish he can begin to see the rightness and beauty of what she has done. The reader too, because her actions, given her premises, are rationally justifiable, noble and not narrowly self-seeking, can at least accord her a tragic dignity, and perhaps even say, if he has no belief in God, that if holiness exists it must be something like this.

Sarah's case, because it is the most intimately presented (through her diary) and articulately analyzed (by Bendrix, the professional writer), is the fullest study of holiness in Greene's novels, but Rose's devotion to Pinkie, in whom she sees a lost and desperate child, is the most conscious and fully human choice of her young life, and the Mexican priest's decision to go on with his mission to his death, to become in another sense an *alter Christus*, are further examples of the same kind of human freedom and dignity. The Skinnerian echo is not inappropriate here, for if one cannot assume that Greene's characters have freedom, the whole aesthetic structure of the novels collapses. To see them as behaviourist paradigms would make them aesthetically meaningless. That would also be the effect of seeing them as examples of a religious determinism in which God, so to speak, pulls the strings to such an extent that the characters' sole function is to think the thoughts He puts into their minds and knowingly or unknowingly complete the robot-like tasks He sets them. Apart from a traditionally Catholic approach, in which man is seen as free to choose good or evil and to be or to refuse to be an instrument of God's will, only an existentialist or a Marxist reading would seem to be adequate. To put the matter simply, seeing them as doomed to choice in a meaningless world or as free and human in the conscious realization of necessity would still leave them with a stature approaching that granted them by the Catholic view, whereas seeing them as conditioned operants or the representatives of the predestined Elect or the Masses would not. Indeed, it is freedom and concsiousness, to whatever degree they may be perceived and accepted, which for Greene are the preconditions of holiness. Sarah is not holy because she has behaved in prescribed ways or thought prescribed thoughts, but because at some point in her life she has seen her true nature and has decided to live in what she sees as accordance with it. Apparently virtuous predetermined ways of living and thinking, habits and established patterns of behaviour may in fact tend to exclude or at least diminish such freedom. In the novels, the habits of religious practice and ecclesiastical and sacerdotal life are sometimes seen as in some ways potentially dangerous, since they can easily blind those who engage in them to the truth of their existential situation.

In that situation, the move towards holiness initiated by freedom and charity is achieved by suffering, which is not removed by faith, the act of will which goes beyond reason, although reason can take it so far and encourage it. Faith does, however, give suffering a place and a potential meaning in human life. With it, man can begin to see what could be a pattern in the apparent chaos of events, a pity in the cruelty of life, a love beyond separation which can, with a certain clarity, see faults and yet still increase in strength. Above all, it enables the individual to stand aside from himself and see himself in new and different ways. It is both the recognition of a previously unperceived ordering of reality and the foundation for a concept of self. Scobie, the Mexican priest, and characters like them see their whole lives in a certain way because of their faith. Querry's loss of faith is linked to his loss of other aspects of his full humanity, and his partial recovery of these might perhaps indicate the first steps towards regaining what he has lost. Sarah's letter to Bendrix indicates the same kind of perception: that the self is a creature for whom God is concerned, who will suffer, who will feel lost and abandoned, but whose life is no longer merely the experiencing of a series of random and inexplicable interior and exterior phenomena.

In none of the novels as far as *Monsignor Quixote* is faith an easy matter for Greene's characters, nor does it provide automatic answers or courses of action. It is never self-evident or coercive. Very often, indeed, it is only when it is confronted by unbelief that its implications are seen. Unbelief, such as that which Sarah finds in Henry, Smythe and Bendrix, which Scoble finds in Helen, and which Monsignor Quixote finds both in himself and Sancho, sometimes helps to clarify what faith involves and offers. Scobie, listening patiently to Helen's comments on what she calls the 'hooey' she supposes he believes in, formulates more clearly, for her and for himself, what that 'hooey' consists of and implies, and sees his own life and himself rather more sharply for doing so. Monsignor Quixote's unpretentious, serious and lucid analysis of his own religious state of mind is illuminating from this point of view. In it he distinguishes, in a reasonably orthodox way, between belief, which is a matter of intellectual judgement, and faith, which is a matter of the direct apprehension of divine truth. Simply but evocatively he suggests all the conflicting perceptions usually potentially and sometimes actually present even within the single individual. He points out 'the shadow of disbelief' that haunts his own belief, stresses that he is 'sure of nothing, not even of the existence of God', although he knows that in this sense 'doubt is not treachery' and maintains that 'belief dies away, like love for a woman'. All this uncertainty is epitomized in the quotation from Unamuno that Sancho mentions to him in Salamanca: 'there is a muffled voice, a voice of uncertainty which whispers in the ear of the believer. Who knows? Without this uncertainty how could we live?' Nevertheless, he hopes to see men 'not necessarily believing. Just having faith ...', the faith that when he disbelieves tells him that he must be wrong.

A Greenean paradox? Perhaps, but disbelief and uncertainty are shown as bringing blessings. Without them, there would be no need for faith. The dream that produces a 'chill of despair' in Quixote is one in which Christ's death on the cross was not necessary and did not take place, since he was saved by a host of angels, Mary wept tears of joy, and the world had no choice but to believe. The faith that makes him say of God 'But he exists, I tell you. I don't just believe in Him. I touch Him' goes beyond belief or disbelief. Even that faith, however, is not certainty. It is a conative rather than a cognitive act, and is seen as such by other characters and the reader, when the book closes with Fr Leopoldo's remarks on the difficulty of distinguishing between faith and fiction and the enigma of Quixote's somnambulistic mass said with no bread or wine to consecrate. But we are left to reflect what the effects of that mass on Quixote and his congregation, and especially the disbelieving Sancho, might be.

The Catholic often encounters disinclination and a refusal or inability to believe which not only throw light on his own faith but sharpen it and to some extent support it and encourage its growth within him. At the end of *The Power and the Glory*, when the hunted priest is finally captured and taken before the lieutenant for interrogation, he is both appalled by his own inability to communicate his faith to his captor and made more aware of what it means for him and of its consequences. When the lieutenant later tries to persuade Padre Jose to hear his colleague's last confession and brings the condemned man a bottle of forbidden brandy, the leader is again reminded of what he has already learned about the apparently nihilistic and ruthless man: that his religious experience has been a powerfully negative one, and that his unbelief is as deep and strong, as immediately and intuitively felt and experienced as the priest's faith:

> It infuriated him to believe that there were still people in this state who believed in a loving and merciful God. There are mystics who are said to have experienced God directly. He was a mystic too, and what he had experienced was vacancy - a complete certainty in the experience of a dying, cooling world, of human beings who had evolved from animals for no purpose at all (Greene, *The Power and the Glory*, 1959, 183).

Such unbelief is a mirror-image of faith, for as Monsieur Quixote says elsewhere, humanism has the shadow of religion behind it, and the charity the lieutenant shows is also a reflection of that virtue as enjoined by faith. He loves his enemies and is not one of the lukewarm whom God, we are told, will spit from his mouth. It might be too much to suppose that he could, like Sartre's Goetz in *Lucifer and the Lord*, change the role he has chosen to play, but it is as well to remember that both the intensity of his vision and the strength of his urge to charity suggest that he is the kind of man to whom faith could conceivably come. He is the classic example in *The Power and the Glory* of what Greene means when he talks about hope as 'an instinct which only the reasoning human mind can kill'. Scobie in *The Heart of the Matter* is the major illustration of the loss of hope for another reason. Greene's aside on him is interesting:

> Despair is the price one pays for setting oneself an impossible aim. It is, one is told, the unforgiveable sin, but it is a sin the corrupt or evil man never practices. He always has hope. Only the man of good will carries in his heart this capacity for damnation (Greene, *The Heart of the Matter*, 1951, 67).

Its interest lies firstly in the fact that it provides a key to the failure of these two intelligent, sensitive, generous, conscientious and hard-working men, who are both to some degree overwhelmed by the inescapable evil and suffering in life. Their loss of hope is a consequence of the perception of the nullity and aridity of a blighted human life and is all the more bitter because both of them have some sense of its potential fullness. Greene's comment is also interesting because it has a bearing on the whole question of human success, which can be called sanctity or the whole-hearted search for good, and of human failure, which can be called sin or the yielding to evil. This dual reflection is a major part of the matter of the novels.

In Greene's work, sin is a negative quantity in the development of the human being. Yielding to evil is a hindrance to his full growth as a human being, and in extreme cases may destroy it completely. If a growth in real humanity means for Greene a growth towards God, the hell that Pinkie and Scobie fear may be in some way the permanent arrest of their still-incomplete humanity, a spiritual abortion of which they may, to some degree and in some sense, continue to be aware. Similarly, although in time rather than eternity, Pinkie's horror of the world, Scobie's weakness, Querry's living death, Bendrix's initially egotistical and unreflecting adultery, Louise's spiritual blackmail in her attempt to use divine means to achieve secondary ends, the Mexican priest's cowardice and refuge in drunkenness, all illustrate the various ways in which the humanity of those characters is imperfect. Seeking its perfection means not merely the practice of noble virtue, but seeing ends and rightful relationships, and seeking, if never totally finding, the tranquillity that come from due order, the peace that Aquinas described as opposed to conflict within oneself as well as to conflict with others.

In so far as these perceptions are achieved - and they are achieved to some extent by many of Greene's major characters - sanctity is possible, and a human being may move towards his true humanity. Such a movement is always difficult, and those who have advanced furthest along that path can see most clearly how limited the progress has been. The Mexican priest sees his own position and in the moments when he reflects on his life as he is about to be executed by the police firing-squad, thinks about what he could in fact have done:

> He felt only an immense disappointment because he had to go to God empty-handed, with nothing done at all. It seemed to him, at that moment, that it would have been quite easy to have been a saint. It would only need a little self-restraint and a little courage. He felt like someone who has missed happiness by seconds at an appointed place. He knew now that at the end there was only one thing that counted - to be a saint (Greene, *The Power and the Glory*, 1959, 273).

That particular tone is at least as typical of Greene as the romantic, doom-laden Catholicism of Brighton Rock. His work is essentially concerned with the growth of faith, hope and charity. This means, within his own terms of reference at least, a growth and deepening of the concept of the self, its nature and destiny and its relationship with other selves. For the Mexican priest, one Indian child is more important than a state or a revolution; for

Sarah, Bendrix is more important than her earthly happiness or all the social work she can engage in; for Scobie, Louise, Helen and the little girl who dies of fever are more important than his own peace and safety. In the novels, the individual person, whether he be lost in the drab, harsh monotony of Mexican poverty, the tropical squalor of West Africa, the London blitz, the slaughter of Indo-China, or the degradation of a Latin-American urban *barrio*, is a world in himself. What concerns Greene is the successful or blighted development of that person as a human being. Proper growth implies an increase in his self-awareness and in the chracter's awareness of others as human beings, arising from his ideas and images concerning the ultimate reality of human life.

CONCLUDING REMARKS

To a large extent Greene's novels, to use Louis McNiece's lines, 'only deal with here and now/as circumstances may allow', that is, with people immersed in a specific, concrete and highly individual human situation, where the extraordinary, such as the inexplicable disappearance of Smythe's disfiguring birthmark in *The End of the Affair* is highly unusual. It is probably true to say that for him, the important task is not the scoring of ideological or metaphysical points, for in that sense he usually seems too tired to argue, but the exploration of certain modes of knowing the individual, of seeing man in a world in which certain ideas and beliefs are taken both as a starting point and as a meaningful and enhancing final frame of reference. What is striking about Greene is the feeling he arouses in the reader that, at least in his own terms, he has told or tried to tell the truth. Part of this truth, and perhaps the major part of it, is the sense of the enormous importance of the individual human being, however degraded, hopeless, sinful or squalid his or her circumstances may be. The *mestizo* who betrays the hunted priest, the Portuguese captain, Coral and Andrews are important not because of what they have or have not, but because of what they are, which is a human person at his own stage of development, each with a potential and a nature which is both common to all of them and yet essentially individual and unique.

Although there are foreground and background figures, there are no Elect and no Masses in Greene's fiction. His characters, at whatever level of narrative or reflective importance they operate, participate in a fictional democracy. The differences between them are ones of degree, not of kind. The child, the adolescent, the immature young man and the older person who has seen the ways of the world and knows his own weaknesses all have the same potential and share in the same situation. None of them will perhaps cope with that situation very successfully, but all of them, at some time, and in some way, will have the opportunity to begin to see and partly to understand both it and the other human lives involved in it, and to learn that the only way in which they can develop is by becoming more human. What this means in effect in the novels is that such characters begin to appreciate the nature and limits of their common humanity and to see human life in a wider and more unifying (and ultimately religious) perspective. The seedy, weary, grey and rather predictable atmosphere of Greeneland notwithstanding, the novels are potentially works in which a kind of acceptance is possible, if not always achieved. Circumstances and human weakness conspire to make of life what, in human terms, can only be called a mess, but there is often an attempt to take that life and live it and make what one can of it, however unsatisfactory the attempt may ultimately be. There are major casualties, such as Pinkie and Scobie, but even in their case there is some movement and growth, and their collapse is due more to their sick or wounded sensibilities than to the total hopelessness of their world. All Greene's major characters make some progress in the direction of accepting both themselves and others as equally and significantly human. Their final situation may illustrate degrees of failure, but it also illustrates degrees of success. Although Pinkie dies a frustrated and angry child, his attitude to Rose has changed and developed, and there is a similar growth of charity apparent in all the major characters. Whatever life has taught them, it is clear that it has given them, to varying degrees of fullness and consciousness, a view of the human person as a separate, distinct, individual and real being, who like them is in many ways unsatisfactory and flawed but nevertheless of great value. Whatever one's views of Greene's religion may be, it is clear that for him our hairs are indeed numbered.

VERTICAL MAN

It will be clear that much of what has been said here reflects a personal reading of the novels, and one which to some extent conflicts with much of what has been written on Greene, particularly by English-speaking critics. It is possible to suspect that this is perhaps so because many of the latter take what may be a kind of guilty pleasure in reading his novels, feeling perhaps that although they enjoy them at the imaginative level of spontaneous response, they are being to some extent manipulated by an inbuilt ideology which they neither fully understand nor fully trust but in which, for aesthetic purposes, they must unfortunately suspend their disbelief. At a later stage of more conscious and systematic analysis of their response to what they have read and of reflection on it, they exorcize the guilt by methodically exposing that ideology for the unsatisfactory and unconvincing thing it is, angry at having been even momentarily seduced by it. If this is true, it says a great deal about both Greene's power as a writer and the natural reactions of critics. The latter in particular deserve some brief consideration here.

A critical reading of Greene's fiction requires not only an intelligent but also an informed response, particularly if the reader wishes to reflect on and understand the religious dimension and the view of human beings presented in it. Much, however, even of the most articulately-formulated criticism of the novels, has been clever rather than intelligent, often using the same sort of rather contrived simplicities of which it accuses Greene, and has often been *uninformed* (see, for example, the collection of critical judgements presented in Pryce-Jones, 1963). Many critics seem eager to detect a sleight-of-hand, a deliberate use of paradoxical aphorisms in his writing. Examples of this are Donat O'Donnell (Conor Cruise O'Brien) with his initially witty but ultimately over-clever and distorting image of the 'quietistic three-card trick' of the false syllogisms allegedly implicit in the novels (O'Brien, 1954, 246-247), Pryce-Jones's simplistically destructive interpretation of certain novels, especially *The Heart of the Matter* and *The Power and the Glory* (Pryce-Jones, 1963, 112-113) and Elizabeth Sewell's perhaps slightly more acceptable contention that Greene simply romanticizes Catholicism as a literary device (Sewell, 1954). The main point of all these strictures is that the religious element in his work is contrived, unconvincing, paradoxical and out of tune with an intelligent humanistic scepticism. This observation may be valid , but is in any case not our essential concern here. What *is* important is the view of man which follows from that religious element, and it is in this area that the assertions of many critics seem both over-simple and wrong. It is insufficient simply to say, with Pryce-Jones, that for Greene in human life 'success equals failure, failure equals success', that 'pity and responsibility become just so many deadly traps', misleading to make him say, as O'Brien does, that passion equals sexual love equals the suffering of Christ, wrong to state, as Pryce-Jones does, that in his novels there is 'the equation of love and lust'. One must ask why the priest in *The Power and the Glory* is in a sense a success, what Greene means by pity and why it is condemned or at least found wanting, why love is in fact so often contrasted with lust and why the latter is seen as unsatisfactory and diminishing. It might be better, as has largely been the method here, to take Greene's work at its face value, to assume that he generally means what he says, and to attempt, on that basis, to produce as reasonably systematic, coherent and comprehensive an account of his views as possible.

In exaggerating the importance of certain of Greene's stylistic idiosyncracies - the apparent paradox or play on words or the use of theological language to emphasize a point of view or underline a perspective - certain critics have almost turned their writings into a parody of his novels. It is perhaps interesting and not too difficult to do that, but the end product should not be confused with the fiction itself, which needs to be read with both intelligence and sympathy. If this is achieved, the paradoxes will be seen to be more apparent than real. It is quite true, for example, that success in one area, and that perhaps an unimportant or trivial one, is often paid for by failure in more profound ways. The satisfaction of ambition, for the Christian or indeed for anyone else, can entail a spiritual impoverishment. Failure in the satisfaction of those ambitions can bring humility, can correct a man's view of himself, can make him apply his gifts to new areas of his life. It is no accident that Monsignor Quixote can say, of the hopelessly incompetent robber he helps, 'I always feel that those who fail are nearer to God than we are'. Virtue, recognized by the self and others, can lead to pharisaism, pride and blindness. Pity can be a self-protective emotion and hide the heart of the matter, the truth of the situation, and can exclude knowledge, understanding and real help.

It is permissible to criticize or reject Greene's view of man and human life, but not to remain culpably ignorant about those views or to misrepresent them. It is permissible to see that Greene is by no means a whole-hearted spokesman for fashionable contemporary opinions in this area and to find fault with him for that, but not, on those grounds, to exaggerate or distort what he says. Greene's own considered view is that one can see that human nature, in the last analysis, is not despicable (Greene, *The Lost Childhood*, 1951, 136). An intelligent reading of his novels will support that opinion. It is hoped that what has been said here will have provided a way of seeing Greene's view of man as an acceptable alternative to the rather condescending and often inaccurate caricature contained in so much of the existing criticism of his work.

Chapter 4

SIGRID UNDSET

Do you remember the old familiar charges against Christianity, especially against the way in which the Church preaches the teaching of Christ? How it was blamed for twisting man's nature, his love of truth and beauty?
Sigrid Undset, *War and Literature.*

Critical views of Sigrid Undset's novels seem to fall broadly into two main groups. The first contains the reactions of those critics who detect in them an atmosphere of harshness and unhappiness. In a canter through Undset's works in his *Six Scandinavian Novelists*, Alrik Gustafson speaks of her 'insistently massive gloominess of spirit' and of the 'sheer brutally consistent accumulation of tragic detail' to be found in them, arguing that for her 'the spirit must eventually triumph over the flesh if man is to be good' and that 'her ultimate conversion is to be looked upon simply as the final, inevitable step in a severe moral discipline growing naturally and directly out of her realistic view of human life' (Gustafson, 1968, 286 ff). The second main group is exemplifed by A H Winsnes. He agrees in the introduction to his study of her life and work that she is of course, in a very fundamental sense, a realist. In contrast to Gustafson, however, he stresses her 'deep love for the normal and eternally human and for ordinary commonsense and her view of the search for a relationship with God 'as a fact just as realistic as any erotic impulse or longing for earthly happiness' (Winsnes, 1953, 7-9).

The most balanced view would probably arise from a reaction to her novels closer to that of Winsnes than to that of Gustafson. The latter finds in them a conflict between flesh and spirit and maintains that for Undset its necessary resolution is a triumph for the spirit. It would seem more exact to speak of the spirit transforming or heightening the flesh rather than subduing its, as even the most superficial reading of *Kristin Lavrannsdatter* or *Ida Elisabeth* would indicate. Gustafson sees her view, presumably unconsciously on his part, as akin to the Nietzschean aphorism that the flesh is an animal to be surmounted, when in fact it is more appropriately to be considered as an expression of the traditional Christian doctrine of love perfecting all things. To say that the novels consist of a brutally consistent accumulation of tragic detail is a distortion. There are few novels fuller of a mature and clear-sighted joy of life than the two just mentioned. Deep domestic happiness, the joy of an ultimately clear conscience and the sense of a life lived, if not always with success, then at least to some purpose, are characteristic of both of them. The joys (as well as the pains) of Kristin's wifely and maternal love, 'all those things by which people make something of their lives', can be seen as bringing a sober but deep and satisfying joy rather than a massive gloominess. A sense of reality, of the pain which human life can and does bring, cannot be simply equated with a sense of the absurdity or squalor of that life. Undset does not suggest that our existence is nasty, short and brutish, or that it is full of sound and fury, signifying nothing, or that it is tragic but ultimately meaningless. The 'moral seriousness' of which Nicole Deschamps speaks (Deschamps, 1966, 7) is not synonymous with lugubriousness or negative pessimism.

To speak of her 'massive gloominess of spirit' is to take an incredible view of the novels, and Gustafson's declaration that her conversion (and hence the portrayal of Catholics and Catholicism and of a whole view of man in her novels) is the 'final, inevitable step in a severe moral discipline' requires so much qualification and explanation that it can only be said to be partly true, and then probably not in the way in which it was meant. One of her own remarks illustrates what the reader must attempt to understand here: that for her Catholicism is both a realistic and hard-headed and yet a profoundly hopeful faith, to which both facile optimism in the human sense and pagan stoicism are equally alien. Two quotations from her essays will illustrate her own ideas on this matter.

The first is from *Saga of Saints*:

> In our days there is a great deal of talk about Christianity being a religion hostile to the joy of life, principally, because it attempted to command and exhort the mighty of this world to take less of its goods than their power would give them. We easily forget that real pagan joy in life was almost always strongly tinged with pessimism in one form or another. The refusal of Christianity to admire Lucifer is, to devout pagan minds, one of its most repellent traits. Christianity will make no concessions to man's longing for the rapture of death and the frenzy of ruin. Its anti-pessmism may have irritated those. who were not naturally simple or naive and incited them to opposition: for optimism does not come easily to one who has delved deeply into human nature, unless he can put his trust in something which is beyond the life he knows (Undset, *Saga of Saints*, 1934, 7).

The second, which is equally forceful and revealing, is from an address which she gave to Catholic writers in 1942, while in exile in New York:

> Tell the truths you have to. Even if they are grim, preposterous, shocking. After all, we Catholics ought to acknowledge what a shocking business human life is. Our race has been revolting against its creator since the beginning of time. Revolt, betrayal, denial, or indifference, sloth, laziness - which of us has not been guilty of one or more of all these sins some time or another? But remember you have to tell other and more cheerful truths too: of the Grace of God and the endeavour of strong and loyal, or weak but trusting souls, and also of the natural virtues of man created in the image of God, an image it is very hard to efface entirely (Undset, *Truth and Fiction*, 1942, 270).

Here she stresses the two major aspects of her work: a refusal to turn away from the harshness of life, and a perception that it is not all harshness. To see in her work the one without the other is to miss the source of their specific quality, which is to combine these two elements into a convincing whole

HUMAN NATURE AND THE WAYS OF SEEING IT

That the human being was a self, a person with an inner, partly-knowable core was axiomatic for Undset. In *The Burning Bush*, Paul Selmer reflects on this fact in terms of that hidden part of each individual which is beyond the judgement of others, the self which is more than the sum of the idiosyncracies, qualities or defects of each individual, and which is only fully meaningful in its relationship with God and other selves. There is frequently in the novel an emphasis on what Schaulach in *Madame Dorothea* refers to as 'the dark side of human mind'. By this he does not mean the diabolical or the exaggeratedly mysterious, but the life of the instinct and spontaneous responses. Significantly, this is not for him an area to be feared or avoided, but rather one which is coequal with the area of rationality and understanding, and indeed whose existence can be comprehended, acknowledged and even allocated to its rightful place by those other aspects of the total personality. It is a part which can be subsumed in an enlightened and understanding whole and which is to be neither ignored, feared nor neglected by the whole man, nor to be allowed to dominate him. To Dorothea's rather self-righteous and prudish unease with regard to this aspect of human life, Schaulach opposes the image of day and night, pointing out that both have their rightful place in the twenty-four hours. To her retort that the night is the friend of no man, he asks - humanely and inoffensively - how she, with seven delightful children, can say such a thing. This particular dialogue, quietly and with a sober humour, emphasises as much as any other in the novels of Undset's characteristic and abiding concern for the deep nature of human experience, even at the most mundane and everyday level. The same perception of the deep drives of our nature is clearly visible in *The Faithful Wife,* when Nathalie and Sigurd discuss Sonja and Sverre. Here, gossip is seen as perhaps inevitable in human life, because it is a means of either hiding or exteriorising one's own unavowed emotions or vices. Scandal-mongering is seen as a kind of vicarious sinning, and as a way of describing, unconsciously and by implication, one's own inner life. The motivation of such behaviour is perhaps less important than what Sigurd suggests is its function. The implication of a hidden life, difficult of access to the person in question and to others, is what is of greater significance here. The notion of the complexity of the individual is again stressed by Sigurd later in the same novel when, discussing the problem of politics, he poses as the first and essential question, that of deciding what one's concept of a human being is, with the corollary that all the others depend on it:

> Nobody is simply Norwegian (...) we're all human beings, and that's more complicated (...) The main thing must surely be one's idea of what a human being is (...) one can't solve any of them unless one knows what one believes a human being *to be* (Undset, *The Faithful Wife*, 1937, 143-148)

The idea of the existence of a human nature is a basic preoccupation in the novels, and the mental picture which those characters most sympathetic to the reader have of it as basically unchanging is emphasized again and again. In *The Burning Bush,* for example, both Paul Selmer's father and Selmer himself find the notion convincing and stress it in their various ways. Our nature is seen as a constant, fixed in terms of external laws govering the whole of nature (by Paul Selmer) and in terms of its own dynamics (by his father). These views are clearly conservative, clearly independent and based upon everyday experience, but they are honest and command respect. They are the kinds of view of his fellow men and himself which Selmer had already begun to form as a young man in *The Wild Orchard.*

Such attitudes contrast sharply with those held by other characters. What might be called contemporary liberal views are held by many of the secondary figures in the novels (in *The Wild Orchid*, for example, particulary by Selmer's mother). They are, no doubt significantly, contrasted with what might be roughly called traditional Catholic views, as exemplified by those of Selmer himself, the potential Catholic convert. In this connection as in others, human beings are to be seen as an antidote to the overdose of the superficial generalities concerning *l'homme moyen sensuel* which the current liberal view would provide, a point firmly made in the autobiographical fragment *The Longest Years*. Undset's concept is traditionally Christian in that it ascribes an intrisic value to the individual quite apart from his social worth, or his lack of it. In *Ida Elizabeth* for example, there is discussion with Sommervold on the worth of human being, both now, when there is still at least a remnant of the old Christian concept of man, and at some future date, when the old view of man, 'the old vision of life', from which we have still not fully liberated ourselves, will have disappeared. Who in such times will bother 'keep alive those who cannot furnish a fraction of what it costs to keep a human body going' when their social usefulness has disappeared, when they are a burden on society and there are no economic reason for their existence? Without a concept of our intrinsinc value, only utilitarian consideration can prevail.

THE INMOST CHAMBER

In *The Longest Years,* Undset describes what she sees as a characteristic of Nordic women: their self-awareness, their consciousness of themseves as persons, as selves. Describing Fru Wilster, she has this to say, evoking an image by means of its opposite:

> There was, in fact, something about her which one does not find in women of Nordic race - she did not seem to know what it was to be self-engrossed. When one says of a Nordic woman that 'she does not think of herself' one means merely that she does not think of her own advantage, she is thinking of how she may best turn herself to account in order to procure advantages for others - but that self is never quite absent from her consciousness. She sees herself, her ego is, as it were, as her capital, whether she be willing to spend it to the last farthing for others, or will rather endeavour to cheat and exploit others in order to add to her ego and avoid spending any of it in life (Undset, *The Longest Years*, 1935, 101)

Their lives are featured and consistent both because of the structure imposed on them by external events such as a marriage or a widowhood and its consequent roles, an assuming of responsibilities or a realization of inner needs, and also because, being what they are, they have a concept of themselves and a fidelity to it.

Although it could be argued that most of her male characters are less well-defined than the women in her work, the observation quoted above, and made about Ida Elizabeth's husband, would also apply to them equally. Paul Selmer, despite his religious and matrimonial vicissitudes, is always aware of his selfhood, aware that he is an entity called Paul Selmer. There is an evolution in his character in the course of *The Wild Orchid* and *The Burning Bush*, but it is a patterned evolution within the framework of a consistent identity. There is nothing random or arbitrary about it. Despite crises, there is a central core, an inner self which remains inviolate and can see itself and realize that it and it alone is the still centre of a human life. In *The Burning Bush*, awaiting his trial, Selmer sees himself in this way:

> But when everyday life returned, he would never again be able to forget that daylight does not merely reveal, it also conceals. Below the surface in himself there would always be a depth which no disturbances would reach.
>
> Fear and uneasiness and indignation might chase each other on the surface. But love was felt as something heavy which sank down and down. However, all this was merely images - whether one pictured to oneself the soul as a house with room within room and an inmost chamber where God is, and the ego as having once found its way in through that door and been recalled to life, and as being changed from what it was, no matter how it may return to its everyday life and live it again. Or whether one imagined oneself like a lake, with a surface ruffled by every wind and deep places where it was always calm (Undset, *The Burning Bush*, 1932, 376-377).

The 'room within room' and the 'deep lake' are the ultimate and abiding images of the self. When the externals of superficial character and adaptation to situation are penetrated, the inner, mysterious, permanent centre remains.

HUMAN FREEDOM

For Undset, it is because of this centre, this self, that man can only be seen as free. Sunnie's apparently imminent death in *The Burning Bush* can, paradoxically perhaps, be seen as an instance of this freedom. After a description of the feverish, painfully-ill child, the reader is given a glimpse of two insights: that of the child, who realizes that she may die, and that of her father, who perceives her knowledge and humbly realizes her lack of fear. Beneath her illness and her pain are calm and freedom, 'the absolute sovereignity over her soul possessed even by so young a child'. The self, despite all the anguish of life and death, of pain and unhappiness in oneself and others, despite all the humiliations and sorrow of all kinds which life offers, retains this essential autonomy to the end. It is itself, independent of circumstances to some extent, even when to the unsympathetic or casual observer there is no sign of its presence. This inner freedom is stressed by Undset on many occasions and in many ways, ranging from the insight arising from the painful circumstances in *The Burning Bush* quoted above to the apparently flippant but really serious remarks made by Uni to Vegard in *Images in a Mirror*, where what is ostensibly a humorous remark contains in essence a careful distinction between will in the sense of appetites and desires and will in the sense of free will, to the less striking - because less immediately connected with moments of major emotional impact discussion of the same topic in *Jenny*.

THE CONSTRAINTS OF SEXUALITY

In a body of works which is largely concerned with heroines rather than heroes, it would be natural to expect to find some reflection on the more specifically feminine dimension of the portrayal of human nature. As early as *Jenny* there is much discussion of the role, concept and nature of women with, typically enough, a robust common-sense prevailing. Women are seen as made for marriage and mating, however talented, independent and successful they may be, as naturally and instinctively monogamous, by desire if not in actual accomplishment, and - by implication, in Jenny's reaction to Gram's suggestions - reserved, cautious and prudent. These characteristics are real, Undset says, because the sensual woman is a myth, the product of a certain kind of limited masculine pride which sees women as simple, vain and stupid, bored unless there is a man to entertain them. For her, their sensuality is, in fact, normally of another, parallel and deeper kind, accompanied by an intuitive but quite clear perception of concomitants and consequence, in particular of their role, potential or actual, as mothers which, far from diminishing sexual love, is in Undset's novels more likely to enhance and increase it. In *Ida Elisabeth*, the kind of sexual curiosity and imaginative sexual explorations to which Aslaug abandons herself, or, conversely, the immature fear of sexuality, really hiding a fascination with it, seen in Ciss Meisling, are shown as an aspect of inexperience, a symptom of puberty or adolescence, rather than as a manifestation of adult female sexuality. Sexual day-dreaming seems to play a very minor role in the psychological make-up of Undset's heroines, who are usually mature young women in their sexual prime. Their sexuality is strong and deep, but it is not frivolous or random. This sexual maturity is seen as the norm, and the reader senses that the young girls in the novels - Aslaug, the young Kristin Lavransdatter and the Ingunn of the early sections of *The Master of Hestviken*, will eventually achieve it and that their nature - broadly human as well as more specifically sexual - will be enriched and deepened as they progress towards it. There is a difference in age of five years between Ida Elisabeth and the young girls on the ferry. The differences between their stages of maturity is hardly reflected in the chronological gap.

For Undset, eroticism - as distinct from sexuality - is perhaps seen as the only kind of communication with men that certain kinds of young women, particularly gentle, faithful and inarticulate ones, can really achieve. This is indicated in *The Burning Bush*, when Paul Selmer is shocked by the way in which the young hospital physician, Hans, makes light of his fiancee Evi, who had 'never possessed any other means of expression than her body' and recalls how radiant she had been when, on one particular occasion, he had seen Hans embrace her. It is not because the language of the body is superior to any other kind that Evi uses it, but because it is all she has. The qualities she can offer - fidelity, love, tenderness, passion - would remain unexpressed without it. The important point is that it is shown as an inarticulate, vulnerable and basically immature response, which will, in most women (if we are to take Undset's heroines as in any sense having universal significance in that they are both individuals and indicative of certain basic imaginative truths about women) be later modified and developed in further ways.

Adolescent or immature female sexuality is usually of relatively minor concern to Undset. Until the sexual energy of her major women characters finds its permanent focus, place and role (which may of course ultimately be very important) in their lives, it tends to be simply a rather uncontrolled and generally disturbing and distracting aspect of their physical and psychic energy. Often there appears to be a strong element of the anti-romantic in her portrayal of the first stages of what are to become extremely important sexual relationships. An example of this is her picture, in the first part of *Kristin Lavransdatte*, of her heroine's reactions after the loss of her virginity to Erlend. These reactions are described with a lowering of the emotional key, and with a sense of anti-climax deliberately expressed by the stylistic devices of the text ('it was as though her body ached with wonder - that this ill thing was what was sung in all the songs') in which a whole tradition of idealized sexuality and *amour courtois* is gently laughed at and deflated. By implication, the more probable truth of such a situation is suggested, just as it is later, when Kristin remembers, in her sexual dreams and longings, her encounters with her absent lover. These are not the dreams and longings of requited or unrequited courtly love, but those of an adolescent country girl in rude health in whom desire is stirring and breathing like the high spring in the countryside around her and who is consequently moody, exhausted and edgy.

SEXUAL REALISM

The element of what might be called sexual realism in the novels is striking. Whether she is portraying an incipient affair, reflecting on the nature of sexual commitment and the roles and satisfactions of both partners, discussing the depth of a sexual relationship or expressing a reflection on what she sees as a universal desire for fidelity, there is always a sense of the newness and individuality of particular circumstances as well as of their universality. The realism lies perhaps in the fact that sexuality is neither romanticized nor trivialized but seen as another aspect of human nature both intensely particular to the individual (and hence subjectively experienced) and as a common characteristic and an objective phenomenon. It is, in every sense of the phrase, a fact of life. On the whole, adult sexuality is what primarily interests her, with her adult heroes and heroines more fully portrayed and analysed than her young girls or young men. It is perhaps significant that in her autobiographical work, *The Longest Years*, childhood sexuality is given some, but not much, attention. What is interesting in that book is not so much the children's interest in their own sexuality, which is real if inchoate, but their interest in that of adults, especially in their sexual roles as mates and parents. It is not too difficult to see that this emphasis persists, for adult sexuality, seen clear-sightedly and without false pathos or sophisticated synicism, is to be her abiding interest. All portrayal and discussion of this major aspect of human life is effected with a combination of understanding and matter-of-factness. The basic fact for her is that sex is not an isolated phenomenon, but is connected with children, worries about them, adjustment to a partner and all the other personal and domestic concerns of a lifetime. It can neither profitably be prettified nor seen as squalid, insignificant, or merely amusing.

The scene in *Ida Elisabeth* in which the heroine, walking to her parents' grave along the Standal Water, reflects on such matters, can be seen as an indication of such perhaps rather stolid but certainly unsentimental views. Human sexuality is far removed from that of plants and animals. The passage is a key one and deserves full quotation:

> She suddenly came to think of some branches of hazel that were passed around the class - it was while she was in the lower school. The mistress explained about male and female flowers, the little round buds with three fine purple filaments at the top - how the stigmas received pollen from the catkins, and how the same process was repeated throughout nature, up to man. - A fierce red flame spread over Ida Elisabeth's face what bosh! Styles and stigmas, bumblebees and nectaries, birds that help each other in building nests and feeding their young, cows and calves and charming little foals - what in the

world had this to do with men and women? She felt this with painful sharpness. The brightness of the spring day, the scent of mould and of all the growth that was forced on by this weather, the trickling of water in the screes behind her - there was a separating gulf between her and all this that was growing and living, unfeeling and lovely. It would change from one beauty to another, the light catkins would become dark and luxuriant foliage, the grass would grow high and full of flowers and be mown and become scented hay. In the little grey beds between the stone-heaps turnips and potatoes would shoot up and spread their rank leaves till the mould was hidden from view. Has this much to do with human beings letting themselves drift from obstinacy, and because they are unhappy and desire to be petted and believe they can force themselves in upon another person - and are afterwards ashamed of having been so naive? One sees that one was mistaken in the other person, but it was one's own doing, and so -. The other one is also human, poor fellow, it won't do to be shabby about it, and one knows that he had *no* idea of what it is like to be me, so that one cannot raise a hand in self-defence.

Animals - they do not know what it means to be in a constant state of anxiety about one's children. They are alarmed when the danger threatens, close at hand. But they do not know the feeling of dread that comes of being forced to think of the future and having children to think of.

What sentimental old maids' talk that children ought to be told frankly and honestly and not be allowed to form ugly ideas about there being anything mysterious or degrading in styles and stigmas, pollination by insects and by the wind, sheep and little white lambs, mama and papa standing hand in hand and watching baby asleep. - Is there anything on earth so lovely as a little child? said Frithjof's mother, as she took the hand of Frithjof's father. It was exactly as if they were *playing* at father and mother, she had always thought. Frithjof's mother was

one of those who were so frightfully given to all this talk
about what was natural and pure and beautiful. And there
was nothing mysterious about it, except in the way of
sacred mysteries. Ugh, people like Fru Söndeled or
Mathilde Baur - but thank God they belonged to an age
which happily was past and gone, when women looked
upon natural cohabitation as something impure and were
so frightfully full of affectation and prudishness.
(Undset, *Ida Elisabeth*, 1933, 32-33).

All the recurring themes are stressed here: the complexity and far-
reaching nature of human sexuality, its central importance, its
essentially humanizing role as it grows and matures. The
similarities with plant or animal sexuality are striking but
essentially superficial, for there are areas of human sexuality
which are interesting and important precisely because they are
exclusively human.

This passionate realism is echoed throughout the novels.
Against the sombre grandeur of fully human love, distractions in
the form of temporary affairs are seen as pathetic and without
dignity, not because they do not bring pleasure, but because,
where sexuality is concerned, pleasure which does not engage the
whole of the human being is no more than a diversion, an
attempted escape from the real and the important. In *Images in a
Mirror*, a potential affair does not begin to take shape against a
background of dying falls or muted chords, or as an illustration of
frank, honest sexual pleasure complete in itself, or in terms of a
liaison with a fashionable strand of sado-masochism, but as part
of an awareness of how easily it could become 'a little
entertainment' and of how fruitless and boring it would ultimately
be. It is seen by Uni - and potentially by Vegard - as almost totally
irrelevant, as merely a moment which forces them to reflect on the
much more complex and mysterious reality of a deeper and more
committed relationship. It is, however, Undset suggests, very easy
to exaggerate and romanticize the importance even of successful
relationships, giving them an excessive importance as 'the
meaning and object of life', as Jens and Borghilda Braatö had
done in *Ida Elisabeth*, assuming superior virtue or status as a result
of them. Nor is mere 'frankness' or 'candour' seen as an ideal

attitude towards human sexuality. It has its darker as well as its joyful side, and to stress the latter at the expense of the former is simplistic distortion. All lasting relationships between men and women - and these are the only ones which really interest Undset - are neither simply sexual, simply romantic, simply domestic nor simply libidinous. They are a form of commitment, of understanding, of the accepting of responsibility, These aspects are not mutually exclusive, but mutually supportive and indeed creative, as they all help to form the total and mature relationship which is the underlying theme of her novels. This is true of both the historical novels and those of contemporary life. Ida Elisabeth's relationship with Frithjof is incomplete because some of these qualities are lacking: she accepts responsibility and commitment and he does not, and is seen, in his immaturity, to be 'taking the children's bread and castng it to dogs', as he either will not or cannot do other than demand a totally maternal and protective love from her. He has not outgrown the egoism of childhood, and has nothing to offer in return. He has none of that natural virtue, much admired by Undset, the instinctive sexual chivalry apparent is so many sympathetic male characters such as Paul Selmer, nor even the potential, harsh and inarticulate commitment of the young Olav to Ingunn in *The Axe*, nor the depth of his feeling for her later.

MARRIAGE AS A FULFILMENT OF HUMAN POTENTIAL

The important aspects of the sexual relationship for Undset are responsibility and commitment and their fulfilment in marriage. The notions of two persons in one flesh, of mutual love, help, esteem and respect, of the perception of the human dignity of the partner and of tolerance where it is needed and justified make married life the natural climate of Undset's novels and that, in a fundamental sense, is what they are all about. Marriage is portrayed as a contract between two people who enter upon it freely and who, if they are Catholics, administer the sacrament to each other. It is also a contract recognized as such by society. Once entered upon, therefore, it brings with it obligations as well as rights. Thus, in *Kristin Lavransdatter*, when Erlend is taken for trial, Kristin is aware that her first concern must be to maintain the loyalty she has promised him, since 'he is her husband and she his wife as long as they both live'.

It is also a relationship which - even in the harsh conditions of medieval Norway - calls for mutual love and respect, as is indicated by Olav's feelings of male protectiveness for Ingunn, by Kristin's felt need to respect her husband's manliness, and by the compassionate and complex relationship between Ragnfrid and Lavrans illustrated so often throughout *Kristin Lavransdatter*, which is no subjective illusion, since it is also perceived by others, notably their daughter. The historical trilogy and tetralogy are indeed not primarily chronicles of bloody, gloomy, grotesque or colourful events, but, basically a study of the developing relationships between husbands and wives. Olav and Ingunn, Erlend and Kristin, owe little of their stature and their compelling presence in the novels to their historical situation or their social function. They dominate the reader's imagination because they are human persons with great potential qualities and are capable of truly human and adult feelings, even if they do not always succeed in achieving what they are capable of, and because they experience the kind of love which is both spontaneous, natural and attractive at the outset and which later grows into a mature and stable bond. Since, in Undset's phrase, 'youth's aim (is) to give its gifts to another', the necessary development in the novels is for the characters, whatever vicissitudes they may encounter, to be seen as moving towards the way of living which, in *The Faithful Wife*, Sigurd describes to Thali:

> But the fact of the matter is, Thali, that every man desires a woman, a wife, whom he can love and be faithful to as long as they live. Most men do, in any case. I believe, too, that if any men don't desire this it is because they have resigned, whether they know it or not... All the same, I believe they will have to fill up a pretty big hole in themselves with phrases and theories before they cease to feel this yearning and fidelity (Undset, *The Faithful Wife*, 1937, 359).

Its more complete expression can presumably be seen in *The Wild Orchid*, when Fr Tangen explains to Paul Selmer the Catholic teaching on marriage, using theology to explain and justify what

Undset clearly proposes as the natural promptings of the human heart. Grace, says Tangen, does not change nature. It makes it perfect again. It is in the indissolubility of the sacramental marriage bond that Undset sees the ultimate expression of her own insights and relfections, which include all aspects of normal human sexuality from the phallic symbolism (so uncharacteristically?) included in *Ida Elisabeth*, to mature married love and clerical celibacy, all of which have their use and their justification.

THE NATURAL GROWTH TOWARDS RELIGION

Growth towards maturity is a major theme in the novels, and the attainment of clear-sighted adulthood can be seen as constituting an earthly *summum bonum* for Undset. The failure to mature (which often takes the form of surrender to the urgent and powerful dictates of selfishness, as with Erlend) is often the immediate cause of unhappiness for the individual and for others. To seek out what one momentarily desires, disregarding other considerations (as Erlend does with Sunniva) leads not to richness but to impoverishment. To go without, to free oneself from distractions, if it is done willingly (as with Brother Edvin) does not mean to be deprived, but to be rich. To be a strong, self-controlled adult (as with Lavrans, Ragnfrid, the adult Kristin, Paul Selmer, Ida Elisabeth) is to achieve a dignity and a deep happiness through love and understanding of oneself and one's fellow men and women. The explicit contrast between Ida Elisabeth's maturity and Frithjof's refusal to grow up, the development in Paul Selmer's character throughout *The Wild Orchid* and *The Burning Bush*, the growth to full and tragic personhood of Kristin Lavransdatter all indicate this. Even ageing is often a synonym for becoming more mature:

> If a man can put up with remaining the same as he has always been and yet undergoing a ceaseless transformation continuing to be the same in another way - then I can assure you that it's exciting to grow old... One gets round things, is able to see them from one new side after another (Undset, *Ida Elisabeth*, 1933, 43-44).

Insight, understanding and the ability to correlate and benefit from a variety of experiences, and not simply physical age, are what make the mature person. All these ways of seeing the human person are of course clearly linked to Undset's religious views, forming a part of a larger view of human nature, history and human life. This is perhaps nowhere more clearly visible than in Paul Selmer's long conversation with his mother in *The Burning Bush* and in his subsequent reflections, where many of the relationships between what the human mind can discover and religious truth are indicated. A suggestion of the kind of view which was Undset's is briefly but evocatively provided when Selmer considers the ways in which his own view of the world and human life has changed over twenty years:

> Twenty years ago the world had appeared to him as something solid, massive, impenetrable to his sight and senses. Firm and solid when he caressed it, firm and compact when he ran his head against it. Now it had gone with him as when one puts bits of matter under a microscope, sees their complexity and knows how infinite it is, even if one pursues it into the interior of the atom. And by way of a supposition one might imagine: what if cohesion were done away with and everything dispersed ? In the same way he saw everything now - all of matter and all of spirit in its place in the procession of things out from the First Cause. But what he acknowledged regarding his own nothingness and his own value, since he too was a mote in this universe, had nevertheless given him another kind of love for men and another kind of love for life, a new way of being happy and unhappy (Undset, *The Burning Bush*, 1932, 200-201).

It is because they are part of this parallel way of seeing life, which is both like and unlike that produced by natural reason, that the religious perspectives of the novels rarely seem extraneous or imposed. Encountered as part of the concrete experience of reading the novels, they are interwoven with fundamental questions and speculations of the kind any reasonably intelligent and imaginative human being might engage in. In purely human terms, men and women are flawed and unreformable, and yet they will always struggle and grow ('the world is always full of good beginnings'). Hope, like faith and charity, is a major Christian virtue. This is apparent in Selmer's, for example, awareness of what he sees as 'the explanation which faith gives of human nature', in Ida Elisabeth's realization that in some mysterious way all the irreconcilables of human nature are reconciled in God, in Selmer's view of the saints as both incorporating and transcending the weakness of their own human nature and in his idea (when he goes to him for instruction) of Harold Tangen's view of man, seeing him as one who

> ... sat there believing that he, Paul Selmer, had an immortal soul which Harold Tangen's lord and master had created. And as his soul had done the same as other souls, run away from its home and lost itself in trackless wastes, its creator had followed it down upon earth in order to save it, had redeemed it from captivity at a price which human thought is utterly unable to grasp (Undset, *The Burning Bush*, 1932, 50).

Undset's faith, in other words, assumes that religion implies not only a clear-sighted view of the flaws, faults and follies of human nature, but also of its final perfectibility, of the fact that it is *capax Dei*. To use her own phrase, man is blighted but beautiful.

These concepts are centred around the ideas of unity and order. Men and women need explanations, which Catholic doctrine ('sober information about absolute truths. Even if the truths in themselves are not sober but fairly wild, and the absolute is infinite and inexhaustible') alone can give. All men, whether Catholics or not, participate to a greater or lesser extent in that view of man which the Church has propagated since its earliest days. Our nature is such that we long for peace, the tranquility which comes from due order, and understanding. Edvin, the monk, makes precisely this point to the young Kristin Lavransdatter:

> For if a man had not any yearning after God and God's being, then should he thrive in hell, and it would be we alone who would not understand that there he had gotten what his heart desires. For there the fire would not burn him if he did not long for coolness, nor would he feel the torment of the serpent's bite, if he knew not the yearning after peace (Undset, *Kristin Lavransdatter*, 1930, 38).

Human nature not only exist for Undset; it is by implication fixed. Those characters for whom she feels sympathy (or who serve as her mouthpiece, if one takes a less favourable view) suggest this by implication. The young Paul Selmer would gladly serve society:

> ... if only he could be lucky enough to come across somebody who had some sensible scheme to that end - who was willing to start from the assumption that human beings are what they are, instead of always operating with human beings as they will be when once they have progressed so fas as, etc - (Undset, *The Wild Orchid*, 1931, 131).

If, in other words, intending reformers would let man be man, and concentrate on ... 'things which are built upon dogmas which at any rate have formed the foundation for the European conception of what each human being is', on that view of man which can be both strikingly individual and in a deep sense universal, on a recognition of truth. Seen from this viewpoint, life, as Ida Elisabeth suggests, 'perhaps hurts more often than not (...) but the good things come first' and, more importantly, the apparently random and transitory events of our existence assume, in relationship with an overall pattern and meaning, a sense and a purpose which, in isolation, are difficult to trace; but which can occasionally, in the course of human life, to some extent at least, be perceived and understood, as Paul Selmer dimly sees:

> It had been as when, one fine day, an unaccustomed light falls upon an old picture on the wall. Suddenly one discovers that there is a unity in it - the two or three details which were all one had hitherto noticed fall into their places as parts of a composition. Things which had happened to him, and thoughts which had passed through his mind years before, recurred to his memory and acquired significance in a new association. It was just the same as with the poems he had had to learn by heart at school - at the time he hadn't even attempted to get at the meaning of them, for of course they were only stuff to be crammed. But it sometimes happened, when one of these poems flashed across his memory after he was grown up, that it came back to him illuminated by one

meaning behind another upon a background of unutterable things (Undset, *The Burning Bush*, 1932, 73).

If human nature and human life are not seen in this way, as dynamic rather than random, as capable of growth and development within certain limits, and as part of a larger pattern of salvation and redemption, then, Undset implies, they will remain incomprehensible and ultimately meaningless, and the result for the individual will always be a sense of having missed some vital piece of knowledge, some clue or code which could have provided the key to a still mysterious but nevertheless significant pattern. Without this concept of man and his nature our question will inevitably be the haunting one which Ida Elisabeth poses: 'Is there something which we ought to have known and have never been told, and is that why we do such terribly stupid things with our lives?' (Undset, *Ida Elisabeth*, 1933, 167). The capacity for religious thought and feeling is an essential dimension of human nature as shown in the novels, and is a major concern. To explore the whole of the religious thought implicit or explicit in the novels would be a major - and separate - undertaking. All we can do here is try to disentangle the elements most important in the formation and colouring of a view of man.

RELIGION AS A FULFILMENT OF HUMAN POTENTIAL

There is a certain matter-of-fact quality about the view of religion and more particularly of the nature of religious perceptions and beliefs which emerge in Undset's novels. They are, so to speak, phenomena like any other. Just as the physical world has density and volume and is subject to certain potentially ascertainable laws which shape, affect and govern it, the human psyche too has certain inescapable characteristics. One of these is a religious response to the questions raised by any reflection on human life. Since she takes the supernatural as a fact, reactions to it and understanding of it, whatever forms they may take in individual cases, are also facts. In her essay *Blasphemy* it is in precisely this way that Undset defines religion: as our relation to the supernatural, whether it be one of acceptance or rejection. For her, this relationship should be a part of a clear-sighted and adult view of human life.

In her novels, the major characters see religion in general and Catholicism in particular as a basis, in the first instance at least, for life rather than for death, as a way of offering some explanation of human existence and of forming the proper pattern for it, and of forming human beings who are capable of doing something for God's sake while they are here on earth. In its essence, it is a sense of reality, a perception, however dim and incomplete, of the way in which human life is organized, of that inner sense of the recognition of truth, the awareness of what Paul Selmer in *The Burning Bush* calls the 'something real that was at work within the reality of sensation, like a body inside a garment'. Its concomitant is a distrust of purely subjective sensation and emotion and a recognition of the need to acknowledge objective and independent truth as a means of achieving sincerity and authenticity and of living in harmony with reality. It is interesting to note in this connection that the unromantic and hardheaded Ida Elisabeth sees the possible nature of an after-life, if one were to exist and some sort of reward or punishment were to be reserved for us on the basis of the way we had lived our earthly lives, as a state in which we might see ourselves *as we had really been*, with the severity of a possible punishment (purgatory or hell) depending on the degree to which we had 'refused to allow the truth to exist' and to which we had decided to accept our own subjective feelings, wishes and imaginings rather than what we knew to be true.

The sense of the need to accept objective truth, a healthy distrust of momentary vagaries and moods in contradistinction to the use of reason are the hallmarks of the ways in which Undset's major characters approach questions of religious faith and of ideas of right based on it. Such qualities are evident in the scenes in which Selmer reflects, both during the early stage of his conversion in *The Wild Orchid* and during his instruction from the Jesuit, Harald Tangen in *The Burning Bush*, on the philosophical basis of his approach to religion. He wants to *understand*, and to explore the consequences and implications of the desired understanding. Given the initial acceptance of the existence of God, they move, as Selmer says, in 'logical sequence, right down to holy water and the blest medal' via the whole of the Church's configuration of dogmas and constellation of symbols. Small things (practices, habits, customs) and large (perceptions, beliefs, ideas) hang together for them because, to interpret the sense of a remark of Selmer's, Catholicism has both a logical basis and a relationship with the material world which goes beyond it: 'Yes' Paul laughed. 'Catholicism is a metaphysical foundation, Puss'. It is perhaps because of this view of religion as something satisfying to the reason as well as to the emotions that, at whatever point in their religious development the novels may finally leave them, Undset's major characters are steadfast. Once their initial commitments to belief have been made, either by accepting the legacy of their childhood and upbringing or by discovering belief for themselves, there is not an apostate or even a real backslider amongst them. The faithful (Lavrans and Kristin, for example) die as they have lived, giving the lie, in fiction at least, to the existentialist view of death as the destroyer of all myths. There are varying degrees of commitment and enthusiasm, but no total lapse once adult decisions have been taken. This is perhaps one of the factors which help to give her characters their remarkable solidarity and opacity, in that their credibility arises from the absence of the random and fortuitous in their decisions and actions. Individual events may not be predictable as such, but the style and pattern of their inner and outer lives is consistent with the fact that they are persons who make choices and accept consequences.

One could not, however, simply say that her major characters seek commitment or are committed to a religious view of the world because they are intellectuals. None of them is a professional thinker, writer, teacher or perhaps even contemplative by nature. The businessman and the housewife (or their medieval counterparts, the feudal lord and his lady) are more typical of her range of major characters than the priest, the artist or the scholar. They are reasoning and intelligent beings with enquiring minds who are busy with the preoccupations of everyday life and try to make some kind of sense out of it. They are all people who are surrounded by life as it is lived by the majority of their contemporaries, and their approach to religion is characterized as much by a consideration of unexceptional experience as by reflection on pure ideas. What impresses the young Kristin Lavransdatter about Brother Edvin is a 'burden of awe' laid on her heart by his spontaneous love of God, his simplicity, gentleness and wisdom in his dealings with people, his deep understanding of them and his 'bright and privy gladness'. For the medieval believers in the novels, the religious dimension of life is expressed in faith and prayer, in the view of the Church as a divinely-founded institution which can incorporate the failings of its human servants and is not dependent on their holiness for its truth and efficacy, and in a sense of the necessity for penitence and the constant need for God.

In neither of the groups of believers, modern or medieval, is religion an emotional matter in any but the deepest sense. Where there is an emotional component, it would not be misleading to adapt Wordsworth's phrase and say that for many of Undset's major characters religion is emotion recollected in tranquillity. Their emotion is the experience of life and spontaneous reactions to it, their tranquillity the later stage in which, when the heat of the moment has to some extent died away, the ability to ponder on that experience and to reflect on its significance or value develops.

The religious experience of many of her characters is more often robust than mystical. They are concerned with life on earth rather than what comes after it and with the implications faith has for human life in their present circumstances. Ideas about God, the nature of the soul and ultimate human destiny are important primarily because they indicate deep truths about human life on earth. There is no character who wonders in anguish whether he will be saved or damned, none who escapes, even temporarily, the confines of earthly existence and enjoys the beatific vision, none who seeks in any way to anticipate eternity. God will provide judgement, salvation, heaven or hell as he sees fit. Kristin Lavransdatter may, as the young mistress of Husaby, be torn by anguish, remorse and repentance for her sins, but she thinks primarily of her present guilt rather than her possible eternal punishment, for she knows that 'when her punishment grew heavier than she could bear, then would she meet, not with justice, but with compassion'. Later, in the convent at Rein where she is to end her days, she may prepare for her death, but she neither seeks it nor is obsessed by it.

What concerns Undset's major characters is their relationship with their fellows in the light of their relationship with God. Each of them is concerned with how to live with his spouse, his children, his fellow human beings in general, because he can see them (or begin to see them, for the progress is not uniform for every major character, nor are the insights identically expressed) in the way in which he sees, or begins to see, himself. That way is, in simple terms, as a being who is of value to God, and who is sustained by him. Consequently he can and must accord to others full human dignity. God is seen not as a subjective experience (which for an Undset character would mean rejecting him), but as objectively true and important, mysterious in the paradox of his own humility and abandonment. Certainly (as Randi Alme declares) he can never be merely an anthropomorphic creation:

> Ah, if you were God! Or if God were like us. What awful rubbish it is, this twaddle about men having created God in their own image! (Undset, *The Wild Orchid*, 1931, 75).

He is omnipresent and we are part of him, never outside his knowledge or attention, never in any real sense, in this life, separated from him. In Gotaa's words to the potential convert, Selmer:

> It's like this - we are in him, everything is, so if you, for instance, leave your room and go past me and speak to me and into the kitchen and back, it's in God all the time (Undset, *The Wild Orchid*, 1931, 39).

The same idea is in Ida Elisabeth's mind towards the end of her story:

> And as she stood here she felt overwhelmingly certain that there was something, as real and invisible as are the stars in broad daylight, and that it was the same for all four of them, the mother and son who were parts of each other's substance, and the old couple who were so infinitely one, and she herself and this man to whom she had been married through error - it was God alone who

really was the same for them all, there was something beyond time and the day, in which youth and childhood and old are one, though here they cross each other like the pattern of a woven fabric (Undset, *Ida Elisabeth*, 1933, 341-342).

God is still the centre of change, the calm at the heart of the universe, the silence at the centre of our fretful human lives, and is to varying degrees individually sensed or glimpsed. Sometimes he is more or less recognized by all collectively, as in the medieval trilogy and tetralogy, sometimes recognized by some, to greater or lesser degrees, as in the 'contemporary' novels, but he is always assumed to be there and sought out by someone. To modify the epithet applied to Nietzsche, Undset's major characters are 'God-seeking' rather than 'God-intoxicated' beings. These ideas of God are immediately important because they indicate an idea of man. Without a sense of God, he is condemned to be himself, condemned 'to become what he must become when he is allowed to follow his own line to the very end', a creature separated from his creator and dwelling in 'an asylum for such as desire to remain for all eternity outside all order and without God above them, sufficient to themselves for ever and ever'. The absence of God can produce both a temporal and an eternal hell for man.

They are also important because they are *explanatory*. Religious ideas imply a view of life, Undset suggests in *Ida Elisabeth*, and the better they are, the greater will be their determining influence on the believer's understanding and explanation of the phenomena he encounters in his own existence. Catholicism, she maintains throughout the novels of contemporary life, is a religion for life, not an opiate or a substitute for erotics but a realistic and to some degree a materialistic religion, bringing to the believer a kind of peace. It enables him to see life constantly and see it whole and provides a framework of reference for his contemplation of the human existence which surrounds him and in which he is immersed. It is thus both a strand in an image of man and formative influence on that image.

What man is like as an individual and in his relationship with God determines to a large extent his way of seeing the natural world about him and relating to his fellow human beings. For

Undset, those relationships are functions of charity, responsibility and natural morality extended by the perception, either complete, partial or fragmentary, of virtue and sin.

THE BASES OF HUMAN MORALITY

There are different levels of moral insight and behaviour in the novels. The first, and in the chronology of the novels the earliest, is that of the natural pagan decencies, expressed perhaps in its simplest and clearest form in the semi-autobiographical *Jenny*. Here we are in the world of the intelligent, sensitive and imaginative person where morality is a matter of sensibility and sympathy rather than of principle, is essentially subjective and emotionally coloured, and is seen precisely as that. Jenny's words to Gunnar Heggen illustrate the quality of such moral views:

> I wanted to live in such a way that I need never be ashamed of myself as a woman or an artist. Never to do a thing I did not think right myself. I wanted to be upright, firm and good, and never to have anyone else's sorrow on my conscience (Undset, *Jenny*, 1921, 265).

Conduct and relationships are simply and immediately seen as honourable or dishonourable, as right or wrong in terms of her subjective ideas, feelings and experiences. In Camus' phrase, her morality and that of most of her circle 'dictates itself' and has no *a priori* objective justification. In this it is typical of the view instinctively held by the other characters in the novel, and, one must suppose, of a stage of the author's own personal development which she felt that she was leaving behind, as there are indications throughout the novel that it seemed insufficient and unsatisfactory to her as well as to Jenny. It is clear that by *The Wild Orchid* and *The Burning Bush* there is a change in the nature of the moral reflections which various characters engage in. There, what might be called the natural decencies are seen through the eyes of a man for whom they are no longer completely satisfactory and are indeed occasionally strange. As a corollary to the notion that merely to be honourable is not enough and that creating happiness for men on earth is, in human terms, the most one could hope for, there is the tentative growth of an idea of an external and normative morality with reference to which one's action can and should be judged. The concept of a different sort of ethical framework begins to appear, and Selmer experiences the:

> ... new discovery that something, some kind of natural moral law, might underlie the laws of conventional morality (...) Till now he had had nothing but his own conscience to go on. Though in a way he had always felt it was something like treason to claim autonomy for it - only he could not tell against whom it might be treason (Undset, *The Burning Bush*, 1932, 72).

This objectivity is seen initially as a separation of moral judgement from subjective likes and dislikes, and more specifically as the realization that liking for a person and approving or disapproving of what he does are separable phenomena. In trying to explain this difference to his wife, Selmer is making a tentative movement in the direction of creating a new understanding for himself, beyond the instinctive morality of his youth and his affair with Lucy, a movement parallel to that made by Jenny Winge when she discovers, or rather rediscovers and re-affirms, that hedonism is not enough. It is the kind of insight epitomized by Ida Elisabeth's realization that she cannot marry Sommervold. Superficially her mind is confused, but beneath the confusion she realizes that as well as subjective reasons for her unwillingness to do so, (the fact that it would radically change the relationship and produce constraint rather than intimacy) there are, however imperfectly she senses rather than sees them, objective ones. She had belonged to Frighjof Braatö, and in some obscure way, the marriage to Sommervold would be unnatural. The fact that the ways in which it would be unnatural remain vague in her mind is unimportant; what is significant is her suggested perception of an external moral order:

> To be married to him would be downright unnatural. And she felt, no matter how she might revolt against nature being thus and thus, no matter what exasperation and despair she might feel at its being as it were closed against her, although she was caught in the midst of it, as in a man-trap - there was something in nature which was not in her, and something in her which it lacked or

escaped. Nevertheless, her place was in it, and when she had raged against it till she was tired, she felt its living warmth, felt that it was full of impulses and exhalations, not good, not evil, but lovely for their own sake. Its opposite, anything that was against nature - something within her offered resistance to the bare thought of it. It was stronger and more obscure than dread; it had some connection with that feeling which makes people say: while there is life there is hope. There were things about which Doctor Sommervold had talked to her - well, in his mouth they sounded clean enough, like sterilized glasses and instruments in his hands. But they gave her the same feeling of invincible repugnance as the proposal that she should conform to custom and have her mother's coffin opened (Undset, *Ida Elisabeth*, 1933, 46).

Inner voices tend to say contradictory things to any major character in the novels and, as those characters change and mature, they realize this. Ida Elisabeth knows quite well that what conscience tells us is often what we want to believe, that what the emotions and affections tell us is often simply what we want to hear and bears no necessary relation to objective truth. She explains this to Tryggve Toksvold, stressing her constant desire for some external source of guidance. Paul Selmer, who is more reflective and more articulate, is also conscious of his own development in this way. There need not necessarily be a conflict between the subjective and descriptive aspect of morality on the one hand and its objective and normative formulation on the other. The latter, as Paul Selmer realizes, will very probably confirm and clarify the former. Virtue, Undset's more mature and intelligent and fully-presented characters are led to perceive, lies neither solely in obedience to external formulations nor in acting upon the impulses of the subjective psyche, but is the result of an honest and clear-sighted attempt to behave intelligently and charitably in the light of both, using each to inform and enlighten the other. A part of the enlightenment is the inescapable truism that virtue brings its own reward and not necessarily any other, as Paul Selmer sees when reflecting on the course of his own life and that of his brother Hans, the womaniser and drug-addict. For

Undset, virtue can be seen as the conscious conforming to the dictates of an informed conscience, which sees both that there is a human nature with its own inbuilt needs and aspirations, and that the human psyche cannot function properly or effectively unless it is guided in its decisions and options by a conscious realization of the objective as well as the subjective factors involved in them. These are of course increasingly seen by Undset, and expressed by her characters, in terms of explicit or implicit traditional Catholic morality. For her, as for Paul Selmer, this implies both a perception that there are lasting laws which govern the right conduct of men and that they are part of that truth which it may be difficult to love, but which one must be able to bear, and that it is easy to accept them pharisaically and negatively.

MORAL PRINCIPLES AND MORAL PROBLEMS

It can be expected that a major element of virtue in a scheme of right conduct like that proposed by Catholicism, which has traditionally stressed spiritual and corporal works of mercy, is responsibility for oneself and for others. With varying degrees of success, Undset's major characters try to arrange their own lives in the light of their understanding of themselves and their situation, and assume they are answerable to themselves, to God, to what they see as right. They also accept responsibility for their fellow men within the limits of their possible field of action, whether it be a family, a firm, or the wider area of society as a whole. Paul Selmer's morality impels him not only to be a good father and husband, but also a good employer. He sees distributism as a defence mechanism safeguarding the rights of the individual rather than as an ideology, since it helps guide and shape the course of industrial development and is not simply subject to it. Like all systems, however, it is merely a means to the end of allowing human beings to be human. Ida Elisabeth reflects on the kind of people whom Toksvold dismisses as 'scrap metal' ('they did form a race apart, the ones who never ceased to need help'), sees that the pursuit of personal and subjective human happiness can exclude them and that if this should ever triumph 'there would be an end of mercy in the world'. The happiness of the couple is not enough. Sacrifice and the acceptance of responsibility for others are needed. This is the point which Madame Dorothea makes when she reflects on her life:

> This lesson she had learnt, however, at the price of seven years of her youth in slavery: we must all fill the position in which we are placed as we are able - otherwise the world would be too terrible to live in (Undset, *Madame Dorothea*, 1941, 75-76).

She realizes that she will never again be able to condemn 'those estimable people who were spoilt by an ill-concealed self-sufficiency' and 'sourness' or 'envy of their more frivolous fellows', for she sees the bitterness of having to do joylessly what has to be done.

If the religious dimension is accepted, then sacrifice has an aspect which in purely human terms may be seen as simply repugnant. Sunnie's plea, in *The Burning Bush*, to her father to offer her death to God and, more significantly, his willingness to do this, seem grotesque and sadistic to Hans, as it must to any reader without religious belief. In Paul Selmer's eyes, however, it is an acceptance of his and her human dignity, of the majesty and providence of God and of the significance and beauty of the girl's inner life. Sucn a scene - unusual in Undset's fiction in its starkness and its sense of the interpenetrability of the temporal and the eternal - is an illustration of the ultimate significance of that acceptance of external and eternal significance in human life.

It is against such a background of the ideas of objective goodness, responsibility, acceptance and sacrifice that any concern with specific moral issues must be seen. If these major ideas are rightly understood, then everything else falls into place, and it is for this reason that specific questions such as contraception, abortion and euthanasia ('parental abortion' in Undset's phrase) occupy relatively so little space in the novels. Ciss Oxley's argument with Sommervold in *Ida Elisabeth* is conducted in such terms of reference, and Sommervold is at least intelligent enough to appreciate this. What the novels do is not so much present an authorial monologue on specific issues (although there is some evidence that in fact Undset's sympathetic major characters act as mouthpieces for her moral views) as provide, through those same characters, a general view of human nature, human relationships, and responsibilities and commitment, of which attitudes to specific questions are a natural extension and development. Clearly, such matters as abortion, euthanasia, contraception and so on are, as far as the Catholic is concerned, questions of dogma, that is, matters on which the Church has a teaching. Yet for Undset, as for many intelligent Catholics who accept it, dogma is acceptable not only because it is taught by the Church, seen as the vehicle of Truth, but also because it is what their own heart and their own reason tells and has always told them, even if unclearly and implicitly. When, in *The Burning Bush*, Paul Selmer reflects on his wife's discovery that she is to have a child, the reader is given a clear picture of precisely this kind of realization:

> And then, suddenly, the ill humour between him and his wife changed - from petty nagging irritation and skirmishes over trifles - to earnest. Björg discovered that she was going to have a child again. She was in utter despair and beside herself with rage. This was about the New Year, 1920. Of course he had always known that this was one of the points on which he and she differed fundamentally. He had tried to silence his own conscience by arguments and quotations of other people's opinions. In this, as in so many other things, it seemed to him that what the Church taught in clear and concise dogma was nothing else than what he himself had divined, in a vague fashion, confused by fear of the consequences, if he put his most hidden instincts into definite thoughts. That was all (Undset, *The Burning Bush*, 1932, 115).

This is what right action is for Undset: action which is in accordance with proper understanding, with the 'informed conscience' of moral theology. Conversely, sin is acting contrary to that understanding, whether it be that of a Christian, a pagan or an atheist. And in Undset's eyes, it is clear that such action is unlikely to bring hapiness, precisely because it implies a suppression, a wilful denial of a fundamental aspect of human nature. As early as *Jenny* the reader encounters such remarks as Gert Gram's:

The experiences which are the results of sin - I don't mean sin in the orthodox sense, but the consequences of acting contrary to your understanding - are always far from sweet (Undset, *Jenny*, 1921, 183-184).

Knowlege - especially self-knowledge - is important, as Paul Selmer realizes. Sin can be both a revelation of impotence and a method of teaching us our own shortcomings. To see, to understand, to conceive of oneself as a finite and fallible being with great potentialities, and not to be content with oneself as one is - in other words, to have a certain concept of oneself as a person - is of paramount importance.

THE SELF AND OTHER SELVES

This is the view of the individual which determines the nature of his relationship with others. To see oneself in a certain way implies that one must see others as selves, as persons in their own right, to whom justice and charity are due, and determines too how one sees that justice and charity. If other persons are ends in themselves, rather than means to the ends of the observing self, then a particular kind of relationship with them is predicated. The specific areas of relationships which Undset portrays and investigates are fairly clearly domestic and marital in the main, with some reflection on wider social and political aspects. It would perhaps be true to say that to some extent at least these wider reflections are an extension of both the concepts of morality which have already been discussed and the specific individual relationships portrayed in the work. 'Confidences between parents and children', said Undset, 'are worthless - a poor substitute for trust', and this is an attitude which underlies her whole view of domestic and family relationships. Trust, insight, understanding and a loving but dispassionate appraisal of the true nature of the family situation are the basic necessary qualities. The various complexities of such relationships are indicated unsentimentally; the nature of material and parental love is examined; the inevitability, and indeed the necessity, of Oedipal instincts seems apparent to Ida Elisabeth; the morality of adult choices affecting children is examined ('am I to take what I want and let my children pay for it?'). It is not, however, the nuances of such relationships that are important, but their underlying nature, which is that they imply taking another person for what he is, letting him be himself, and struggling against anything which is likely to vitiate or undermine his personhood. In the passages mentioned above, Undset neither idealizes nor demeans family relationships. They *are*, rather than are attractive, or disgusting or boring. They are good in that they exist and are part of the created pattern of human life, as much a part of the inevitable texture of that life as are hard stones, cold water or warm fires. What is, is *ipso facto* good. It becomes wrong or evil if it is misused, sentimentalized or degraded, and the first essential for right use is not divine revelation or prescriptive morality, but perception of the real nature, of this as of everything else. For Undset moralities arise from understanding, the understanding proper to our mode of being as persons further enlightened, in the case of the fortunate, by the teachings of the Church. Such understanding, Undset implies, does not primarily derive from the minute compilation of data or observation. It comes from something parallel but deeper: the insight which one human being can have into the life and being of another. Thus, despite the fact that Paul Selmer had been separated from his father at an early age and had known, as he said, little about him, he was certain that he knew all that was of significance. He felt that he had known his father well. Simon Darre's understanding of Lavrans and of other characters in Kristin Lavransdatter is a further example of this insight.

The same kind of views is implicit in what Undset has to say about marital relationships. In that of Paul and Björg Selmer, it is clear that the former is the one whose relationship with his partner is in a sense 'right' and that the latter's is 'wrong'. This is not because, or not primarily because, Selmer is a Catholic and his wife is not, but because he understands and accepts and can see the difference between what is inevitable and what can be changed and she cannot. Paul Selmer is an adult who accepts the implications of being an adult, Björg is an adult who wants to remain a child:

> But what made his married life a little wearisome at times was precisely the fact that she was not a child; she was a person of full age without the charm that a child's

childishness possesses - the ceaseless development, the everlasting and spring-like surprises of growth. She had simply stopped growing at a certain early age, and she was no more amusing than any little girl would be who was kept back in a school class below her age (Undset, *The Burning Bush*, 1932, 77).

There are many parallel situations throughout the novels: Ida Elisabeth and her feckless husband, Kristin Lavransdatter's acceptance and fidelity, Jenny's tragic understanding and Nathalie's humility in *The Faithful Wife*. The most striking aspect of such characters is their wisdom, understanding, patience and firmness. The task they have is that of accepting responsibility and of understanding and guiding those they understand. They are the characters who in the phrase in *Ida Elisabeth* see the differences between 'thinking of' and 'thinking about', and realize that what we truly perceive of others and our superficial opinions of them are not necessarily identical, and who can go further and accept that comparison and anitpathy are often both inevitably present in our attitude to them. For such people, Torkvold's easy evasion of trouble and unpleasantness is *too* easy. As a result of their nature, their experiences and their understanding, they are forced into Paul Selmer's position, that of having to accept other people and to worry about other people's opinions of them not out of arrogance, but out of a kind of humility, because they have seen that other people - all other people - are not simply 'all and sundry', but individuals and persons just as much as they themselves are. For them, Hell cannot be other people, however uncomfortable, antipathetic or uninteresting others may be. In their own way, they have seen and experienced the brotherhood of man (or, in Christian terms, the mystical body) and realize that it is the fact that men are brothers, both literally and figuratively, that leads to so much strife and evil amongst them. Ida Elisabeth arrives at this stage through a realistic and clear-sighted love of her children, and sees that love of them as individuals is inextricably bound up with the love of all human beings as individuals. Love and understanding increase each other, and neither can ever be static or quantifiable.

CONCLUDING REMARKS

From these views there follows a major implication for Undset's heroes and heroines. Any view of man which reduces his dignity is evil. Paul Selmer sees this clearly, and realizes that many ideologies which loudly assert the importance of the individual in fact condemn him to passivity and slavery. Given human nature ('... the fundamental difficulty, that human beings are human') there can be no clean breaks or totally fresh beginnings. There is nothing new, only previously unnoticed things. He discovers, or rediscovers, the ideas of St Thomas Aquinas, and realizes in a fresh and striking way the deprivation of the proletariat in modern industrialized society, forced into a vegetative, uncreative and unreflecting way of life. For him, as for Harald Tangen, the Jesuit who has given him instruction, political ideologies with a materialistic basis are not enough ('materialism is never anything but (...) an accident in a view of life which in its essence is the cult of humanity').

Whether seen as an individual or in his relationship with his fellow men, the human being is, for Undset, *important*, a real and vital person, rather than a cluster of random impulses or a schematic representation of dogmatic concepts. In her novels there is a genuine coincidence of faith, reason, reflection and moral gravity, so that the reader feels that whatever her view of his ultimate nature, her picture of the human being is intelligent, solid, credible and convincing, because she sees men and women as having precisely these characteristics themselves.

Chapter 5

GEORGES BERNANOS

And he knew what man is in reality: a big child, full of
boredom and vice.   Georges Bernanos, *Star of Satan.*

For a leading Swiss theologian, Bernanos's fiction establishes
an image of man based on the highest Christian reality and
provides the key to the essence of our humanity and the measure
of man (von Balthasar, 1956, 24). His English biographer also
stresses that even more important than his idea of France is his
idea of man (Speaight, 1973, 19). My aim here is to consider the
concepts of human nature, of the imaginative and intellectual
ways of seeing and depicting human beings which underlie and
inform his novels.

Bernanos was never a philosopher in the formal sense of the
word and composed no treatise specifically devoted to a study of
human nature. He did, however, have a great deal to say about it
implicitly and explicitly in both his polemical works and his
novels. The former deal with the question in terms of historical
patterns, sweeps of events, ideologies or views of life, the latter in
more specific and individual terms, with the reflection and general
observations arising from the concrete situation of a particular
human being. Perhaps we can try to work towards the kind of
statement which might be made about individuals if the same
techniques of generalisation and synthesis which Bernanos used
to a large extent in his polemical works were to be applied to an
examination of his novels. In the latter, there is comment on
human nature which is frequently and forcefully made, although it
is necessarily scattered, diffuse and unsystematic. The reader

certainly receives a general impression of Bernanos's mental picture of human beings, and it seems worthwhile to try to bring this image more sharply into focus.

THE ILLUSION OF ORDINARINESS

For Bernanos, the idea of the 'ordinary' man, the convenient fiction of a readily-comprehensible creature whose hopes, fears, pleasures and pains are observable, classifiable and foreseeable and who is consequently to a large degree predictable and manageable, is an illusion. 'The average man we never meet' exists not only in theological, sociological or psychological textbooks, but also as a picture in the imagination, deadening our perception of the complexity and depth of the human person. Such is the sense of the words of the subtle, articulate and wise old priest Menou-Segrais in *Star of Satan*, when he explains to his gauche young assistant, Donissan, whom he understands, his own way of seeing human nature and the simplified diagrams of it we have drawn. Our inner life, he says, is taken to be merely the dreary battleground of our instincts, morality a hygiene of the senses, and grace no more than an argument addressed to our reason, which temptation or carnal appetite tend to lead astray. This means, he continues, that we can barely account for the most mundane aspects of the struggle that goes on inside us.

Such explanations may be valid for the non-existent creature our systems postulate, but in terms of our real lives they explain nothing. In a world of feeling and reasoning animals there is no room for the saint, and often of course we find him insane. The truth of the matter, however, is that each of us is sometimes a criminal and sometimes a saint. At certain moments we are drawn towards goodness, not because we have carefully weighed up its advantages, but by a whole thrust of our being, an effusion of love that makes sacrifice and renunciation objects of desire. At others, we are tormented by a mysterious longing to degrade ourselves, to taste ashes and to exult in the vertigo of animality and our incomprehensible nostalgia for it. Evil like good, Menou-Segrais maintains, is sought and served for its own sake. Whether this notion is expressed explicitly and eloquently, as it is in *Star of Satan*, or implicitly and hesitantly by such characters as Malvina, the wife of the neurotic and deviant mayor in *The Open Mind*, it underlies the whole of Bernanos's fiction. There are no ordinary human beings, only those shown at a greater or lesser depth. Man is an insoluble enigma if not seen in the light of the divine and interpreted by reference to God, an enigma both to himself and to others. This central mystery at the heart of any human being might, like so many others, be expressed in the simplest of phrases, but its complexity soon becomes apparent. In *Star of Satan*, for example, Bernanos makes his priest-hero, Donissan, describe human beings as grown children, full of vice and boredom. Although that particular formulation may sound like a simple piece of old-fashioned clerical cynicism, it haunts the reader as the novel progresses and he begins to have some idea of what vice and boredom mean to Donissan and Bernanos. The complexity of Bernanos's view of human beings soon begins to become apparent. In the priest's strange encounter with Mouchette Malorthy, he reaches the inner reality of another psyche, the dark, porous rock of the hidden self. What he sees is the inner life of a young woman who has just killed her lover. He does not know her, has indeed never met her, and is not, given her radical and anti-clerical background, likely to evoke sympathy or confidence in her. Directly and intuitively, he experiences her hidden thoughts and feelings and penetrates to that deepest layer where, says Bernanos, instinct roars like an underground river, that region in which she is herself.

THE HIDDEN CORE OF BEING

Such passages indicate a whole attitude towards the perception and understanding of the nature of human beings. There is a source from which all our most significant deeds arise, those deeds which shape and determine a dimension of our lives or decide our final destiny. Two examples of this intimate link between the inner core of a character's being and his external observable actions will serve to illustrate this point. These are the growth of the idea of committing murder in the mind of Simone Alfieri *in Night is Darkest* and the final desire of Mouchette Malorthy in *Star of Satan* to die in the local church.

In the former, Simone's mind entertains the idea of murder at first as an intellectual possibilty, as a notion to be explored in the way that she is accustomed to explore possibilities of such a kind in the course of her work for Ganse, the novelist. There is of course the possible incentive of increasing the wealth of her lover, Olivier, by murdering his aunt and so releasing her fortune, but it is clear that initially at least the project is no more than a potential development of an existing situation, an option to be kept open. The 'obvious' motive of self-interest and gain is not the overriding one. Gradually, as she investigates the situation, her real motivation, which is hardly capable of definition or analysis, begins to come to the surface. It is the 'rêve' of the original French title (*Un mauvais rêve*) which dominates Simone and her actions, the 'dream' which is the concept which she has of herself and her life, her choice of mystery, of withdrawal, of falsity and secretiveness. Committing the murder and keeping it as her secret is what drives her, not the simple possibility of material benefit. The passage in which Bernanos analyses her decision to kill, which must be read in conjunction with what we know from other parts of the novel - her domination of Olivier, her intelligence and subtlety, her love of manipulation and of guiding events secretly, her will-power and determination - indicates something of the nature of this motivation. There is no distinction between will and desire, a 'mysterious instinct' makes her choose the circumstances of the crime, and she is caught up in a 'dream', knowing absolutely that a cold decision to do what she has moved inexorably towards doing will shape future events, and that she is now stronger, more cunning and more capable than at any time before. She is equally aware, however, that along with this cold determination to go to the heart of the lie - from which there will never be any escape - there is a certitude that in some way chance will betray her. Bernanos's final comment on her state of mind is interesting. No strong person, he suggests, is ever swayed by an intuitive fear, and indeed their fate is sealed by the sadness and foreboding that go with their insights.

The deviousness of her action and the nature of its deep and hidden motivation make it akin to Gide's 'gratuitous act' of the kind committed by Lafcadio Wluiki in *The Vatican Swindle* and discussed at length by him and Julius de Baraglioul. One striking difference, however, is that the characters in that latter book are figures in a satirical farce, and are clearly not meant to be realistically convincing, whereas those in the vast majority of Bernanos's novels are precisely that. They have a force and a life which arise from the fact that in all respects they are, to a reader of sensibility and imagination, totally credible creations. What we have here is a picture of a woman acting in an unpredictable way, if we judge by superficial character traits, and yet in total consistency with what we perceive through our own intuition and Bernanos's commentary as the deepest strata of her being.

Similarly, the official, discreet, diplomatic interpretation of the events culminating in Donissan's carrying of the dying Mouchette Malorthy into church in *Star of Satan* omits dimensions of the reality of that occurrence which are emphasized in the narrative of the mental events which precede it. The fuller version suggests whole ranges of inner experience which are ignored by the later, carefully-edited account. These include the intuitive awareness of a family history of vice and moral squalor, of generations affected by the same cancer, the realization that Mouchette's own actions are not, as she had thought, magnificently idiosyncratic, but part of a drearily-repeated pattern of corruption in which the individual acts out gestures already performed by others in other circumstances. They also include a self-awareness and self-knowledge which are, Bernanos indicates, produced by a consciousness heightened by an extreme situation. The emotional crisis is basically a crisis of identity bought into being by a fuller perception, a new view, of the nature of the self. In Mouchette's cases the impulse to suicide is only the culmination of a whole series of graphically-evoked mental states which contribute to her new and compellingly convincing way of seeing herelf. The carefully-edited and readily-acceptable version of her final moments, incorporated with connivance and deliberate simplification into both the official and personal attitudes of limited and fearful men, is no more than a shorthand form passed off as a whole truth.

In *Star of Satan* particularly, perhaps because it is the most problematically and overtly 'supernatural' of Bernanos's novels, the question of the immense complexity of human nature and experience assumes great significance. Individual comprehension, perception and motivation, Bernanos indicates, are always so hidden as to defy classification. Our interior experience is deep, secret and ineffable. The incidents of Donissan's spiritual crisis in his encounter with the horse-dealer related both as he experiences them and as a commonsense observer later reconstitutes them, and his attempted resuscitation of the dead child at the Plouy farm are examples of this suggestion of hidden complexity. The individual undergoes inner experiences which are beyond the perception of the external observer. Bernanos's novels represent an attempt to express what ultimately cannot be verbally expressed - the essence of the human psyche and the complexities of its individual experience - and he himself was aware of the great difficulties presented by the task:

> The most elementary emotions spring to life and take root in impenetrable night, where they blend or sunder according to secret affinities, like thunderclouds, and we are only aware of the surface flashes piercing through the blackness of those inaccessible storms. That is why the most accurate psychological hypotheses may help to reconstitute the past but are of no use in predicting the future. They merely serve - like many other assumptions - to dissemble a mystery of which the bare idea is a load upon the spirit (Bernanos, *Star of Satan*, 1940, 39).

That observation is not primarily a comment made by Bernanos on any individual character in *Star of Satan*. It is indeed a reflection induced by a contemplation of Mouchette Malorthy, but one which also extends to the whole of mankind and is of general rather than particular application. Any of Bernanos's powerful characters - Cénabre or Chantal de Clergerie in *Joy*, the parish priests of Ambricourt or Torcy in *Diary of a Country Priest*, the eponymous heroine of *Mouchette*, Simone Alfieri in *Night is Darkest* - could all serve as particular instances of the kind of mystery indicated by Bernanos's words, without in any way excluding each other or any other character. Even Ouine, the shadowy but major presence in *The Open Mind*, the incarnation of a spiritual and psychological vacuum, a man who has chosen negation and consequently total simplicity, transparency and emptiness, is an illustration by antithesis of the fact that living people are complex and opaque. He is not distinct from the objects of his curiosity. Both he and his pallid, prurient curiosity are:

'Pure water, you say?... Not pure, insipid, colourless, without freshness or vitality... Steel is less hard and lead less heavy, no-one could ever bite into this! This water is not pure but intact and changeless, as polished as a diamond looking-glass. And my thirst is like this water! My thirst and this water are one and the same'. (Bernanos, *The Open Mind*, 1945, 217).

SELF-CONCEPTS

The way in which characters are seen by Bernanos and by the reader is linked with the way in which they see themselves. Indeed, they need their self-concepts: if these are thrown into disarray or destroyed their life loses its meaning and they become no more than uncoordinated, gesticulating puppets whose apparently random actions lead towards their disintegration or death.

Perhaps the clearest way to show the importance of these self-concepts is to outline what happens when they collapse. Pernichon, a minor character in the untranslated (but see Bibliography) *L'Imposture*, offers a good example of this. The first ten pages of the novel are devoted to a study of the way in which the priest Cénabre, subtle, intelligent, sardonically curious and himself undergoing a crisis of identity, convinces the dreary journalist Pernichon of his emptiness and insignificance and, by means of the shock of making a vain man see his own feebleness and futility, sets him on the road to suicide. He thus hastens a process of disintegration which, because of his victim's idea of himself was founded on his weakness rather than his strength, was already latent within him. By making Pernichon see this, Cénabre starts to destroy him. The nature of the questions he puts to him, 'How do you see yourself?' and 'Do you think you are alive?' illustrate the fundamental nature of the attack: Cénabre wishes to destroy the most vital part of the inner life of a fellow human being. The result of the onslaught is that Pernichon's whole idea of himself, his whole way of seeing himself as a person, is shown as irrelevant and meaningless:

What of itself was enough to lay brutally bare the total chaos reigning in a normally extremely ordered mind was its invasion by the suddenly very plausible notion of a life with no spiritual reality. So many of us, even though we examine our actions fairly critically (...) fail to take into account the direction of our will or our perverted instincts (...) What is to be dreaded is not the strangers whose paths cross ours, but our own countenance, that our uprooted souls suddenly see face to face and do not recognize. (Bernanos, *L'Imposture*, 1963, 323).

As already suggested, it is because Cénabre's own sense of identity is disintegrating that he attacks Pernichon so violently:

The priest's sudden revolt was moreover simply a delayed defensive reaction ... And yet the thought born in his mind some time ago and stronger every day thrust itself constantly upon him and thwarted his efforts to avoid it. He would push it aside only to find, to his amazement, that it was now everywhere woven into the fabric of his daily life. In his sudden fit of anger against Pernichon, he recognized it yet again. (Bernanos, *L'Imposture*, 1963, 327-328).

His constructed self, acquired over years of self-discipline, austerity and scholarship, crumbles, and he is faced with the fact that he is a stranger to himself:

The conviction that his distress was pointless and unreal was the final blow cutting the last link between the present and the past and leaving him in a void. His faith had vanished as though it had never existed, and at that moment he felt as if he had never lived. He would have given everything to feel even the most painful resistance or heartbreak, to feel anything but the silent disintegration of a being he had thought real and that was now replaced by emptiness ... but he now seemed marked forever by a supernatural silence (Bernanos, *L'Imposture*, 1963, 335).

The result of this is to be the complete transformation of his inner life, and indeed his final total breakdown. As his self-concept disintegrates, he abandons himself to nothingess, to the interior void left by the dissolution of his idea of himself:

> It was the same dizziness ... the same burning forehead, the same feeling of hollowness in his chest, of icy cold on his shoulders. The one thing that could best express the blind violence of his thoughts would have been a shriek, and yet the silence was total and solemn, becoming denser and shriller around his despair with each moment that passed. At such times, the whole body is aware of pain and death, and in every fibre of his being he felt that he had gone beyond the point of no return and that his fall would of its own accord grow faster and faster. He had no hope, nor could he even imagine a return or a halt in his vertical descent. (Bernanos, *L'Imposture*,1963, 371).

Observations of this kind are frequently encountered in the novels. They are expressed, for example, in *Night is Darkest* with reference to Simone Alfieri, where once again, as a persona crumbles under the impact of reality (in this case, the shock of killing), an inner void becomes apparent, and the character becomes an actor, functioning outside her own personality. Her actions, as Bernanos has already pointed out, are the result of the deep self-hatred which all falsity ultimately produces:

> At a certain pitch of nervous tension when panic itself may be said to have found its point of balance, a terrifying immobility, the living creature's strongest instinct, self-defence, seems in fact to be submerged. The wretched victim is then no longer able to escape from his pain or distress; he can only exhaust it. Madness in all its forms ends by stripping man to the last layer of his soul, his secret hatred of himself; the most deeply hidden thing in his life, probably in all life (Bernanos, *Night is Darkest*, 1953, 173-174).

Here, she has reached a final stage where the emptiness and nothingness are accepted and welcomed and the heightened sense of the imminent dissolution of the self produces a cold, detached and sombre state of exaltation. She experiences the same clear awareness of one kind of ultimate situation as that earlier Bernanosian epitome of the lucidly despairing protagonist, the austere and intelligent priest Cénabre:

> Father Cénabre thought that he had been courageous enough to empty himself of both hope and despair. Now that he had gone as far as he could, there was nothing left. The thought exhilarated him, and he turned it constantly round in his mind, as one does with a delightful memory known to oneself alone. His soul, long imprisoned in the solitude created by his wrong action in the past, was now willingly and irrevocably abandoned to it. The only thing between himself and nothingness, he was aware, was his flickering life that could be snuffed out by something as insignificant as a burst blood vessel. That realization immediately made him feel as if his heart was surrounded by flames of fire.
>
> We usually accept the idea of nothingness as the only possibility left when all the others have been destroyed, simply because by definition it cannot be tested and our reason can tell us nothing about it. Most of us do so with despair and repugnance. Cénabre, however, truly gave that nothingness his faith, his strength and his life (Bernanos, *L'Imposture*, 1963, 443-444).

AN INFINITY OF MASKS

There are constant references throughout the novels to masks, roles, falseness and hypocrisy, and it is clear that Bernanos sees the choice and pursuit of a lived lie as a basic fact of at least certain kinds of human experience. In the final part of *The Crime* the words of the supposed priest of Mégère to the half-comprehending young altar boy who has accompanied him in his fight explore the heart of this fundamental kind of falsity. Deception, deliberate bad faith and the conscious creation of a false persona are a major component of the Bernanosian image of man, even though such undertakings are the prerogative of an intelligent and lucid elite. *Corruptio optimi pessima*. The world, the 'priest' tells the boy, is full of people who hide nothing because they are nothing. They can know themselves only through the view of them that others have, and are condemned to live and die with the identity given them, like ships sailing under a foreign flag. Few people, he continues, are capable of 'dreaming', which means lying to oneself after one has first learnt to lie to others. In an attempt at self-reproduction, he suggests to the acolyte that if he had stayed in Mégère he would have had to put on a mask or masks, an infinity of masks, one for each day of his life.

These remarks too are made by a character at a time when the lie at the centre of his life is no longer possible, when events force out the truth and he sees himself in its light. The accretions of a lifetime fall away, and his real inner life, which he has for so long stifled and vitiated in order to support an external persona, withers in the face of an unbearable reality. Characters in such a situation (and there are many of them in the novels) are all in fact victims of the danger which Simone Alfieri sees in *Night is Darkest* and which they think they can escape: 'We are all play-acting, but one must have time to choose one's part - a part that allows us to act a lie before other people without completely losing touch with ourselves' (Bernanos, *Night is Darkest*, 1953, 102). The contact *is* lost to a great extent, and it is this that produces their ultimate breakdown. The lie feeds on their inner life and flourishes whilst that life weakens and fades. The fundamental tragic error of such people is their belief and that the self can live on and from itself, can feed on its own contemplation, can so to speak *create* itself in the eyes of others, achieving this self-creation by the selection of a personality, the putting on of a mask. Sartre's idea of the human being as condemned to be what others see him to be must perhaps be without meaning here, for Bernanos's characters willingly *choose* to create that image in their own fashion. Their pleasure is to know that it is false and implanted by their own efforts, and to feel themselves infinitely more varied and complex than any image of themselves which they create for others to perceive. The active nature of the vocabulary and metaphor which Bernanos uses to describe their actions - choosing a role, wearing a mask - is significant. The very deviousness of certain Bernanosian characters can in fact be seen (paradoxically, perhaps, as it leads ultimately to their personal disintegration) as an affirmation of the plenitude and complexity of psychic life. What they create may be false and short-lived, but the frequent recurrence of such psychological strategies in Bernanos's novels does indicate a concern to show that man is an intricate and mysterious being.

THE 'VORACIOUS MAW' OF SELF-ABSORPTION

It would, however, be quite untrue to suggest that Bernanos saw self-knowledge or self-exploration as an ideal. The opposite, which is implicit in what has been said so far, would be nearer the truth. It is Ouine himelf, the anti-person incarnate, the fat, sick, pale, sweating retired professor of modern languages, who more than any other Bernanosian character preaches it as a goal. Although he can say that there is no end of the world, but that we can all go to the end of ourselves, finding there enough substance to nourish a whole life, his own final state is one of total nothingness, of a complete interior void:

> 'But now nothing will ever fill me, (...) It would need tremendous labour to fill me, and this labour as yet hasn't even begun. Life has run through me like a sieve. I've opened myself, dilated myself, to nothing. I was a mere orifice, an intake, a swallowing up, both my body and soul wide open on all sides. Among the many pastures from which I could choose, smothered like an ox in provender, with what careful patience I always selected the most nutritious, the most succulent, the apparently poor and at times repellent, and usually despised by fools. I was in no hurry. I flattered myself I knew how to wait. I quietly assessed my pleasure beforehand, and my profit too. I worked out the exact point of succulence, the point of that complete maturity which comes invariably, just before decay sets in. And always alone! So as not to have to share my pleasure or pain. Alas! what could I ever have shared? I longed, I puffed myself up with longings, instead of simply eating my fill. I made no substance, either good or evil, one with myself - My soul is no more than a leather bottle full of wind. And now, young man, just see what's happening to me! The bottle is sucking the whole of me into it. I can feel myself melting away and

vanishing down its avid throat. My very bones are melting away!' (Bernanos, *The Open Mind*, 1945, 212).

In his essays too, Bernanos has given his opinion of those who see the exploration and extension of the personality and self-knowledge as ideals. What he says about Proust in *Le Crépuscule des vieux* is harsh but not uninteresting:

> The awesome introspection we see in Proust's work goes nowhere. For a while it may lead us breathlessly on, constantly opening up new vistas and creating an illusory lesson that it is always about to yield up and never in fact does. Trying to track down its message is a staggering and perhaps even a hopeless undertaking. His characters are lubricious animals endowed with reason, as polished and complicated as surgical instruments, creatures for whom Christ died to no purpose. I am saying not only that God is absent from Proust's work, but that there is not even a trace of Him, and that it would be impossible even to speak His name (Bernanos, *Le Crépuseule des vieux*, 1956, 78, 79).

Introspection for its own sake is sterile. In a mirror, one sees neither God nor man, but, inevitably, a distorted image of oneself. Man is complex, fascinating, mysterious and unknowable and cannot be fully or truly perceived or understood through a fascinated and indulgent self-contemplation or self-analysis. Our concept of ourselves as persons is totally independent of such activities and, can in fact, only be weakened by them in the long run.

We need to see ourselves, Bernanos implies, in quite a different way. What is important is not that we should explore what we might see as the mysteries and delightful idlosyncracies of our own fascinatingly various and immensely subtle personalities, but that we should have a concept of ourselves as independent, autonomous beings with a deep nature, an inviolable central core of being which cannot be manipulated, dissected or even fondled out of existence. This central reality may be whole, intact, integral, totally itself, as it possibly is in Chantal de Clergerie in *Joy*. If we achieved that situation, we should, because we should be fully human, be saints. Or it may be distorted, weakened, starved as in the case of Chantal's father in *Joy* or of Ganse or Olivier in *Night is Darkest* and of the vast range of mediocrities in any of the novels. Or, if it is totally shattered, as with Cénabre or Simone Alfieri, our lives will become empty, sterile and devoid of all meani ng, and we shall live outside them, spectators of our own futile and empty actions, watching the lies at the centre of our lives evaporate and unable to fill the emptiness and deadness left in their place.

The nearest Bernanos approaches to a clear statement about the real nature of our inner lives seems to come in the words of Menou-Segrals in *Star of Satan*. We are sometimes and in some ways a criminal or a saint, sometimes impelled towards good not by a judicious estimation of the calculable benefits which a particular orientation may offer, but by a movement of our whole being, in which we are sometimes drawn on by a sense of beauty and peace, sometimes tormented by a mysterious enjoyment of our own degradation, our longing for the taste of ashes in our mouth, the traces of our animal nature still present in us, and our nostalgia for it unappeased. The currents of our being, Bernanos contends, run deeper than moralists or psychologists would have us believe. We cannot define ourselves clearly, because all definitions are simplifications and therefore falsify. The only ultimately meaningful concept of man is that which takes account of the self-contradiction arising from our fallen nature, of what Newman called our 'aboriginal calamity'. Any attempt to explain man in other terms, says Bernanos, provides an apparently acceptable definition, but man is more complex than any definition, is not reducible to it, and goes beyond it:

> Outside the hypothesis of original sin - that is, of a deep contradiction in our nature - the idea of man becomes clear, but it is no longer an idea of man. Man goes beyond any definition of him, as a handful of sand runs through our fingers. (Bernanos, *La Liberté pour quoi faire? (Freedom for What?)* 1972, 252-253).

THE PERMANENT AND PRECARIOUS SELF

It should perhaps be stressed that although in Bernanos's eyes man is necessarily flawed, he is not flawed beyond the possibility of redemption. Although he is a being in whom the image of God has been distorted and clouded, it has not been totally obliterated, and in his heart man senses this.

He is a creature perhaps 'full of boredom and vice' but still 'a big child', who needs a concept both of his own guilt and his own goodness if he is to survive as a person. Although it is possible to weaken such concepts and, superficially at least, to move beyond them, this can only be done at the risk of producing a crisis of identity and of being whose cause may be obscure to the observer but whose consequences for the person enduring them will be extremely grave. There are several reflections on this theme in, for example, *The Open Mind*. The parish priest of Fenouille, in an anguished discussion with the local doctor, stresses the result of destroying man's view of himself and his nature, for then, without the sanction of the supernatural, the natural (in this case natural virtue, a natural desire for decency and purity) will be weakened and forced undergound, to surface again in unsuspected and perhaps malignant and destructive ways.

'All the same' said the priest, 'one day you'll get proof that you never reckoned enough with the supernatural. Yes,' he resumed after a silence, in that voice which every time it was heard contrasted so strangely with his usual manner and way of speech that it might have been the voice of another man, 'yes, when you've managed to stifle in human beings, not merely the speech but even the sense of purity, that very faculty in mankind which distinguishes purity from filth, there'll still always be instinct left. Instinct will be stronger than you and your ways. And if ever instinct should be atrophied, suffering will still remain - a suffering men will have ceased to be able to give a name to, a poisoned thorn in the heart of man. Suppose one day you manage the kind of revolution which biologists and technicians keep invoking, so that you do away with any hierarchy of the needs of man, so that lust seems merely an appetite of the loins, which need only be kept from sating itself to the very uttermost by a strict hygiene - yes, then you'll see mayors of Fenouille springing up everywhere, turning their hatred against themselves, against their own flesh, a hatred which then will always be blind, since then its causes will lie buried deep in the darkest layer of inherited memory. While you may flatter yourselves on having reconciled this basic inner contradiction, secured the mental peace of your wretched slaves, reconciled humanity with the thing which at present still torments, puts it to shame - I prophesy a plague of suicide, against which you'll be powerless. So you should go in fear of our human longing to be clean, you should fear it far more than obsession by lechery. It pleases you to see in men's blind revolt against physical lust, fear, kept alive through centuries by the Churches, those cunning servants of judges and law givers. But our love of purity there lies the mystery! - love, in the finest men and women, and in the rest sadness, regrets, that indefinable, poignant bitterness which rakes cherish more closely even than desire. Good enough for cowards, whipped on by death or the torment of pain, who come begging the doctor for a reprieve. But I've seen, - yes, seen! - in eyes looking up into mine, something quite different. In any case, the time for persuasion is over, the immediate future will show us all just where we belong! At the pace the world is going now, we shall soon know whether man can ever be reconciled with himself to the point of forgetting once and for all, what we priests know by its real name, our ancient earthly paradise, our lost joy, our lost Kingdom of Joy. If piety were only an illusion, even though it had lasted thousands of centuries ... (Bernanos, *The Open Mind*, 1945, 190-191).

Such ideas, whether one considers them to be visionary, prophetic and deeply convincing, or rhetorical and empty, the noisy rattle of a morbid and dying view of the world, speak for themselves. Whatever the reader's view of the way of seeing human life which inspires them, their import is clear. If we have a reductionist view of man, if we see the psyche as a balance of impulses, happiness as an epiphenomenon of the satisfaction of our urges, then, without any capacity for healing shame, the greatest hope left for our fallen nature, we are doomed. Secular man, in sexuality as in everything else, is for Bernanos man without hope in either theological or human terms.

Rather surprisingly perhaps, Bernanos has little to say about the precise way in which we see ourselves. Presumably, this is because we are ultimately as much a mystery to ouselves as we are to others. There is an indication, powerful and convincing, in the novels that we have a deep sense of ourselves as persons, but, except when this idea of our independent being is endangered or weakened, either because the specific manifestation of it in our own minds or that of other is destroyed, or because it is a false one, or because external circumstances combine to weaken it or to distort it, there is no detailed exploration of it in depth beyond an indication that it consists largely of our awareness of its complexity, indivduality and irreducibility. Thus, in the case of the second Mouchette, for example, the fourteen-year-old who dies largely because her concept of herself as a person, however inchoate, amorphous and clouded it may be, is challenged and the whole integrity of her being is slighted and threatened, there is a series of negative or indefinite statements, or at most statements which illuminate a specific notion in her mind without doing more than suggest one aspect of the way in which she sees herself. We are told, for example, that her thoughts are vague and disconnected, and that her image of herself as one of the very poor and deprived is made up of a number of separate dissociated images:

> Of course, thoughts never passed through Mouchette's mind in such a logical way. She was vague and jumped quickly from one thing to another. If the very poor could associate the various images of their poverty they would be overwhelmed by it, but their wretchedness seems to them to consist simply of an endless succession of miseries, a series of unfortunate chances. They are like blind men who with trembling fingers count out the coins whose value they cannot calculate. For the poor, the idea of poverty is enough. Their poverty is faceless. (Bernanos, *Mouchette*, 1966, 16).

We also learn, in a succession of rapid and evocative images, a great deal about the way in which she sees both her own individual purity and purity in general:

...Perhaps in this way the innate knowledge and pride for which she had doubtlessly been born had awakened. Any talk of virginity would simply have made her smile stupidly. Purity meant scarcely more to her than the physical image of clear water or - even more naively - the memory of the pretty girls who visited the big houses of the district each summer, with their fresh, clean clothes, their soft, laughing voices and their long hands lingering on carriage doors. Thus her hungry pride, so long unrewarded and joyless, but secretly nourished in her own innermost being, had at last found in this childish and brutal revelation of her physical integrity what it needed to blossom.

She had no vanity about her body. It bore the marks of blows and the scratches of brambles; it was tanned by winter winds and dressed in ridiculous dresses made from cut-down garments of her mother's. Her fierce modesty had nothing in common with that other sentiment which throughout the centuries has owed more to painters and poets than to the deep instinct of defence from which it is supposed to derive. It was not that false modesty with which the beautiful girl, preoccupied with the worship of her body since before her senses were wakened, confuses her sense of delicacy, and which she feels to have been offended when, despite the concerted efforts of her perfumer and her dressmaker, she must submit to the humiliating violation of her idol (Bernanos, *Mouchette*, 1966, 63-64).

We are also aware of a fierce and uncompromising pride which is very closely linked to her way of seeing herself:

She was not aware of despising anyone because, in her innocence, this seemed outside her capabilities, and she thought no more of it than she did of the other more material characteristics which the rich and the powerful reserve for themselves. Indeed, she would have been amazed if anyone had told her that she despised Madame. She simply saw herself as a rebel against an order which the schoolmistress typified. When Madame told her from time to time that she was no good, she never contradicted her. She was no more ashamed of that than she was of her rags. For a long time she had delighted in a savage indifference to the disdainful comments of the other girls and the mockery of the boys.

Often on a Sunday morning, when her mother sent her to the village for the week's bacon, she deliberately let herself get muddy on the road and reached the square just as people were coming out of Mass. And yet, suddenly, something had happened ... (Bernanos, *Mouchette*, 1966, 30-31).

At no point in the novel, however, does Bernanos synthesize these various elements of Mouchette's concept of herself. The reader, in fact, must make the imaginative effort to see the whole, and to link all these and other separate elements of one inarticulate individuals way of thinking of herself into an overall perception. This he will, no doubt, largely do subconsciously, intuitively, and imaginatively, as Mouchette herself, or Bernanos, would do, rather than consciously and methodically. Reflection and analysis are later processes.

Even when such means are within the grasp of a particular character as a result of his intelligence, education or training, they can only offer limited help in the process of self-understanding. Indeed, Bernanos hints, those who use them as a means of exploring themselves may find something quite different from what they expect or hope to find. The self they see may in a sense be a parallel one, a forgotten one, perhaps the one which lies at the basis of the present way of seeing themselves but which is even more mysterious. This is the experience undergone by the hero of the *Diary of a Country Priest*. Ultimately his idea of himself must, despite his experience of the interior examination so essential to his vocation, remain as imprecise, as partial, as diconnected as Mouchette's is to her. At this level, there are no words to define and illustrate perceptions. Images and a communication of immediate reactions are all that is available. What is perhaps even more important is an awareness of the possible dangers of introspection. Seeing ourselves as only God perhaps could or should see us might lead to a melancholy and tender self-indulgence or towards a certain rather weepy self-concept, and such traps could only be avoided by rigorous honesty. A short passage from the novel seems to suggest the nature of such processes and the dangers inherent in them. The young priest is well aware of the difficulty of examining ways of seeing himself and is clearly impressed by the ultimately enigmatic revelations which they often bring. His reflections contain suggestions of many recurring Bernanosian themes, notably those of lost childhood, of the harshness of individual fate, and (more relevantly here), of the dangers of self-absorption and of the mystery at the heart of all human existence and experience:

> It isn't exactly a question of scruple; I don't think I am doing wrong in jotting down, day by day, without hiding anything, the very simple trivial secrets of a very ordinary kind of life. What I am about to record would not reveal much to the only friend with whom I still manage to speak openly, and besides I know I could never bring myself to put on paper the things which almost every morning I confide to God without any shame. No, it is hardly a scruple, but rather a sort of unreasoning fear, a kind of instinctive warning. When I first sat down before this child's copy-book I tried to concentrate, to withdraw into myself as though I were examining my conscience before confession. And yet my real conscience was not revealed by that inner light - usually so dispassionate and penetrating, passing over details, showing up the whole. It seemed to skim the surface of another consciousness, previously unknown to me, a cloudy mirror in which I feared that a face might suddenly appear. Whose face? Mine, perhaps. A forgotten, rediscovered face ...
>
> When writing of oneself one should show no mercy. Yet why at the first attempt to discover one's own truth does all inner strength seem to melt away in floods of self-pity and tenderness and rising tears ... (Bernanos, Diary of a *Country Priest*, 1937 (rep 1975) 15-16).

And yet self-doubt is wrong, and a morbid tenderness towards oneself the sign of a serious lesion of the interior life. The dangers of self-observation are those of a certain kind of vicious pride, of the possibility of self-destruction arising from despair and self-sickness:

> To doubt oneself is not to be humble, I even think that sometimes it is the most hysterical form of pride, a pride almost delirious, a kind of jealous ferocity which makes an unhappy man turn and rend himself. That must be the real truth of hell (Bernanos, *Diary of a Country Priest*, 1937 (rep 1975) 264).

This is because what we call moods or states of mind or, in more technical theological terms, dispositions of the soul, are, says Bernanos, the soul itself, and our flawed nature has as its very basis sadness, anguish and despair. Without the presence of grace, acting in some way or another, a total and uncompromising awareness of oneself would mean, it is clearly and unequivocally stated, the disintegration of the human being. This is the great danger which is shown to the reader in the priest's diary, and the one which the great sinners in the novels, those who destroy their own humanity, such as Cénabre and Simone Alfieri, encounter as the result of a sudden and overwhelming perception of the lie at the heart of their lives. It is the ultimate complexity, the ultimate mystery, at the heart of the human being:

> Nevertheless as I read these pages, and though I can find no real fault with them, they appear very futile. No reasoning yet has ever created real grief - grief of the spirit. Or conquered it, once it has come into us, God knows through what gap in our being ... Such grief did not enter, it was within us. More and more firmly am I convinced that what we call sadness, anguish, despair, as though to persuade oursleves that these are only states of the Spirit, are the Spirit itself. I believe that ever since his fall, man's condition is such that neither around him nor within him can he perceive anything, except in the form of agony. (Bernanos, *Diary of a Country Priest*, 1937 (rep 1975) 213).

When there is no concept of or desire for the pity of God which the country priest mentions, it is this sudden glimpse, as the result of a crisis, of the ultimate truth about themselves which pushes individuals to destroy themselves, to hasten the process of returning to dust. The collapse of the psyche, the final madness of which Bernanos speaks, will produce a violent, acute and accelerated form of the 'sickness unto death'. Simone Alfieri's state of mind at the moment of the murder she has long premeditated is extremely relevant. All she can accept at that point is her own death, her own removal from the meaningless society of her fellow-men. Anything else would be incongruous and ridiculous, and Bernanos stresses the suicidal aspect of her situation, her desire for her own dissolution as a living entity. The culminating scene of her life has produced both a desire for death and a moment of lucid calm followed by a dull, self-destructive rage, a vivid sense of the simplicity of death, an impatience for it and a curiosity about it, emotions which she had already felt in a similar situation at another time and in another place. To live with herself, as to live with others, would now be grotesque, cheap and ultimately impossible. The result of her actions and the final crisis of her life is:

> ... a kind of suicide but lacking the immediate fall, the dizzy descent into oblivion. At least it allows a respite, however short; even if it is only long enough to allow a brief enjoyment of that blissful solitude, the solitude of happiness or genius.
>
> She was enjoying this even now, and she reflected not without a certain satisfaction that this enjoyment was precarious, that wronged society would not delay its revenge. The disproportion between the gravity of the deed she had committed and her meagre joy mingled with satiety and disgust - like the joy that follows any great emotional effort of one's being, first the fall of man, then the infernal circle, followed by derision - was beginning to arouse in her heart a dull rage that was being gradually directed against herself. Just then she would not have made the slightest move to get away and in truth any notion of flight already seemed futile. Her imagination had not seen beyond the murder, and now, with the murder accomplished, as if she had come to a crossroads, a new prospect opened before her. She must finish off what she had begun; it needed this last scene

to give the drama its meaning. In a sudden flash she saw herself standing before her judges just as she stood now before her puny victim, motionless, silent with her eyes half-closed, answering the accusation with a scornful, inflexible silence. The idea of resuming her old way of life at the point where she had left it - in the odious little apartment, or, why not, at old Ganse's desk - seemed too ridiculous to be worth considering. And suddenly nothing seemed simpler, wonderfully simple and easy in fact, than to await the return of the housekeeper. Deep in her heart she had already felt that faint stir of curiosity and impatience which she knew so well and which she always felt in every crisis: face to face, for example, with another corpse, that of the handsome lover, with his head broken in, lying in the palace room with the dark bloodstain on the blue carpet, a smell of stale air mingled with the scent of amber and English tobacco (Bernanos, *Night Is Darkest*, 1953, 179).

Such quotations illustrate, it can be argued, specific examples (in different circumstances and in different crises, but with the same underlying insight explicitly formulated), of the essential philosophical or spiritual perception expressed by the country priest. When a human being sees himself as he really is, when he perceives the fundamental truths about his existence and his nature, when he clearly sees the 'movements of the soul' which are in some sense *himself*, he needs more than merely human strength if he is not to succumb to anguish and despair. Without the watchful divine pity, the country priest tells us, a real knowledge of ourselves might be unbearable.

This idea of the potential dissolution of the self is latent in all of us and can overwhelm us when we are lucidly aware of our own mortality, our own weakness, our solitude and our apparently ephemeral and contingent existence, or when a moment of crisis throws the true nature of our lives sharply and pitilessly into focus. Anguish is a precondition of any real knowledge, either of the self or of what is outside the self. It may lead finally to the kind of illumination which we presume the young priest has as he is dying in the squalor of his renegade colleague's flat in Lille and which is indicated by his final words ('Grace is .... everywhere') or it may lead to a direct or indirect form of suicide, fully and immediately accomplished or not, as in the cases of the two Mouchettes or of Simone Alfieri. In these cases, the actions of the individual, because they spring from feelings or motives so deep within him, are in a sense inexplicable to the outside observer and consequently seem sudden and gratuitous. For Bernanos, however, their seeds have lain germinating throughout a lifetime and finally, as a result of circumstances, have been brought inevitably to fruition. He speaks of a predestination to suicide, and it seems probable that it is in this sense that the word must be understood. Human life carries within it the seeds of its own potential destruction and in certain lives, once a particular orientation is established, the only eventual way out is a death of one kind or another, whether it be death in the literal sense, or the kind of death-in-life where nothing more than a basic biological flicker is maintained and which is so often portrayed in the novels.

Such a contention would seem to be borne out by what Bernanos says in other places. The Mouchette of *Star of Satan* is to do what she does because of her bitter disappointment and scorn when faced, after her killing of Cadignan, by another 'yokel' in the form of Donissan. Given her idea of herself, her experiences, her attitudes, her motivation, the whole 'movement of her soul', the whole etiology of her situation, what was to happen seems, as the author says 'already written within her'. Indeed, in more general terms, Bernanos has already spoken in the novel of the deep self as the container of the driving force of an individual life, or the destiny that shapes its end, both of which are often incompatible with what external appearances would suggest:

> There are some who seem made for tranquillity, yet tragedy lies in wait. You would never have thought it, you could not have foreseen it. For the facts are nothing: the tragedy is within (Bernanos, *Star of Satan*, 1940, 22).

If we take here 'facts' as external, verifiable, observable events and actions, we have a statement which sums up the whole of Bernanos's view of human nature, of character, of relationship with the external world and, in the sense mentioned above, of predestination. It is a rather more profound expression of Novalis's alleged dictum that character is fate, and is illustrated in such creations as Cénabre, who, by being what they profoundly are, in a sense *choose* their fate rather than are subject to it. The mystery of that fate for the external observer is explained by the very fact that he *is* an external observer:

> It is not of course that this remarkable man was born marked with such a dreadful curse. Whatever part of his youth had been devoted to a lie, there had come a time, outwardly indistinguishable from any other, when indifference had become a deliberate, conscious and lucid choice of negation. What cannot be known is when that time was (Bernanos, *L'Imposture*, 1961, 443).

THE SHADOW OF THE PAST

As well as being the result of an inner, unknown choice, however, this element of predestination in human life is linked to what we might loosely call heredity. The sins of the fathers are indeed visited on the children. No man is an island, for there is a solidarity in sin in the novels just as there is a solidarity in sanctity. Good and evil for Bernanos are not a private matter between consenting adults, for every action and every choice is complex and unpredictable in its ramified and scattered effects. As well as being potentially sanctified by others, each individual is also potentially flawed by them. Those others may be people with whom he comes into contact during the course of his life as, for example, Chantal encounters Chevance and Cénabre in *L'Imposture* and *Joy*, or people who have left this world and whom he has perhaps never met, such as the dead generations who have preceded and produced the second Mouchette and the Steeny of *The Open Mind*. One of the recurring themes of the novels in fact is precisely that of the legacy of evil bequeathed to each human being as a result of the flawed nature of his forebears, and we see in them specific and suggestive existential examples of the effects of original sin, perpetuating itself from generation to generation. Mouchette Malorthy in *Star of Satan*, for instance, is shown as having been shaped to some extent by her ancestry, and as having, in her encounter with Donissan, an insight into the dreariness of generations of petty evil. In a similar way, the various kinds of weakness apparent in Steeny's ancestors in *The Open Mind* although they are less striking and more amorphous, have combined to produce a 'different' Philippe, a child deeply affected by them, who will one day shatter the calm of the ordered, leisurely vice of his mother's household.

But not all the evil contained in the ancestry of the present generation is simply to be seen or described as morally blameworthy acts. It is what the ancestors have *been* rather than what they have *done* which represents the deadening weight of the past on the present. The deprivation, squalor and ignorance endured by generations of the second Mouchette's ancestors are at least a contributory cause of her rebellion, leaving her with an inheritance of 'unreasoning, animal revolt' and both her present situation and her reaction to it have been shaped by such factors.

In *Diary of a Country Priest* too, much incidental comment is made on the young priest's alcoholic inheritance and of the squalid scenes he has witnessed in his aunt's bar as a child, and such things have clearly influenced him very deeply. His abilities, his self-confidence, his very view of himself, have all been in a sense diminished and his freedom consequently lessened by such antecedent influences. What an earlier generation either freely or involuntarily has made of human life determines to at least some extent what a later one will make of it. Cénabre's father was an alcoholic killed by drink at an early age, the Evangeline of *The Crime* is the illegitimate child of an ex-nun and (probably) an unfrocked priest. Tainted ancestry is a blight on human life throughout the novels.

LIFE AND CHOICE

And yet paradoxically human beings in Bernanos's novels can be free. We should not take his use of the word predestination in any absolute sense. For Bernanos, freedom means fundamentally freedom from evil, active or passive, and the ability, within a given situation or frame of reference, a given predicament perhaps, to see that there is a way out. Again paradoxically, that freedom depends on acceptance and not on refusal. The country priest, in this sense, is free enough to accept his suffering and death and to offer his vitiated constitution to God. In *Star of Satan*, Bernanos stresses through Menou-Segrais, a character of whom he clearly approves, the inescapability of moral choice in all human life: 'There's no end to arguments and theories, but to live means you've got to choose' (*Star of Satan*, 1940, 83). That existentialist echo, together with many other references in the novels to the choices made by various characters and their commitment to good or evil following from them, is strikingly reminiscent of Thomist thought, in which desire might be unfree, in the sense that it is inbuilt, predetermined, influenced or indeed tainted by nature or heredity, but the ability to choose between a number of possible actions or responses in a given situation is at least to some extent free and undetermined and may in fact be in direct opposition to desire. These two contrasting strands run through the whole imaginative texture of the novels. Where there is 'predestination', it is because desire, demanding and imperative, is accepted and freewill ignored, and impulse rather than direction is chosen. When the possibility of choice is heeded, there is freedom. Where deep drives are dominant, when options cannot be seen or can only be partly seen, or cowardice reigns, freedom disappears or is attenuated.

EXCEPT YE BECOME AS LITTLE CHILDREN....

Such freedom is, for Bernanos, to be achieved by the confrontation of two irreconcilables: adult corruption and the innocence of childhood, and by respecting and loving the latter. This is exactly what the childlike saints in his novels do and thus free themselves and their associates from the stifling and deadening burden of sin. It is the great achievement of lives which on the surface appear wasted, such as those of the country priest and Chantal de Clergerie. Because they choose to accept their sufferings and to give their joy and their lives for others, they become free, and by the redemptive value of vicarious suffering can free others. Because they are childlike, they have the generosity and charity to act in that way.

Childhood was of prime importance for Bernanos, representing freedom, spontaneity, generosity and perceptiveness and seen clearly as the essential precondition for entry into the kingdom of heaven. Although it is a major and recurring theme in his novels, it is not treated sentimentally. Its importance is emphasized again and again, for it represents a kind of paradise lost, a mental and emotional climate which is vitally necessary in human life. It is something which can never be left entirely behind, and for the country priest, the Bernanosian character who above all others has retained his childhood, it is the gift of God which will vitally shape a man's life:

> And I know now that youth is the gift of God, and like all His gifts, carries no regret. They alone shall be young, really young, whom He has chosen never to survive their youth. I belong to such a race of men. I used to wonder: what shall I be doing at fifty, at sixty? And of course I couldn't find an answer, I couldn't even make one up. There was no old man in me.
>
> This awareness is sweet. For the first time in years - perhaps for the first time ever - I seem to stand before my youth and look upon it without mistrust; I have rediscovered a forgotten face. And my youth looks back at me, forgives me.
>
> Disheartened by the sheer clumsiness in me which always kept me back, I demanded of my youth what youth alone can't give, and I said it was a stupid thing and was ashamed of being young. But now, both weary with our silly quarrels, we can rest awhile, silent by the road, and breathe in the deep peace of evening where we shall enter together. (Bernanos, *Diary of a Country Priest*, 1937 (rep 1975) 309).

This is the Christian equivalent of Nietzsche's dictum that what matters is not eternal life but eternal vivacity, and in Bernanos's novels this eternal vivacity is wholeness, purity, holiness. With sanctity comes an abundance of life and freedom, and the candour and insight of the child both precede and are contained in sanctity.

As an innocent, though deprived and brutalized child, the second Mouchette has these latter two qualities. She can see in Arsène something which no-one else could see in him, and which she could see in no-one else. For her, he represents salvation, in human terms at least, because he is a human being to whom she could have given herself. At the level at which she sees him (that of another independent, autonomous, mysterious human being, despite all his vices and his irresponsibility), this is a valid insight, one of those immediate and intuitive perceptions on which so much of human destiny depends. The world of no longer innocent adults, of which Arsène is already a part, destroys any such possibility, but the potential, which she and only she is able to glimpse, fleetingly and fragmentarily, is nevertheless there, however briefly.

THE BLESSING OF SHAME

Childhood is a constant point of reference, a light in which our adult lives are seen and judged. However naive or subtle a man may be in his awareness of himself, the memory of his childhood will always, Bernanos suggests, be one dimension of his self-understanding and self-judgement. In the novels it is often a memory of a lost innocence which produces a deep shame. From this sense of shame may arise varying states of mind, ranging from the self-disgust of the mayor in *The Open Mind*, where there is no faith or hope to counterbalance the shame, to joy and acceptance in the country priest who can see it as a means of starting the return to God by way of a rediscovery of the innocence and sincerity of childhood and as an aspect of that fortunate fall (*o felix culpa*) which necessitated the tremendous act of love accomplished by Christ in his redemption of humanity. Speaking to the Countess, he says that those faults that leave us with shame are blessed, and hopes that she will experience it, for shame is a potentially liberating human experience, another element in the intricate play of predestination and freedom which lies at the heart of all human life. It can be the object of interested but detached reflection, savoured for its own sake as an interesting experience, and its possibility as a means of salvation can be rejected, as is the case with Cénabre, or it may be an instinctive, incoherent, nebulous and naive movement, simply an instinctive modesty, as with the second Mouchette, but in both cases it is decisive factor in an individual destiny. It is a major element of human self-awareness, a constant of the inner life of the person, and a key factor in any understanding of his being and his actions.

Clearly, for many human beings, conflicts arising from their own sexuality will often, although by no means always, lie at the origin of shame. This is the case in the novels with Séraphita Dumouchel in *Diary of a Country Priest*, Mouchette Malorthy and Saint-Marin in *Star of Satan* and Arsène in *The Open Mind*. For Bernanos, sexuality, or rather, to distinguish as carefully as he himself does here, lust, is one of the great wounds in the human psyche. Indeed, in his view of man, there is an important distinction between these two related phenomena. In a very real sense it is the perception of this distinction and the consequent ability to separate, isolate, cultivate and refine sensation, to substitute a means for an end, which mark man off from the rest of the animal creation. It might be possible to define evil actions as those which wilfully introduce disorder into human life. If this is so, the attraction of lust, like that of all evils, is that it can create a superficially convincing counterfeit of the good of which it is essentially a deprivation. Bernanos seems to suggest this:

> What do we really know of lust? What do we know of their hidden connections? Lust is a mysterious wound in the side of humanity; or rather at the very source of its life! To confound this lust in man with that desire which unites the sexes is like confusing a tumour with the very organ which it devours, a tumour whose very deformity horribly produces the shape. (Bernanos, *Diary of a Country Priest*, 1937 (rep 1975) 135).

That he makes a clear distinction between the natural and the exaggerated and depraved is obvious. It is a distorted, artificially heightened and maintained sexual greed and not natural appetites with their inbuilt controls and natural order that he sees as both a distinguishing mark of fallen man and one of the chief sources of that other specifically human quality, shame. Bernanos maintains that we are all guilty of complicity and connivance, of sentimentality and of a desire to foster such distortions at the expense of 'young human dignity' and, in a whole series of images, illustrates the depth of our semi-playful, semi-serious desire to break down the natural modesty and reticence of the young:

The world, helped by all the glamour of art, takes immense pains to hide away their shameful sore. It is as though with each new generation, men feared a revolt of human dignity, a desperate revolt - the sheer refusal of still unsullied human beings. With what strange solicitude humanity keeps watch over its children, to soften in advance with enchanting images this degradation of first experience, an almost unavoidable mockery. And when despite all this, the half-conscious plaint of flouted young human dignity, outraged by devils, is heard again, how quickly it can be smothered in laughter! What a cunning mixture of sentiment, pity, tenderness, irony surrounds adolescence, what knowing watchfulness! Young birds on their first flight are hardly so hovered around. And if the revulsion is too intense, if the precious child over whom angels still stand guard shudders with invincible disgust, what cajoling hands will offer him the basin of gold, chiselled by artists, jewelled by poets, while soft as the vast murmur of leaves and the splash of streams, while the low-pitched orchestra of the world drowns the sound of his vomiting! (Bernanos, *Diary of a Country Priest*, 1937 [rep 1975] 135,-136).

Lust is not to be confused with virility, with natural pleasure, with creativity or joy, for it is their opposite and destroys them. It is a lesion, a cancer, a major source of human misery, a blight on all human life, a sickness which distorts and destroys human nature. No-one who has any experience of sin, says Bernanos, can help but see lust for what it is:

We priests are sneered at and always shall be - the accusation is such an easy one - as deeply envious, hypocritical haters of virility. Yet whosoever has experienced sin must know that lust, with its parasitic growth, is for ever threatening to stifle virility as well as intelligence. Impotent to create, it can only contaminate in the germ the frail promise of humanity; it is probably at the very source, the primal cause of all human blemishes; and when amid the windings of this huge jungle whose paths are unknown, we encounter Lust, just as she is, as she emerged forth from the hands of the Master of Prodigies, the cry from our hearts is not only terror but imprecation: 'you, you alone have set death loose in the world!' (Bernanos, *Diary of a Country Priest*,1937 (rep 1975) 137-138).

This of course contrasts completely on the one hand with what one might, anachronistically, call the radical chic view of sexuality propounded by Gallet, the medical officer in *Star of Satan*, in which human sexual and emotional life becomes a matter of hygiene and mutually convenient temporary relationships, and virtue consists only in the respect of the autonomy of one's partner, and on the other with the Freudian view of morbid sexuality expressed by La Pérouse in *Joy* and also, it should be noted, with the merely symptomatic value accorded to sensuality by Cénabre in *L'Imposture*. Of these opposing views, only that of La Pérouse, with its alternative if curiously parallel imaginative concept of repressed and often unrecognized sexuality as a blight on full humanity, has anything of the complexity of the insights and intuitions suggested by Bernanos or can offer an equally disturbing image of one of the great shaping or distorting factors of human life. The main point of difference between the two is of course that whilst Bernanos sees lust as ubiquitous but not as an original and essential part of human sexuality, precisely because it is a lesion of that sexuality, La Pérouse sees morbid sexuality as one more manifestation of man's incongruous presence in the universe, part of the whole infection which will one day be removed from the purity of stellar space. For Bernanos, lust is the corruption of good which grace, often reaching us through shame, can heal. The most that La Pérouse can hope for, presumably, is the state which Freud described, in which an irrational melancholia is changed into a rational unhappiness. Cénabre speaks as a man who seems never to have known sexual problems, and although in a sense his dismissive and supercilious comments may be valid, they are so, one feels, only at the superficial and pragmatic level, and Gallet's observations, in the light of the imminent developments in his relationship with Mouchette, strike the reader, as Bernanos presumably intends them to strike him, as merely sterile and pathetic.

For Bernanos, the complexity of all human emotion is reflected in human sexuality. Sexual relationships and situations are not simple. As one would expect, that of Simone and Olivier in *Night is Darkest* is mysterious and ambivalent, for they are complicated and cerebral people. But the same is true of the 'simplest' characters in the novels. There is always a suggestion that sexuality is deep and mysterious and that, if it is subjected to a merely superficial examination and classification, it can only be misunderstood. Bernanos's treatment of the sexual element in the relationship of the young priest and the twelve-year-old Séraphita Dumouchel in *Diary of a Country Priest*, for example, illustrates this point clearly. For the priest, lust is a source, in a complex sense, of fear, and his own understanding of the girl's sexuality shows him the danger of meddling, even with the best intentions, with such a complicated pattern of actions and emotions. In common with all those other drives which motivate humanity, sexuality is mysterious and never isolated. It can, as we have already seen, be associated with shame, or with hostility and mockery, as is clearly the case with Séraphita in the scenes in the catechism class, and also with her mother, as she speaks to the priest while Séraphita waits in church. Nor can one argue simplistically for a concept of sexuality as a force which in itself is either purely good or purely evil. Woman, for Bernanos, for example, is neither an impure vessel nor an angel of sweetness and light. Nor is she simply both. On different occasions in the novels a different emphasis is perceived. Sometimes the country priest can speak in terms such as these:

> ... that quiet fury, which seems relentless, the whole female creature reaching out grandly for evil, and for her prey. And such freedom, such naturalness in wickedness, in hate, in shame was almost beautiful, a beauty not of this world, and yet immediately realize that they do not convey the truth.
>
> I have since endeavoured to thrust this thought away. An absurd and dangerous thought which seemed rather lovely at first when I was feeling vaguely for it. (Bernanos, *Diary of a Country Priest*, 1937 (rep 1975) 143).

This is precisely because such notions represent a received idea, a speciously attractive image which is a simplification and

159

consequently a distortion. In a similar way, the picture of Mouchette's outburst of sexual mysticism in *Star of Satan* indicates a perception of the complexity of her own nature rather than simply an analsyis of her sexuality, and is the presentation of a person rather than the indication of a role. Bernanos's comments on her reactions when her mother suspects that she is pregnant also suggest an instinctive female desire to increase a natural element of mystery, even if only for immediately practical purposes. The different strands of pity, compassion and protective love woven into female sexuality are also apparent and also mysterious, sometimes appearing in a natural and wholesome form (as with Séraphita Dumouchel or Dufréty's woman in *Diary of a Country Priest* or in a perverse and suspect one (as with Simone Alfieri in *Night is Darkest*). Again, all that can be said is that here as elsewhere the central fact about any person is his mystery and that central integrity which includes apparently opposing elements.

HUMAN RELATIONSHIPS AND THE RELATIONSHIP WITH GOD

Relationships, of sexual and other kinds, between individual human beings in Bernanos's novels are not isolated and independent phenomena. Their complexity and interdependence derive to a great extent from a more primary, more inward and less tangible factor, that of the relationship of each individual with God. How one person acts upon or reacts to another, and what intellectual or emotional attitude he adopts towards him is largely determined by (although it also determines) what we might call the state of his soul. If he accepts, however dimly and with whatever difficulty and uncertainty, a concept of God and of the consequent dignity and holiness of man, he sees the other as a *person*, with a dimension of being which passes beyond immediate, observable data. In some sense, however obscurely it is felt, the other is seen to be partaking in the ultimate mystery at the heart of life, and as in some obscure way to be sharing in the divine being and will. If this is the case, then attitudes and reactions are creative and accepting. If not, they are destructive and rejecting. In *Diary of a Country Priest* the actions and reactions of Séraphita and the Countess illustrate, at various points in the novel, a movement between these two contrasting dispositions and concepts. The former, despite the initial vindictive slyness and sexual hostility she shows towards the priest, does in fact later see him as someone whom she has injured, and she makes reparation in her own way. The latter, because she cannot accept God's will, has rejected in her heart human life and her fellow human beings. The death of her child has isolated her from God and frozen her emotions. It is only when, in the climacteric encounter at her house, the priest reconciles her to her loss that he creates for her a new way of seeing the world and helps her to love her family, or at least removes the obstacles which have prevented her from doing so. The symbolic act of throwing the locket into the fire is not simply melodrama. It will not make her dead child any less dead or any less dear to her, nor will it 'please' God. Her action is an emotional response to an insight into the way of freedom from rancour and bitterness.

Such reconciliation is not always achieved, however, for the opportunity for grace can be rejected, mocked and distorted. Fiodor, in *Joy* for example, who is subtle, intelligent, imaginative and determined, not only rejects God. At the human level, he in a sense usurps him, using his own considerable gifts to vitiate and destroy the lives of those around him. He and others like him - Cénabre, Simone Alfieri, Ouine - experience a cold joy in the lucid destruction or distortion of another human life, and other less extreme characters in the novels also help to create the grey world which follows an impoverishment of humanity. For Bernanos, life for those who reject God and Christ is hopeless: the opposite of a Christian people, Torcy tells the country priest, is a people grown sad and old. In the novels this grey, sad mass is composed of such people as the characters of *Night Is Darkest*, *The Open Mind* and the minor figures of *L'Imposture* and *Diary of a Country Priest*. In their case, life has often been reduced to the merest basic biological flicker and their full humanity diminished. The images Bernanos uses in writing of them indicate the concept he tried to communicate. Like Ouine, they have passive, parasitical qualities, floating and absorbing rather than living, jellyfish in the depths of the sea.

They live a half-life, characterized by petty, selfish calculation and become, in fact, the 'insects', rather than the 'real people', of whom Fiodor speaks. Theirs is the world of half-heartedness, compromise, accommodation where any commitment is more apparent than real, where in the words of the country priest:

> ...many men never give out the whole of themselves, their deepest truth. They live on the surface, and yet, so rich is the soil of humanity that even this thin outer layer is able to yield a kind of meagre harvest which gives the illusion of real living (Bernanos, *Diary of a Country Priest*, 1937 (rep 1975) 120).

There is a missing dimension, a gap in their lives, a profound futility and emptiness of the kind described to the parish priest of Fenouille by Ouine:

> 'No man ever yet shared human boredom and still managed to save his soul. Human boredom will get to the end of everything. Monsieur l'Abbé, it would even crumble the earth!' (Bernanos, *The Open Mind*, 1945, 129).

Such reactions to human life and to one's fellows may not necessarily arise from lucid or very cerebral decisions. They do, however, represent a more or less conscious movement of the heart and mind away from the demands of full humanity. With Bernanosian characters, it is not observable, enumerable, classifiable characteristics that are important, but the direction and quality of a life. Characteristics are an outward indication of an inner disposition, and when that disposition is in some deep way wrong, the resulting lesion prevents the individual from loving either himself or others. When we encounter such limit cases as Ouine or Cénabre, we know that we are in a world where the phrase of the country priest, 'hell is when we cease to love' is totally meaningful. In such a world, they share a prison with others whom they cannot love as themselves and can only desire or hate in terms of the image they have of them. It is a world where they and we see that, in Cénabre's words:

> The good thing about vice ... is that it teaches us to hate human beings. Everything is fine until we begin to hate ourselves. Hell is hating one's own kind in oneself. (Bernanos, *L'Imposture*, 1963, 437).

To a varying degree according to the individual predicament, this world is that of evil as Bernanos understood it, negative, parasitic rather than symbiotic, destructive not merely of one way of living, but of life itself, in which evil is 'not a way of living but an attack on life itself'. Its negative and detructive power its ability to consume a person and destroy his core, to make the whole of life pointless, boring, empty and nauseating, is stressed again and again throughout the novels in similar terms to those used in the diary of the country priest:

> The world of evil is so far beyond our understanding! Nor can I really succeed in picturing hell as a world, a universe. It is nothing, never will be anything but a half-formed shape, the hideous shape of an abortion, a stunted thing on the very verge of all existence. I think of sullied translucent patches on the sea. Does the Monster care that there should be one criminal more or less? Immediately he sucks down the crime into himself, makes it one with his own horrible substance, digests without once rousing from his terrifying eternal lethargy. Yet historians, moralists, even philosophers refuse to see anything but the criminal, they re-create evil in the image and likeness of humanity. They form no idea of essential evil, that vast yearning for the void, for emptiness: since if ever our species is to perish it will die of boredom, of stale disgust. Humanity will have been slowly eaten up as a beam by invisible fungi, which transform in a few weeks a block of oakwood into spongy matter which our fingers have no difficulty in breaking.
>
> And the moralist will dissertate on passions, the statesman redouble his police, the educationalist draw up new courses of study - treasures will be squandered wholesale for the useless moulding of a dough which contains no leaven. (Bernanos, *Diary of a Country Priest*, 1937 (rep 1975) 157-158).

Sin is seen as a layer of unknown depth and complexity, an incrustation on the soul, and the human psyche as the secret agent of its own destruction, nourishing the seed of evil within itself. The country priest reflects that man is always at enmity with himself - a secret, sly kind of hostility. Tares scattered anywhere will, he says, almost certainly take root, whereas the smallest seed of good needs more than ordinary good fortune, prodigious luck, not to be stifled. The result is that once our vision of a world of grace is lost or abandoned, we share in that consuming boredom which for Bernanos is a fundamental characteristic of flawed human nature and which both creates and reflects a major dimension of our experience:

> The world is eaten up by boredom. To perceive this needs a little preliminary thought: you can't see it all at once. It is like dust. You go about and never notice, you breathe it in, you eat and drink it. It is sifted so fine, it doesn't even grit on your teeth. But stand still for an instant and there it is, coating your face and hands. To shake of this drizzle of ashes you must be for ever on the go. And so people are always 'on the go'. Perhaps the answer would be that the world has long been familiar with boredom, that such is the true condition of man. No doubt the seed was scattered all over life, and here and there found fertile soil to take root; but I wonder if man has ever before experienced this contagion, this leprosy of boredom: an aborted despair, a shameful form of despair in some way like the fermentation of a Christianity in decay.(Bernanos, *Diary of a Country Priest*, 1937 (rep 1975) 10-1 1).

In such conditions, the self destroys other selves and is destroyed in its turn. The major manifestation of evil in the novels, as the reader sees with the insights of such characters as Cénabre, Fiodor or the country priest, is this destruction of the human person.

OPENNESS TO GOD

Bernanos's characters are perhaps fully comprehensible only within a Christian, and more specifically a Catholic, frame of reference. Whatever their own personal beliefs, doubts, refusals or alternative systems of belief, unbelief, or denial may be, such characters only make full sense as fictional creations in relation to a certain way of seeing the world. The psychiatrist La Pérouse in *Joy*, with his desire for a dead, brilliant, aseptic universe free of the corruption and contamination of human life ('a cunning detestable maneouvre against the purity, the majesty of death') embodies the opposite of the Christian hope of having life and having it more abundantly, and his deepest psychic drives attempt to destroy it in those around him. But Bernanos's characters, whether they are fully or residually Christian or post-Christian, have all been infected to some extent by the virus of religious belief and a religious view of life. It is part of their inherited mental and imaginative apparatus, and to that extent they are caught up in a Bernanosian 'predestination', for they can no more ignore its implication in themselves or in others than they can any other aspect of their mental make-up. Some have rejected faith, others have 'lost' it in the sense in which Bernanos understood the expression ('We do not lose our faith. It simply ceases to inform our life') which is that it no longer has any meaning for them, although the fact of faith, as an element in themselves or in others, is a real, objective pehenomenon.

In the novels, religious belief as a *hypothesis* is unbearable and unstable. That is, for example, the source of Cénabre's tragedy perceived when he examines his conscience, for on that occasion he sees clearly that he does not believe, and finds hatred inextricably mixed with his loss of faith. That cluster of ideas, imaginative concepts and emotions once called faith, hope and charity are of paramount importance and closely interrelated in these novels. If affirmation becomes denial, despair and hatred follow. If despair triumphs, faith and the capacity to love disappear. If a character hates his fellow men, he cuts himself off from the acceptance of God and the possibility of salvation. Whether the reader sees any of these concepts as corresponding to objective realities is perhaps of secondary importance. What he must accept is their validity as emotional, intellectual or psychological concepts within the framework of an individual writer's view of the world. For the non-Catholic, the reading of the novels perhaps requires an effort of the imagination rather than a suspension of disbelief.

The consequences of belief or disbelief assume major proportions in Bernanos's fictional world. Faith may be many things: a certainty, as with Chantal in *Joy*, a cast of mind produced by the inheritance of generations, as is possibly the case with her father; an anguished search for a hidden God, as sometimes with the country priest; but it cannot be a hypothesis, an 'as if' situation. The 'as if' soon becomes a 'yes' or a 'no'. Because belief shapes the lives and relationships of his characters so profoundly, Bernanos has much to say about it. He makes explicit or implicit comment on, for example, mysticism and dementia, the temptation to despair, and priests and the role of priesthood. Most of the novels contain such reflections. Even in *Mouchette*, where an implicitly religious stance largely replaces discursive reflection, the religious perspective is still striking. Here, however, we shall consider only those aspects of it which bear fundamentally on his concept or image of the human person. That he sees man as an *anima naturaliter christiana* is clear. Equally clear is the importance of religion seen in its widest sense as a cast of mind and a collection of beliefs and predispositions concerning the nature and destiny of the individual, rather than as a set of practices or observances.

The importance is epitomized, as has been suggested, in its effect on the links between characters and their relationship with one another. In the last resort two alternatives are open to them: unity in charity or separation in despair. In short, they either live, to varying degrees and in varying ways, in an enriching relationship with the sources of the potential fullness of human life, or they do not. In all that he wrote, Bernanos was fundamentally concerned with human dignity and freedom, grace and the interplay of good and evil within the human community. These concerns underlie all his novels from *Star of Satan* to *Mouchette* and are interdependent. They all centre on sanctity, which is accepting life because it is good and precious and comes from God. Bernanos is brutally simple, for he implies that it is only by being holy that we can be human. This seems on the face of it a highly disputable assertion. However, it was for Bernanos an observed fact of life and not a piece of theological speculation. To understand what he has to say, it is necessary to move away from the idea, which is implicit in the ethos of our times, that sanctity is somehow abnormal and unusual, and remember that for him it is the state for which man was made, and it is a positive, not a negative value. It means living both within and beyond oneself, rejecting nothing which is natural and human (although one can, as a freely accepted sacrifice, deprive oneself of the use and enjoyment of natural things, as Chantal and the country priest do in certain ways). It also means recognizing that our life depends utterly on God.

What Bernanos *shows* in his novels is that when a character is in a state of grace - that is, is not spoiled by sin, the deliberate turning away from his true humanity - he is most truly himself and most completely a *person*. The true saints in Bernanos's novels are not superhuman. They are the most natural, the most alive, the most human of his creations. They have their life, and a mysterious extra dimension, a luminous quality which somehow adds meaning and completeness to everything they do, even to their apparent failures. We might consider as an example Chantal in *Joy* who is a very attractive girl who does not find sanctity incompatible with singing, whistling, enjoying cooking and driving her father's car fast. Such people are completely human because the supernatural fits them perfectly and forms them. Their 'joy', founded on something deeper than a well-adjusted psyche, is too profound to be totally shattered, although it may be impaired by the frequently distressing events of their lives. Such qualities are hard to describe, but easy to recognise, whatever name the reader gives them in his personal vocabulary.

Man can, however, according to Bernanos, also be so devoid of warmth, and hope, of everything beyond the basic biological flicker of life, as to be almost sub-human. This dehumanization of man is the chief evil of life, and because it is an insidious and, humanly speaking, an almost irreversible process, it is terrible and disheartening, perhaps as near to a vision of despair as we can approach. The characters of *Night is Darkest*, with their rejection of any real human emotion, of all warmth, all commitment of themselves, perhaps approach this state most closely. With their deliberate coldness and aloofness, their conscious choice of a created, empty death-in-life, they epitomize the real sinners Bernanos portrays. With the amorphous group of the cowardly, careful, calculating mediocrities, their pale reflections in other novels, who refuse life and will not accept its challenge, they are constantly judged. The narrative of the fiction is often interrupted for this purpose, for Bernanos saw the novel less as a distinct literary form with its own rules and conventions than as one way of expressing a total vision of the world.

Those characters who represent a failure of humanity are nevertheless only one aspect of that vision, and Bernanos has a great deal to say about sanctity as the fulfilment of human nature. Although it is evident that his saints are sometimes exceptional creatures (for example Donissan and to a lesser extent Chantal), they are often striking at least as much by their natural as by their supernatural qualities. Their naturalness is enhanced rather than diminished by the supernatural element in their lives, in the sense that the movement towards sanctity is often accomplished both in some special, privileged way and within the domain of the normal and ordinary. Even Donissan, Bernanos's first and most extreme attempt at the portrayal of a saint, operates for much of the time at this latter level. In *Star of Satan* Demange's analysis of sanctity and Bernanos's own exploratory paragraphs both stress the ordinariness of the spiritually great. The two major 'supernatural' episodes in that novel are both exceptional, and in any case capable of other interpretations. In *Joy* Chantal's 'ecstasy' presents a similar though less striking phenomenon. It is as much as fact, a *datum* of the novel, as Donissan's encounter with the horse-dealer is in *Star of Satan*. Although it is mentioned, it is her naturalness rather than her exceptional experience which is stressed. She is candid and frank, hating subterfuge and mystery, and is made unhappy and uneasy by the nature of her experience and doubly so by what can be made of it by others. Naturalness and genuineness are all she wants, and those qualities produce in her a clarity of vision and a charity great enough for her to offer the joy created by such spontaneity in exchange for Chevance's happy death.

But within the novels these exceptional beings, if we choose to see them as such, are precisely exceptions. The saints are on the whole ordinary zealous Christians, of whom Torcy in *Diary of a Country Priest* might be seen as a prototype: honest, hard-working, with a job to be done conscientiously and thoroughly. Bernanos himself, in that same novel, compares the exaggerated literary-hagiographical view of sanctity with the everyday qualities of such people. Indeed, many of his saints are striking by virtue of their rather pedestrian characteristics. Chevance in *Joy* and Dufréty's woman in *Diary of a Country Priest*, who will not marry her lover in case he might eventually wish to return to the priesthood, are precisely the sort of person extolled by Torcy. Their virtues are often the heightened natural ones, such as a feeling for natural justice and the need for restitution of the kind that Séraphita experiences, or the concept of honour and military virtue explained by Olivier. When their faith is clouded or diminished, they can still, like Delbende, try to face up to life.

They are people who can see a distinction between a greater good and a merely utilitarian ethic and who, like the country priest, sense the mystery and depth of their ties with other people. Indeed, from this point of view, the most striking figure in the novels is neither simply an example of *'homme moyen sensuel'* nor, perhaps, totally an admirable person. Donissan rarely experiences what are known as the consolations of religion, and occasionally there is a rather suspect element of the merely heroic, the flagrantly exalted in his make-up. At the time of the attempted ressuscitation of the dead child at the Plouy farm, for example, when he is described as having the face of a hero, not of a saint, there is a quality of hard, egocentric determination in him which jars with sanctity. Rather than a transfiguration or perfection of the self, the reader perhaps occasionally wonders whether he just detects something of the very different quality of the going beyond the self which Ganse describes in *Night is Darkest* and Bernanos himself analysed in the same novel.

Certain kinds of morbid or suspect religious elevation may contain that hatred. It is perhaps going too far to suggest that it is present in Donissan, but the reader feels that for Bernanos a genuine ecstasy contains quite different elements. We have no suggestion that Chantal's, however disturbing it may be to her afterwards, contains pride, self-hatred or despair. Whatever its origins or its results, it seems to offer no dangers while it lasts. The whole set of experiences is presented simply as a fact, not described in any detail, except in the case of the occasional phenomena (the precision of the perception of an object, for example) which give the first hint that it is imminent, and as there is no analysis of it, the reader is left to make of it what he will. In most cases, it probably remains for him simply an unexplored dimension of Chantal's personality and is accepted as such.

The essential difference between these two major characters is that in such circumstances Donissan is less and Chantal more open to God, a difference indicated by the former's violent efforts and the latter's calm receptivity. It is this latter quality which, in the novels, ultimately characterizes the most fully human of Bernanos's characters: the country priest, Séraphita in the later stage of her relationship with him, the Countess after her period of crisis, Mouchette Malorthy in her dying moments, and perhaps Cénabre at the instant of his final collapse. In a sense, it is at such times that they find themselves most completely. In Bernanos's world, human beings, because they are selves, are condemned to some degree to selfishness, but it nevertheless seems that it is at moments of the greatest openness and renunciation that their selfhood is most pronounced.

HUMAN SOLIDARITY

Despite the conflict and destruction apparent in the fictional situation of most of the novels, they contain an illustration of the inescapable fact of human solidarity. Whether we wish it or not, our fates are inextricably linked. We see in Bernanos's work what, in the language of the theologians, has come to be called 'the mystical body', that is, the community of man in Christ, of which the members, bound together in their common humanity, can individually further or hinder his work of redemption. The saint is not alone in his sanctity, for by his existence, his thoughts and his actions, he affects the life of the whole community. Nor is the sinner isolated in his sin, since his rejection of grace has repercussions which pass outside himself and beyond his perception and control. As the country priest tells the Countess, 'I don't suppose if God had given us clear knowledge of how closely we are bound to one another both in good and evil, that we could go on living, as you say'. The idea of the mystical body and of the communion of saints is deeply embodied in much of Bernanos's writing, and is clearly present in many of the novels.

By an act of love, one human being can accept the sufferings and unhappiness of another, or give the other his own peace and joy. This is precisely what happens between Chantal and Chevance in *L'Imposture* and is a major factor in establishing the situation in *Joy*, its sequel and companion-piece. Chantal does not simply sit patiently and gently with a dying man to comfort his last hours on earth. Although this was her original intention - charitable enough as it is - her real gift, which Chevance accepts with knowledge and gratitude, is the gift of the joy which comes to her as a result of her ability to accept God's will. In *L'Imposture*, the reader expects to encounter such overtly theological insights, however embedded in the matter of the novel they may be. In other novels, events of this kind occur less visibly and from the aesthetic point of view perhaps more effectively. Very often, the creation or transference of some kind of happiness is part of the ordinary traffic of human relationships and not necessarily an event reserved for ostensibly solemn and special moments. The incident of the ride on Olivier's motor-cycle in *Diary of a Country Priest*, an event in itself quite banal and of no great external significance, a mere gesture of friendship, is nevertheless an important psychological and spiritual experience for the priest. As a result of Olivier's spontaneity and charity, he sees, or sees more clearly, a dimension of human ideas and emotions which had hitherto been more or less meaningless to him, and both he and Olivier are richer and more aware after the incident. When this charity fails or is suppressed, the effects of its absence are visible. *In Night is Darkest* Jambe-de-Laine, for example, is depersonalized and reduced to the status of an object by the doctor. In *L'Imposture*, Cénabre's haughty self-absorption produces in him cold pride, and a deep instinctive fear has sharpened in him, long before the later crisis in his life, the capacity to dissemble, to create an isolated, private, manageable world, and, above all, has intensified a deep and visceral loathing of all who lack his very real intellectual and imaginative refinement and subtlety. The examples could be multiplied almost indefinitely, but the point however is perhaps already sufficiently clear.

THE ELEMENTS OF OUR KNOWLEDGE OF OTHERS

These differing relationships are very closely linked to the way in which the characters see other persons. There are two extremes in the novels. At one end of the spectrum, others are seen in the light of love (that is, with charity, compassion and understanding), as other selves, other living souls. At the opposite extreme, they are seen as the 'other' in the Sartrean sense, as the prisoner of a '*regard*', who see their fellows in turn not as persons but according to their own image of them, distorting and simplifying them without perceiving their real being. It seems that for Bernanos we can only know what, in this sense, we love, and love what we know. In *Joy*, for example, the only person whom de Clergerie understands is his mother, because she is the only person whom he really loves, 'with a profound animal sympathy akin to passion'. Conversely, it is what we do not love or what we love incompletely that we destroy. De Clergerie's lack of understanding of his daughter, and secondarily of any of the other people who surround him, is an important contributory factor in the tragedy which is to take place in his house.

One of the most striking aspects of Bernanos's novels is precisely this question of knowledge of the other, of insight and perception. In human terms, it is perhaps what marks off, in Fiodor's phrase, the real people from the insects, the compelling character from the mediocre. The central figures of any novel (Donissan, the first Mouchette, Cénabre, Chevance, Fiodor, Chantal, the bogus priest in *The Crime*, Simone Alfieri, the country priest, Ouine, even the second Mouchette), are all people who to some extent see in their fellows, who have, to varying degrees, a perception of what is really happening in the core of their being. In a sense, the novels are about this central core of the person and the way in which it is seen or not seen by other people, with the reader perhaps assuming some of Bernanos's sacerdotal function, or even being permitted to see the characters as God might see them. From this point of view, it is a dimension of the human mind which Bernanos illuminates, showing its importance its unsystematic, unpredictable and varying nature and extent. For him, the fully human person is one who has knowledge of other human beings. The ability to see the real nature of another is both a higher function and a criterion of our humanity. Without it we are as insects, imprisoned in our own narrow and unfree lives, the slaves of cliches, half-truths and diagrammatic and oversimplified ideas.

Donissan, the first, is also of course the most striking example of this ability to perceive the real being of others. In his case, that of a man of apparently rare spiritual experiences, we are given to understand that this gift is a function of his sanctity in the narrower sense, as another saint might have the gift of bilocation or levitation. When he meets Mouchette Malorthy, he sees a human soul, knows the thoughts, fears and hopes therein, and penetrates to the centre of another person's being. It is not simply a case of understanding her background, the circumstances of her case, or her psychological and sexual history, but of knowing what in human terms must be unknowable (events which have occurred in secret, fears and thoughts which she has confided to no-one, a whole sociological and spiritual history) and of making Mouchette *see herself* as she has never done before. Donissan, she, and the reader, see her story from within, as a result of a sudden and total insight which is the opposite of a painstaking study:

> For nothing was less akin than this to the slow investigation of human experience, going from one observed fact to the next, forever hesitating, and nearly always impeded in its advance, when it is not made the dupe of its own sagacity. Father Donissan's interior vision, preceding every train of thought, imposed itself by its own quality; this sudden evidence was such as would confound the intellect, but intelligence, though already conquered, could only find its way back slowly, by a twist, to the reasons for its certainty (Bernanos, *Star of Satan*, 1940, 180).

Bernanos stresses that what Donissan perceives is something which cannot be described, about which no idea can be articulated - a human being:

> The human tongue cannot be forced to any adequate expression, in abstract terms, of the certainty of a real presence, since our certainties are all deductions ... And yet the thing which in that instant revealed itself to the eyes of Father Donissan was neither a figure nor a sign - it was a living soul, a heart sealed to all other eyes (Bernanos, *Star of Satan*, 1940, 185).

From Bernanos's treatment of this episode the reader might assume that Donissan is a privileged creature with special gifts and that such insights are closed to ordinary human beings. This would be to overstate the case. It would be more accurate to say that Donissan's gift is greater than that of others, but not that it is different in anything but degree. There are many passages in the novels which support this view. Menou-Segrais, for example, has something of the same sort of insight into Donissan. One has only to read those scenes in which he interviews his curate both before the latter's encounter with Mouchette and later before his enforced five-year monastic retreat to realize the depth of perception involved. The old priest has an intuitive perception of Donissan's nature, a deep understanding of the problems that face him, a subtlety and sympathy that also come from the perception of a living soul which in its turn is perhaps also sealed for everyone except himself.

Bernanos here, it seems, presents us with an illustration of St Thomas Aquinas's dictum that the known becomes part of the knower. Menou-Segrais accepts Donissan and makes him part of himself. This knowledge of the other is at what is very evidently a fully human level. Man can know man at that level, perceive his mystery, his dignity, his suffering. Olivier and Laville in *Diary of a Country Priest* recognize something of themselves in the priest, just as he in turn sees something of himself in them. Chantal's understanding of her father, of Fiodor, of her grandmother, of La Pérouse, is striking. The reader's instinctive reaction is to accept her insights as valid rather than those of (say) La Pérouse. One is meant to know, as she knows, that their 'knowledge' is somehow both more suspect and less complete than hers. As the situation in the novel changes, so her perception of people assumes a new colouring, a new quality. Here, as elsewhere, knowledge of the other is not simply an awareness of his goodness. It is a total, clear sighted if indefinable knowledge, and perceives the bad as well as the good. In *L'Imposture*, Chevance sees the emptiness of Cénabre's heart: 'Revolt and blasphemy would be infinitely better for you .. Oh, in blasphemy, Canon, there is some love of God, but the hell you are in is the coldest of all'. (Bernanos, *L'Imposture*, 1963, 356).

Where goodness is involved in such knowledge, it is not necessarily the goodness of the observer or the knower, which is quite independent of that of the observed or known. The former, however, is the more important, for where it is absent, perception is destructive. This indeed is the major temptation which Donissan has to face, and which is described in what must be one of the most important passages in the whole of the novels:

> To him whose flesh had so long been his slave, lasciviousness at last showed her true face, all one quiet smile. And yet not even such an image nor any other could trouble the senses of this lonely old man, since now another lust had been aroused in his obstinate, childlike heart, the delirious hankering after knowledge which drove to perdition the mother of men, when she stood erect and wondering on the very verge of good and evil. To know in order to destroy and, in destruction, to renew knowledge and desire - oh Light of Satan! - the craving of the void sought for its own sake, abominable effusion of the heart! The Saint of Lumbres had no longer the strength to do more than evoke this fearful repose; divine grace cast a veil before these eyes which only a little while ago still had been filled with divine mystery. And now the clear gaze had become hesitant, it had lost the knowledge of where to look ... A strange youthfulness, a simple avidity, something like the first wound of the senses, warmed his old blood, beat within his bony chest. He sought hesitantly, he caressed death, through so many veils with a dying hand (Bernanos, *Star of Satan*, 1940, 238-239).

As Michele Estève, the editor of the standard collected French edition of Bernanos's novels, points out, the lucidity of Bernanosian heroes is ambivalent in that it both enables the 'saints' to see the soul of the sinner and free it and also constitutes a great temptation. What he says of the saints, however, is equally true of others who have a similar gift yet no sanctity. The temptation is clear, for example, in Cénabre's destructive analysis of Pernichon, and is perhaps the foundation of Ouine's whole life, where curiosity and a total absence of charity have produced an empty, colouriess, insipid world. His description of his own curiosity provides a parallel with that of Cénabre and to some extent of Fiodor and of Simone Alfieri. It is worth quoting at some length as it reveals one extreme of this tendency:

> Monsieur Ouine continued: 'My curiosity is devouring! At this very moment it gnaws, it hollows me out - what little remains of me. Such is my hunger! Oh, why could I not be curious about things? But my only hunger was for souls. Hunger - how shall I put it? What is hunger? I coveted souls in a way the word "hunger" doesn't fit. Authentic hunger grinds its teeth, the eyes of famine burn like fire! And why did I never prey upon souls? Alas, I didn't crave for many of them - one, the most wretched - would have sufficed me. I could have shut myself up with it all my life, in perfect solitude, as a physiologist shuts himself up with the stray dog which is to serve as his material for experiment, or as a boy in his teens with his first grotesque mistress, picked up on the pavement. But I watched their sufferings and rejoicings as He who created them might have watched. I caused them neither pleasure nor pain, I only flattered myself that I gave them imperceptible impetus, just as one turns a picture towards shadow or light. I felt myself to be their providence - a providence with designs as inviolable, as far above suspicion, as the other. It pleased me to think how old and gouty I was. I opened out like a flower at the very sound of my own voice, whose tone I was careful to over-emphasize, like a nasal bassoon contrived to reassure the brats. With what pleasure I entered their modest consciences, all so alike, so common and commonplace, and their small inglorious brick dwellings, as grimy with habit and stupidity and narrowness of mind, as they were with soot! I took my place in them with dignity, I filled them with my own benevolence, my discreet solicitude, and at once they yielded their secret entire. But I was in no hurry to take it! My eyes gloated on all the things which that kind of house presents to the stranger, the casual visitor, so innocently - their absurd

"home-comforts", the lace doylies, the photographs hanging on the walls, the cruet capped with a plaster girl, the looking-glasses black with fly-blow, more mysterious than forest paths, the one carpet glistening with dirt, the canary-bird! Yes, my eyes pierced all the barriers, behind which sheltering mediocrity consumes itself in peace and quiet, and I appeared to do nothing whatsoever to disturb or interrupt the process of reabsorption. I only made it, without their knowing it, impossible by slow degrees. The safety of their souls lay in my hands, and they never realized it! I showed and hid it from them by turns. I played on that kind of gross security as I might have played on a delicate instrument, from which I drew a special harmony, superhumanly sweet. I indulged myself with the pleasures of God, since certainly that is how He amuses himself in His leisure hours. That is the way their souls were made. I was very careful never to change them, I showed them to themselves with as many precautions as an entomologist unfolding a butterfly's wings. Their Maker knew them no better than I did, no possession by love can be compared with that infallible handling which gives the patient no offence, which leaves him intact, and yet quite at one's mercy, imprisons him, yet preserves his most delicate shades, such iridescence, such variegation of life! Those souls were thus and that is what I had to accomplish in this old house, which should keep the memory of me, since my pleasure impregnates every stone. Yes, I moulded the coarsest paste into bubbles, into something even lighter, still more impalpable! These big clumsy fingers performed that miracle! (Bernanos, *The Open Mind*, 1945, 218-220).

This is the limit of human knowledge and control of other human beings, but there are, of course, intermediate stages. Saint-Marin in *Star of Satan*, for example, represents one. He has the same curiosity, the same parasitical destructive impulses, but not the gifts and subtlety of Cénabre, Simone or Ouine. This range of insights of varying depth and subtlety is one of the major components of the view of man implicit in the novels. He is

177

capable to varying extents, with varying motivation, with varying success - of seeing his fellows directly, intuitively and in depth. He has gifts which defy analysis precisely because they operate directly and intuitively and without the intervention of reflection and ratiocination. From the point of view of verisimilitude, the portrayal of such processes of insight perhaps raises problems, but that is not our major concern here. It is at least arguable that given the insidious persuasiveness of such words as those which Bernanos gives to Ouine, their imaginative power and the force of their impact, the ideas which they implicitly or explicitly contain are bound to carry, initially at least and even for a sceptical or unsympathetic reader, an immediate conviction which may not be supported by subsequent introspection and reflection, but which, during the actual process of reading, certainly compels attention and possibly assent, or at least the willing suspension of disbelief.

It can be suggested that Bernanos deals with human life at such deep levels that almost everything he creates is likely to appear unacceptable to those who, even imaginatively, cannot share his viewpoint. At the level at which he portrays people, behaviour, to the perceptive reader, is perhaps both strange and yet somehow expected. To those who never see beyond the distant flashes of lightening, the storm they indicate will necessarily be incomprehensible. The ability to choose and the power of insight he describes will perhaps not surprise or astonish the sensitive and open-minded reader, however he might himself define them or to whatever causes he might ascribe them.

CONCLUDING REMARKS

The concept of man contained in Bernanos's novels is created less by the subtle, highly-conscious and painstaking psychological analysis characteristic of the grand tradition of the novel in France than by the emergence, out of the turmoil of a haunted mind and an obsessive imagination, of a powerful way of seeing or imagining the deeper layers of the human psyche. The characters in his novels grow rather than are depicted. They evolve and develop and are never static and finished. This is not simply because the reader sees 'more of them' as a given novel progresses, but because they themselves, by their conscious or unconscious choices and attitudes, help to create or destroy themselves. Like Sartre's characters, Bernanos's heroes and heroines have a kind of freedom. Their destiny is fixed only in terms of their decisions, whether they be ratlonal or irrational, subtle or intuitive. Determination for them when it arises is not direct and mechanistic but springs from a reluctance to reject sin and to accept their freedom as a result of a loss of faith or a surrender to despair, from seeing, as Bernanos expresses it in an image in the country priest's diary, creation the wrong way round, of living against life and the deepest human wisdom:

> Sometimes I think of Satan as trying to get hold of the mind of God, and not merely hating it without understanding, but understanding it the wrong way round; thus unknowingly struggling against the current of life, instead of swimming with it: wearing himself out in absurd, terrifying attempts to reconstruct, in the opposite direction, the whole work of the Creator (Bernanos, *Diary of a Country Priest*, 1937 (rep 1975) 81.

Perceiving and making radically different choices in the general orientation of their lives is what separates so sharply such characters as Simone Alfieri and the country priest, Chevance and Cénabre, Ouine and (however hesitatingly the latter may act) the parish priest of Fenouille. What they choose shapes the whole cast of their humanity and determines the fulness or emptiness of their being. At the same time, however, this suggests a common characteristic, for in whatever direction his options may take him, man for Bernanos is dynamic. He has a centre, a core, a bedrock of self which is neither rigidly static nor fluidly amorphous, and which can be perceived if not defined. Paradoxically, it is the mystery and depth of the characters which produces the impression of fidelity to observed and experienced psychological truth. Human beings, at the level at which Bernanos portrays them and which in real life can only be glimpsed occasionally, are perhaps as fundamentally enigmatic and irreducible to simple statements as he would have us believe.

One can hardly use the word 'technique' when talking of Bernanos's writing, but the ways in which he presents characters combine to create this total impression of mystery and depth.

Within a general pattern of the creation of individual characters and wider comment on human nature, the reader can detect three ways of reflecting on human beings. These are firstly, an often rather ruthless direct authorial analysis, as for example in *Joy*, where de Clergerie is treated in this way. Secondly, there is a kind of 'internal' analysis, achieved by means of comments passed by one character on another or on others, as when, in the same novel, Fiodor describes the other inhabitants of the house or La Pérouse talks about Chantal, or when the examining magistrate in *The Crime* comments on what the presumed priest of Mégère *is* rather than on what he does or does not do. Thirdly, there is the dramatic technique which Bernanos uses to show a particular individual, as when he depicts Mouchette Malorthy's searingly painful development in *Star of Satan*. From this amalgam of narrative, comment and explanatory and reflective analysis arises the overall impression of complexity and conviction which characterizes the novels. It is, of course, this complexity that is the major characteristic of the idea of man which Bernanos presents. The human being is a largely unknowable creature whose motivation lies far beyond the observable and classifiable. His own concept of himself is striking and important, for he sees his own individuality, his own life, and is a 'self by experience'. This concept is sometimes fragile, and can crumble at moment of crisis. If it is false, it vitiates his true nature and sometimes destroys it, for when the false persona collapses under the impact of reality, the true self, after its long erosion, lacks strength and disintegrates. There is often a lie at the centre of a life and such concepts as masks, roles, falseness and hypocrisy are key ideas in any understanding of Bernanos.

The cult of the self and the pursuit of self-knowledge are not however a prophylactic for this or a good in themselves. For Bernanos such concerns are largely sterile. The need is not for self-exploration, but for an idea of oneself as an autonomous, independent, free human being. This concept is fundamental to any human dignity and freedom, and if it is destroyed, the consequent dangers are grave. Introspection and self-consciousness can be very dangerous, for without grace the self-contemplating self can collapse. With grace and its consequent charity, the anguish which is a pre-condition of deep knowledge of one's own self and that of others can be fruitful. The precise way in which we see ourselves and others is left unclear and mysterious. It can only be described as insight, and is, as Bernanos stresses in *Star of Satan*, incomplete where there is no charity involved, for it is the charity and supernatural compassion of the spiritually great that takes them straight to the secret places of other lives. Every human being has this potentiality within him.

In the human soul there is often an element of 'predestination' which follows either from an inner (and unconscious?) choice, or from heredity. But this slavery to a conditioned desire can be broken by awareness, and by grace, as with Mouchette Malorthy in *Star of Satan* or the country priest, for sanctity equals true freedom, the freedom from the stranglehold of sin which, for Bernanos, is total freedom. It is of course here that the 'guilt' which has been ascribed to Catholic man comes in. It would be better to call it 'shame', which for Bernanos was a liberating experience. It is not sexuality which so often lies at the basis of this shame or guilt, as the clichés about Catholic literature would have it, but lust, a perversion, distortion and aberration of that sexuality and it is significant that those characters in the novels who despise and reject sexuality (La Pérouse and Cénabre for example) are condemned by themselves. Here, Bernanos's ideas are perhaps realistic rather than puritanical or idealistic.

Relationships between human beings are not isolated, random affairs determined by the arbitrary play of 'character' and events. They depend on a more fundamental relationship, that of a character with God, and upon a disposition of the whole being. Faith, however dim and tenuous it may be, entails charity, hope and life. Despair destroys life. These dispositions are not always the result of conscious decision, and very often they follow from the kind of semi-conscious choices typical of man's fallen nature. For Bernanos, a vision of human goodness, righteousness, and naturalness is rejected at the risk of a corrosive boredom and the disintegration of the self. The men and women portrayed in the novels only make sense when seen within a Christian and more specifically a Catholic frame of reference, and whether they are Christian, marginally Christian, or post-Christian, they all have a

Catholic virus or its remains in their blood. Man is an *anima naturalita Christiana*, even in a 'Christianity in decay'. Religion is in this sense a dominant, perhaps the major, factor determining the human person, determining the nature, self-concept and destiny of each individual. Sanctity means true and full humanity, for when the supernatural is removed, the natural crumbles. Hence the saints in the novel are fully human. Their experience may be extraordinary, heroic and variously interpretable, but it is a fact of the novels. They may equally well be 'ordinary' people (Torcy, Chevance, Dufréty's woman) undergoing 'ordinary' experiences. In neither case, however, are they characters who suggest anything less than a fully human stature, or the widest and deepest range of human potentiality.

Bernanos's image of man is not original in the sense of being novel, but it is original in the sense of being highly personal, idiosyncratic and profound, and consequently strikes the reader with the freshness of new insight. Apparently paradoxically, it is both a personal, instinctive image and a highly orthodox one, for like Chesterton's, Bernanos's instinct for orthodoxy (which is not merely assent to a certain number of theological propositions, but an acceptance of a whole view of man and his place in the universe that will colour and inform a total personality) was deep and forceful.

In his polemical works Bernanos discussed the men of his time and explored human nature and experience in collective and general terms. In the novels, he explores such questions in terms of individual existential experience. Bernanos's fiction is not primarily important as a grouping of dynamic character-studies, however forceful and striking individual characters in it may be. The importance of the novels lies rather in their creation of myths, of patterns of insight into human nature and experience and into the common fund of humanity and inherited patterns and ways of life as seen by one writer and presented to some extent in an explanatory way. Since Bernanos is a deeply French and a specifically Catholic novelist, the extent to which the reader foreign to those traditions might need to make an imaginative leap to share in or even to understand his way of seeing man is open to argument. That there is a complex, poetic and profound view of man in them, is undeniable. That 'certain idea of man', like so many of Bernanos's ideas, political as well as theological, seems best defined by its opposites. It is the antithesis of any reductionist view (Catholic or otherwise), of any conceptually diagrammatic system, of any simplistic way of seeing a phenomenon of which our knowledge and understanding must in the first place be direct and intuitive. The concept of man which Bernanos presents in his novels is one of a nature which is partly given, in which the individual perhaps knows himself better than he knows others, but which is infinitely more complex, mysterious and indescribable than we can guess and, significantly, one in which charity as well as reason is an element of any possible knowledge of the human person.

Chapter 6

A PICTURE EMERGES

We may state therefore as a provisional conclusion: "Christianity and humanism are not opposites." (Hans Küng, *On Being a Christian*.)

It is not surprising to find that the fiction we have examined contains both a series of images of the human person and some evidence of reflection on them. Although the concrete image precedes and is perhaps more important than the element of discursive analysis contained in such novels, a way of seeing human beings is often, if intermittently, quite explicitly proposed. Both a fairly consistent 'literary Catholic' concept of man and a reflection on what kind of creature he is both emerge from their work.

Central to all three novelists is the conviction that there exists an inner self and a reflection on our knowledge of that self. These concerns are of prime importance both as constitutive elements of the view of man contained in the novels and as the sources of the action and developments which feed the narrative. In this connection, for example, Undset writes of the self which is beyond the judgement of others, the 'room within room and an innermost chamber of 'the deep places of the lake, always calm when the surface is ruffled', Bernanos of the central core of the personality, Greene of 'the deepest mind, the plane of memories, instincts, hopes', where the human being is inescapably and most profoundly himself and the real drama of his life follows its course. In Bernanos, either a character emerges as more fully himself or a *persona*, a false understanding or a false presentation of an inner reality, is destroyed. In Undset, there is often a greater movement towards self-knowledge and a consequent re-ordering of a life. Greene shows the self as a *datum* and the source of reflection and development. In all three, the idea and the image of a central and vitally important inner core of being, of a depth and complexity of experience and reflection not suggested by external characteristics and actions is forcefully present. The external reality of their heroes and heroines is sometimes a rough guide to this inner area of emotions, reflections and choices and sometimes obscures it. Either of Bernanos's two Mouchettes, Undset's Paul Selmer, Dorothea and Evi and Greene's Pinkie and Sarah (whom he once described as one of his best-drawn women characters) can all be seen as illustrating, in their various ways, this difference between their readily perceivable characteristics and the inner space in which they are themselves.

In Catholic literature of the kind we are looking at here, the notion of the average sensual man is seen as a falsifying and distorting simplication. The beliefs, ideas and emotions which make up the mental, spiritual and psychological climate of these novels propose a view of man in which all human nature is paradoxically both simple and complex. It is simple because it is a core of being, where the person simply *is*, and resultant action, which is only comprehensible in terms of that central core is seen as a series of expressions of the potentialities within it. It is complex in the sense that although one can begin to make statements about it, every individual instance of it is different, new and unknown in its specific uniqueness, neither fully communicable nor fully reducible to diagrammatic formulas. Personhood and individual being are matters of recognition rather than of definition. This is a valid if rather clumsy description of the unstated but fairly clear starting-point of these three writers. For them, as for Augustine, man is an abyss. All three assume that the complexity of human nature must be seen as a basic fact of our experience. Our inner self is obscure not only because of the difficulty of comprehension but also as a result of an apparently intrinsic quality of human nature: its ability to enrich or diminish itself. This element of mystery and complexity is seen by Bernanos as both fundamental to our nature and probably outside our conscious control, if not necessarily outside our direct and intuitive knowledge. For Undset, it is capable to some extent at least of being perceived, comprehended and allocated to its rightful place by our rational understanding mind. Greene posits it simply as a fact of experience. Even for Bernanos, the most extreme of the three from this point of view, insight into oneself, if it is of the right kind, is necessary, even if it is fraught with danger. For Undset, the most matter-of-fact, insight is important for oneself and for the proper conduct of one's life, and for Greene it appears to be a major factor in our growth towards fuller humanity. It is, however, important to notice that for none of them is the understanding, appreciation or cultivation of one's indivduality an end in itself. The cult of the self has no place in their work. Self-knowledge, in so far as it has a purpose, is a way of becoming more human, which means in essence the recognition of the equally important humanity of others. As an end in itself it is meaningless. Proust's introspection, Bernanos tells us, goes nowhere.

The perception of oneself as a person leads to the perception of other human beings as other valuable and significant selves. Such a movement, it is implied, represents a growth of wisdom and is seen as both a possibility and a necessity of human life. Human solidarity is impossible without it. Where it is absent, there is aridity and despair and the individual is isolated, introverted and self-consuming. Where it is present, life is more fully human, more rewarding, richer. The known then becomes part of the knower, and when both knower and known are knowing subjects they are even more closely united. For all three writers, the concept of personhood can be seen as the basis of honesty, justice and charity in human relationships. Conversely, when we do not or cannot see human beings in this way, as persons or selves in their own right, we are always potentially and often actually destructive towards them. Abolishing their subjectivity reduces them to the status of objects.

This, it is implied, is precisely what must not happen. What for Bernanos is the overwhelming mystery, that of another person's being, of the inner reality which makes him fully human, can and must be recognized. In so far as the perceiver is himself a conscious human being, it *can* be so recognized. The ability to perceive or sense, however dimly, the separateness and autonomy of another person is a human mode of understanding and a criterion of full humanity. To be able to see what Greene calls 'the human stature' of another, to appreciate that, in Undset's words, 'human beings are human' and to see that they are mysterious to each other implies two major insights. These are that in some sense other human beings have a personal autonomy which is as important as our own, and that they are ultimately as unknowable and unique as we see ourselves as being. This is the normal mode of visualizing human beings in Greene, Undset and Bernanos and, with all its limitations, represents the limit of our understanding. Even with Bernanos, any insight which goes beyond a perception of the complexity of another person and a general insight into him (whether it be the kind evident in Fiodor, in Cénabre, in Ouine, or in Chantal or the country priest) is exceptional. Donissan's total comprehension of Mouchette Malorthy in *Star of Satan*, in which he sees her whole being, is a unique event in his fiction and is not matched in any of Greene's or Undset's major characters. For the most part, the characters of all three novelists have a more modest and restricted, if equally direct and intuitive, perception of the inner reality of others. The recognition of the mystery rarely implies a complete understanding of it. Despite the differences, however, it is important to note that there is a major similarity. Striking as it appears, Donissan's gift implies a difference in the perceiver rather than in what is perceived. The scholastic tag which holds that *quidquid recipitur secundum modum recipientis recipitur* - i.e. whatever is received (known, understood or assimilated) is received according to the mode of the receiver - is appropriate here. Donissan's mode of reception is different in degree (but perhaps not in kind) from that of Greene's Scobie or Undset's Ida Elizabeth, but what is received, the hidden nature of another human being, is the same. The Mexican priest's knowledge of the half-caste Indian who betrays him, Bendrix's knowledge of Sarah or Henry and Kristin's knowledge of Erlend is less complete, but its incompleteness suggests the mystery that still lies outside that knowledge, which in Bernanos's phrase, is that of another 'living soul, a heart sealed to all other eyes'.

A feature of the view of the human person which emerges from these novels is the sense that what people do is ultimately considerably less important than what they are and less important than the image which they leave in the reader's mind. The external and verifiable actions of Scobie, Bendrix, Sarah, Smythe, Ida Elisabeth, Paul Selmer, Kristin Lavransdatter, Simone, the country priest, have their origin in what those characters *are*. Their essence precedes their existence, in that they are before they act or react. Their choices, actions, acceptances, refusals, however important they may be, however far-reaching and of whatever nature their consequences for themselves and for others, are an extension or expression of their inner selves, which events may influence in certain ways but never create, and are seen as realizing or frustrating an existing potential rather than as producing a being.

What the characters do is the expression of an already existing interiority, a reflection of the general orientation of their lives. The country priest's interview with the Countess, the second Mouchette's suicide, Paul Selmer's conversion to Catholicism, Kristin Lavransdatter's acceptance of her adulterous husband, the Mexican priest's decision to stay in the anti-clerical state or Scobie's taking Communion while in mortal sin do not make the characters, do not in the Sartrean sense create their essence. They have an identity apart from what they do, and are more than the total of their actions. Being, in Catholic literature as in the tradition of Catholic thought (*operatio sequitur esse*), lies behind action, just as it lies behind the outward, describable aspects of 'character'. Mouchette, Scobie, Kristin and the two priests are themselves, and would still, without these actions, remain themselves. In Bernanos, Greene and Undset, what is done or thought suggests the nature of being rather than defines or creates it. The major characters in these novels do what they do, within the limits of their freedom, because they are what they are. Whatever their experience may be, they remain unique and specifically themselves in the face of it. It is difficult to imagine that a different range of options would change them in any significant way.

Nor are they prisoners of the gaze of others, fixed by the image which the latter have of them. Their being is not determined by other people's views of their lives and actions.

Louise, Scobie sees, is a person in her own right, whatever his view of her may have been. Bendrix's view of Sarah, as he fully realizes, cannot include all that she has been and has done, and he knows that he will never 'get to the end' of her. Kristin Lavransdatter as a person is not determined by what her feudal peers and superiors see as her role, function or nature, but by her own view of herself, her duties and the meaning of human life. One of the most striking aspects of her personality is that when she is old, poor and living from day to day, waiting upon the will of the God to whom she has abandoned herself, beyond human judgement and in a sense living a life which is emptier than at any other point of her existence, the fullness of her being is at its greatest. Mouchette Malorthy is also a great deal more mysterious, independent and autonomous than the Count, Gallet or her family can conceive, and their images of her are all shattered. The novels are in one sense a development of the theme of the growing perception of the personal reality of other people.

Most of the major characters move towards a lived, rather than a purely conceptual, recognition of such virtues as loyalty, responsibility, understanding and compassion. They also move towards the acceptance of a pattern, however dimly perceived, of values which go beyond their personal desires. Greene's characters can be (and have been) criticized for the confused nature and general wrongness of their values, Bernanos's for being over-dramatized and superhuman, Undset's for being illustrations of a massively gloomy and severely Catholic morality, but apparently none has been condemned for having no values. It could be said with some accuracy that Undset's heroes and heroines illustrate, as a result of a natural sense of what is right, a growth towards the idea that what is good is desirable, perhaps achieved slowly through the perception that what is truly desirable is good. Realizing that natural decencies are not enough and rejecting a utilitarian morality, they gradually perceive the possibility of making objective moral judgements by means of an attempt to separate personal likes and dislikes from decisions about their own conduct. They are aware that, although their inner sense of what is right can help them, subjective promptings may be confusing and contradictory. In moving towards a view of what goodness is, they see that sacrifice, responsibility and loyalty are part of it and that 'moral issues' of the kind that are often the subject of debate in the novels are to be seen in the light of this enlarged concept. Bernanos's ideals of personal loyalty, sanctity, sacrifice and charity form a major and inescapable strand in his fiction, and his characters are judged on their success or failure in achieving them. His characters tend to *see*, and are judged on their acceptance or refusal of the consequences of that perception. Greene, like Bernanos, seems to share what might be described as Aldous Huxley's doctrine of intelligence as a virtue (see the latter's *Ends and Means*, London, 1948), although he does not appear to be as aware as Bernanos of its possible dangers. For Greene it is 'innocence', by which he means a dangerous simple-mindedness, the inability to perceive human deviousness and the complexity of human motivation, that poses grave risks. Wisdom would avoid so much unnecessary suffering. One major aspect of this wisdom is the ability of his characters, despite their often rather simple and squalid failings (there are no lucid and deliberate sins of the spirit in his or Undset's novels) to move painfully through self-criticism towards a sense of responsibility for others.

For all three novelists, the ability to grow and develop in these and similar ways is an integral part of being human. Circumstances may perhaps dictate the pace at which this growth can occur, but it is always an element in the total image of the human person. In all their novels, human relationships are not isolated, independent phenomena of interest only to those who are engaged in them, but elements in a wider and deeper nexus of lives. Their effects are not predictable and will have repercussions outside their own immediate and limited area. Bernanos, with the wealth of interspersed theological speculation he provides, could perhaps be seen as the prime example here, with Undset and Greene as the providers of detail. His suggestion, for example, of the potentially saving or destructive nature of such relationships, of the possibility of human unity in charity or separation in despair, can be seen as parallel insights to those in the view expressed by both Greene and Undset that there is a need for responsibility in human relationships, for answerability for the well-being of others, and to the latter's suggestion that right (i.e.

charitable, loving and understanding and at the same time realistically perceptive) conduct is the only way in which human happiness can be achieved. Here too, self-concepts are important, for the way in which a character sees himself will help determine the way in which he sees others and consequently the way in which he will treat them. It would be simplistic to say that they impose an ideal. Their characters are, like all human beings, necessarily imperfect. Complete charity is unobtainable in human life, and none of them attempts a fictional portrayal of it. Donissan's is flawed by spiritual pride, or a temptation to spiritual pride, and a certain suspect heroism. The Mexican priest's life is full of weakness, remorse and bungled good intentions. Paul Selmer is to some extent a failure in his relationship with his wife. Too much cannot be demanded or expected of human beings. They will falter in their resolutions and often fail to achieve what, with a little more effort, could have been within their grasp, or they will be reluctant to accept the chances of sanctity which life offers them. Like Simone Alfieri, they may in full consciousness choose a life of negation or, like Cénabre, simply accept it. Like the country priest or most of Greene's and Undset's characters, they may seek, with varying degrees of zeal and effort, a way out of such a life. Virtues, and particularly faith, hope and charity, are not thrust upon them. Whatever progress may be made is achieved at great cost and with great effort.

This is largely because the area in which those virtues must be practised is that of human relationships, and in the portrayal of such matters all three authors evince a rather hard-headed realism. Undset accepts family, marital and sexual relationships, which are the basis of the subject-matter of her novels, as what they are: simply facts of life. For her, what is, is good, and evil lies in the misuse of such relationships by the idealization or degradation of them which can arise from a misunderstanding of their nature. It is our human brotherhood and sisterhood, which is quite a literal one, that leads to strife, and one necessary element in a reduction of that strife and its replacement by a fuller humanity is what she would call adulthood and what Greene would see as the opposite of 'innocence'. Neither solutions based on a false idealism nor those based on a reduction of human dignity can be accepted. In this connection, Greene's explicit or implicit reflections are more difficult to analyze. This is partly because they are less systematic than those of either Bernanos or Undset and play a relatively minor role in the movement of the novels, partly because they occupy a middle ground between the theological and often visionary insights of the former and the pragmatic and more or less immediately intelligible comments of the latter, and partly because the scope of the more fully developed relationships in his novels is often largely limited to only one of the possible forms such relationships might assume, that of the man-woman sexual partnership. Those of Bernanos embrace certain limit-situations or moments of crisis in which sexuality is almost irrelevant, and Undset's, although they lack Bernanos's sense of crisis, cover wider aspects of family and domestic relationships than those of Greene.

And yet in all three writers, sexuality and its expression can perhaps be seen as an epitome of human relationships, a microcosm and example of all our dealings with each other. It is a modern commonplace to assume that none of our relationships can be separated from our sexuality. Bernanos, Undset and Greene suggest, as many other writers would not do, or not do so forcefully, both this idea and its corollary: that our sexuality and our sexual roles are not separable from other aspects of our humanity. For all of them sensual and biological urges are important, but do not exist in isolation. Persons are no more simply sexual than they simply are economic or social units, but human beings in whose lives these (and other) specific attributes and functions are incorporated. Our sexuality is straightforward neither in itself nor in the way in which it forms a part of our whole life. Sexual appetites do not exist merely as isolated phenomena, but are woven into the stuff of our whole being, along with other concerns, other needs and other desires. Sexuality and sexual relationships are both so complicated in themselves and linked to so many other experiences that they cannot be described or discussed in isolation, or expressed in neat shorthand terms. To do so, or to suggest simply that they subsume all other relationships, or to simplify them by assuming that sexual gratification is their only component, is to dehumanize them. Bernanos speaks on the one hand of the degradation brought about by lust and on the other of the desire that brings the sexes together, using terms similar to those in which a distinction between greed and a healthy appetite might be made. Lust is a cancer which destroys natural desires, creativity and joy. Greene, in the reactions of Scobie, Bendrix and the Mexican priest, also suggests that lust in isolation and the reduction of human beings to sexual objects is diminishing both to the other human being and to oneself, and points out that more complex and more human relationships will preclude and inhibit 'simple lust' both within and outside them. Only people who are not fully human, he suggests, who are incompletely adult, can be satisfied with an impoverished variety of sexuality. In the case of Undset, in whose novels the more brutal male passions play, even in the medieval cycles, a rather restrained role, reference to female sexuality is made in robust and uncompromisingly traditional terms. It is false and unrealistic, she implies, to see women as basically other than marriage partners and mates, basically monogamous, cautious, reserved, prudent. She suggests that female sexuality is far deeper and more complex than essentially male myths about sensual women can ever suggest, and like Bernanos implies that such myths and attitudes are part of a certain prurience, a certain connivance, a 'strange solicitude' which can only harm 'the majesty of youth'. For Undset, who had lived her early adult life as an educated, emancipated and free-thinking young woman, sexuality alone, in isolation, is perhaps the only language which certain women, painfully inarticulate, know how to use with men. It is not that it is the best, or necessarily the most natural or obvious one, but simply that because such women are immature and insecure, they can find no other. They are not more, but rather less, womanly as a result of this incapacity, even if they are apparently more feminine. In her commonsense way, she sees sexuality as a fact of life, and not as its 'meaning and object' or as any more a liberating and enhancing experience than its concomitants of marriage, domestic commitments and family life. What she would see as the childish attributes of sexuality - a movement towards irresponsibility, the cult of the momentary sensation, the short-term relationship - are for her incomplete, unserious, unsatisfying. Stability is more important and, significantly, more desired and desirable. In her novels it is adult sexuality which is important and satisfying, because it is humanizing as it grows and matures. Sexual distractions are precisely that: irrelevant, escapist, pathetic. In her fictional world, sexuality must be consciously and willingly accepted, but it must be adult and related to the whole of life. For her, as for Greene, human relationships depend for their success and plenitude on humility, trust and the concomitant acceptance of responsibility. More forcefully than his, her novels imply that relationships of this kind are capable of being stable and lasting, although Greene too, despite the nagging and ever-present suggestion of insecurity in his fiction, offers them as examples of human dignity and charity, in which the partner is seen in his or her full humanity as another real and autonomous person.

The extent to which the major characters of the three novelists are caught up in the day-to-day business of human living and to which they are 'in the world' differs considerably. In one sense, the matter of their work is human life here and now, with all its complications, its immediacy, its apparent or real confusion and its extensive and dense web of human relationships. On the other hand, the 'world', although it is difficult to describe how this happens, assumes a different level of ultimate importance for each of them. There is a difference of focus and to some extent of interest, and consequently existential human life is seen in a different way. Undset's chief concern is to write about the daily lives of a number of intelligent, attractive and often thoughtful, but by no means extraordinary, men and women whose chief concern is to live their lives properly and in a way which will in all respects be as deeply satisfying as one can reasonably expect, with proper regard for their own nature and that of their fellow human beings, at peace with themselves and their neighbours. What Greene shows is men and women of very varied backgrounds and temperaments and from very different cultures, living in a world which, even in comparison with her medieval settings, is much crueller and more violent that Undset's. His contains men and women who either try in their various ways and with varied success, and sometimes with spectacular failure, to come to terms with life or even to make something of it, or else as in the case of

Pinkie, his most extreme character, reject it violently. For Bernanos, the world is very much present, powerfully real and recognizably an image, albeit a highly personal one, of France and French society at a particular time. Nevertheless, there is a powerful sense that it is something which will soon pass away.

The natural centre of gravity of Undset's and Greene's novels is in a sense lower than that of Bernanos's, and for much of their time their characters are concerned with life here and now and a consideration of its immediate implications. On the whole, eternity on the part of both Greene and Undset, and more particularly the latter, is left to take care of itself, even by Catholic heroes and heroines. Their lives are lived out largely in local and temporal terms, and even Pinkie's suicide is a protest against this world rather than against any divine or eternal order. On the other hand, many of Bernanos's characters are often shown at a period of intense crisis and, whether they themselves know it or not, are already focussed upon the eternity that will soon resolve it. Even when death is imminent for Greene's and Undset's protagonists the world is still much with them, whilst for Bernanos's (the country priest and Mouchette, for example) it is already in process of becoming simply what they will soon leave behind them. Despite these differences of emphasis and atmosphere, however, and the different modes of human experience they portray, all three novelists are to a greater or lesser degree concerned with man as a creature among his fellows, whose life is inescapably linked with other human lives. The destiny and ways of being of each individual are so enmeshed with those of others that every human action can, in ways which are not necessarily perceived but are nonetheless real, have effects throughout the whole human community. This inescapable human solidarity, as Bernanos's country priest realizes, arises from the consequences for other people of what a given individual is, what he thinks and what he does, and will always be mysterious and probably indirect and unknowable, and it is fortunate that this is so. Charity, the genuine love of one's fellows, is essential, for without it human beings destroy others as well as themselves.

With Undset, the same vision is less intense, more immediately practical and limited. Her characters see the need for charity, for a sense of commitment to other human beings, for responsibility, and can also see that the likely consequences of a refusal of such obligations will be 'an end of mercy in the world' and 'a world too terrible to live in'. They know that no brotherhood exists without strife, but they are also aware that brotherhood is there, inescapable and compelling. Greene in his turn suggests the link between religious belief and love for other human beings, an idea which is given vivid expression in the thoughts of the Mexican priest, Sarah and Leon Rivas.

For Bernanos, man is the product of centuries of unknown ancestors and the inheritor of a legacy of good and evil. He is shaped by the accumulation of evil, and the sins of the fathers are visited upon the children. His appetites and desires, moulded by this inheritance and by the framework of his nature and circumstances, are often corrupt and sometimes unconscious, but man is not seen as totally unfree. The reader can sense a certain imprisonment in sinfulness, but is led to believe by words such as those of Menou-Segrais, for whom life is primarily a matter of choice and the consistently made decisions of the major characters, that free will is not an illusion and that human beings have the ability to discern possible options. In Undset and Greene, these options can be clearly seen. In Bernanos, they may, because they imply a directing of the whole mind and heart, be less immediately nameable and classifiable, only revealed by a return to a certain simplicity and acceptance. For Undset and Greene, freedom is simply a fact: in a given situation, a character can do this or that. For Bernanos, it is primarily a liberation from the stranglehold of sin which results in new, fresh perceptions, a regaining, in a sense, of the spontaneity and directness of childhood. Unless we become as little children, he implies, we shall not enter into the kingdom of heaven. The ability to see our lost innocence will produce a liberating sense of shame.

This is the area in which Bernanos's emphasis differs most, and most clearly, from that of the other two novelists. Greene suggests the innocence of childhood and its inevitable loss, its transience and fragility, and Undset, at least on occasions, its sharp-eyed perceptions. Neither, however, directly returns to the theme of the adult perception of that lost innocence. This is the dimension which, in two writers who suggest the need for adult wisdom and understanding, is less immediately visible. In their case, however, there is an indication that a fully adult wisdom must necessarily include the freshness and direct perception of childhood. There are scattered and unsystematic indications of this in, for example, the refusal of any of their major characters to wear the spectacles of political ideologies, of currently fashionable views, of simplistic (rather than simple) views of human life and human affairs, in their perception of natural justice. It is perhaps here that they come closest to Bernanos's concept of the direct vision of childhood as being all-important as a means of seeing life truly.

The ideas of God present in the novels are of crucial importance here because they suggest in their turn an idea of man. If man has no sense of God, or rejects notions of God as an all-powerful creator and the centre of man's life, there can be only one consequence. He will be condemned to that situation, so graphically described in existentialist literature, in which he will be doomed to be himself with no possibility of salvation, in either temporal or eternal terms, condemned in Undset's words 'to become what he must become when he is allowed to follow his own life to the very end', to inhabiting 'an asylum for such as desire to remain for all eternity outside all order and without God above them, sufficient to themselves for ever and ever'. The same perception is apparent in Bernanos. Hope and charity are inextricably linked with faith, and if the latter disappears the former will become vitiated or perverted.

As with Greene, love of God and love of man are very closely related. Belief is the source of the other great virtues, and it is not seen as a perhaps rather interesting and subtle subjective experience, but as the acceptance of a difficult and seminal objective truth, namely that human life is linked to the existence and life of that being who has commanded men to be still and know that he is God, who has told them that to reject him is folly, and has let them see that his ways are not their ways and his thoughts are not their thoughts. All men have some sense of the possibility of God and can either accept or refuse him, and both choices will have consequences. In neither case need such decisions be formal, explicit or public. They may sometimes be sensed by other characters, as Chevance in *L'Imposture* senses with terror the depth of the denial of God as the heart of Cénabre's life, or as Harold Tangen in *The Wild Orchid* appreciates the direction in which Paul Selmer's is moving, or they may be made in isolation and unknown to others, as are the negative choices of Simone Alfieri *in Night is Darkest* or the positive one of Bendrix in *The End of the Affair*. The major characters in such works, whatever their individual position in this respect, must however be seen by the reader, as they are by the author, in the light of such an acknowledged, ignored or rejected relationship with God and in the light of what follows from it. For the former believer, such as Querry, all is futility and aridity once the results of a loss of faith, or rather, as Bernanos expresses it, of the failure of faith to inform life, become apparent. For the philosophical atheist such as the Mexican lieutenant of police, little remains except a bitter anger in the face of the squalor and pain of human life. For these who, like Bendrix and Sarah, begin to see and sense their relationship with God, the world and human life are seen in a new perspective.

In relation to these novels, sanctity could be described as the state for which human beings were made and in which human nature moves towards its perfection. It implies living first in a proper relationship with God and consequently with one's fellow human beings. To be good is to experience the plenitude of one's own being, both in itself and in its relationship with others. That, in essence, is what the hunted priest sees at the end of *The Power and the Glory* and what Bendrix can begin to imagine in *The End of the Affair*. It is also what Bernanos's country priest and Undset's Kristin Lavransdatter come to understand more clearly as their lives progress. Such characters, for all their faults, can still criticize themselves and see, although not without difficulty, both their own worth and that of others. Each, in his own circumstances and in his own way, comes closer than before to obeying the second great commandment which Christ laid upon those who wished to follow him, that of loving one's neighbour as oneself.

There are clearly differing areas of major interest, different emphases and, in each case, a rather different personal vision of human life. There is also, however, a major coincidence of shared perceptions in certain areas. For each of these writers, man is a person, and hence a mystery, with a nature which is in some sense given, but which has a potential for development and perfection. He can see himself, and when he reflects on his own being he is faced with a creature who is difficult to analyse and understand and is more complex and elusive than the structures or concepts which he or others may try to impose on it. For his proper but by no means inevitable growth, man seen in these terms must begin to have an idea of the kind of relationship to be established with the creator of this kind of being and with his fellow men and women. Good and evil will quite literally be their own reward. Man, like Bendrix, Smythe and Scobie, cannot rest until he finds the completion of his being which exists only in God. Nor, like Cénabre, Pinkie and La Pérouse, can he rest in the denial of being which is what evil really is. His nature is flawed and his free will vitiated by sin, but man remains, in Undset's image, beautiful as well as blighted, a creature for whom faith, hope and charity are the preconditions of real life.

Human nature in these novels is thus neither totally static nor totally dynamic. It might in fact be reasonably accurately described as having a *dynamic stability*. The characters, or perhaps more specifically the heroes and heroines, of Greene, Bernanos and Undset certainly have the potentiality to *become* (which is the dynamic aspect of the concept of man they illustrate), but not to *become anything at all*, simply to become more or less fully themselves, and this is its stability. They cannot create themselves, for in that specifically Sartrean sense they are not 'free'. They can struggle to perfect their essence, or to abandon the attempt in weariness or despair or pride, but they are not free to create it. They can change within limits, and it is this sense of limits which helps constitute a concept of human nature. Usually, Bernanos's characters simply want to be themselves, and it is interesting to note that it is only those characters in his novels whose selves are in some way blighted, such as Evangeline or Ouine, who are tempted by masks and roles. An Undset heroine could become a kept woman, a mistress, an efficient businesswoman. In the event, she often chooses to be a wife, a mother and a mate, because she knows that by doing so she can be more fully herself and at the same time help others towards their full humanity. In Greene, the Mexican priest could be comfortable, safe and respected elsewhere. In another part of Mexico he could, in a sense, be a different man. To do so, however, would also in a sense mean being a lesser man, for he too knows, wearily and with resignation, the demands which he can and should make on his own humanity. He is persuaded into what he knows is the trap of hearing the mortally-wounded American gangster's alleged confession because he chooses to try to further his own redemption and that of another human being. It is more fully human to do so than to opt for safety and ease.

This growth, as has already been indicated, is clearly a major factor in the image of the human person seen in such literary works. Characters either develop into more significant human beings within the frame of reference adopted by the novelists or, by a refusal of their humanity, become negative and regress, losing what both makes them most distinctly themselves and unites them more closely to other persons. In Bernanos, the clearest examples of this are Cénabre, La Pérouse, Ganse and Simone Alfieri, who all finish with their fullness impaired and blighted. The mediocre characters in Undset (Frithjof, Sommervold, Björg Selmer) could be seen in a similar way. They are less extreme and dramatic cases than those encountered in Bernanos, but their failings (coldness, egotism and a lack of psychic energy and vitality) are of the same kind. Greene too shows many characters who, like the Henry of the period before Sarah's death in *The End of the Affair* or Fellows in *The Power and the Glory*, have stifled their potentiality for growth, or who would willingly do so, and for whom happiness is a second-best alternative to changelessness.

It is also apparent that this growth is from the *individual* in the sense in which both Vann and Mounier used that term, towards the *person*. All selves are inescapably tied to selfishness. It is a condition of their existence, and in some sense egocentricity is inevitable. In the kind of Catholic novel discussed here, however, the interest of a given major character often seems to lie less in a process of increasing individuation and of subjecting the world to his desires and needs and more in a growing awareness of his personhood. This is produced by an increase in charity, in the acknowledgement of the full human status of other individuals and a more or less conscious diminution of egocentricity. The capacity for growth is, in this fiction, as much an inbuilt component of human nature as any other. That nature may be frustrated, unfulfilled, distorted, as it is with Bernanos's second Mouchette or Greene's *mestizo*, but it is there, even if embryonically. Sin is what prevents it growing towards its potential perfection (i.e. being more truly itself); charity and grace are what encourages growth, as happens for Chantal, Ida Elisabeth and Paul Selmer. Like the 'individual', the 'person' will have aims, and the acceptance of the existence of such drives, needs and potentialities constitutes a major dimension of this particular concept of human nature. Men and women need certain psychological goods: an acceptable notion of themselves, satisfying relationships with other human beings, a sense of purpose and of (at least) potential achievement, a sense that they are unique and autonomous selves amongst other such selves, and a sense of their responsibility for others and of others' responsibility for them. This latter aspect is the most human and the most specifically Christian of all, and it is largely that area of human relationships which Undset, Bernanos and Greene portray and illuminate, because it is part of the basic and almost unavoidable material of fiction. It is also the aspect of the way people are depicted in these novels which comes closest to the idea that there is some similarity between the divine nature and human nature, that in some way man is created in God's image.

The inescapable fact is that the essence of Catholic images of man is this notion of the analogy of being, which both gives the human being a significance beyond the bounds of the existential, and also means that human life without the idea of the fatherhood of God and the consequent brotherhood of man will be meaningless. In so far as these ideas are only imperfectly reflected in human life, we are to a greater or lesser extent exiles. What must be a major element of any Catholic view of man is epitomized in Augustine's phrase *'Fecisti nos ad te et inquietum est cor nostrum donec requiescat in te'*. ('Thou hast created us for Thyself, and our heart is not quiet until it rests in Thee.')

CONCLUSION

This concept of man as a personal subject whose essence is
to be, or to construct himself in freedom by giving meaning
to a world of people and things, is one to which we shall
assume from the outset as a forward-looking, open-ended
definition of man in which believers and non-believers alike
can find a common ground for dialogue

Edward Schillebeeckx, *God and Man*

What has been said so far can reasonably be seen as offering a
picture of the general cluster of ideas about humanity traceable in
Catholic literature around the middle of the century and as
providing a general indication of the ways in which such ideas ran
parallel to similar developments in theology. Both are intended
primarily as illustrations of the ways in which certain Catholics
appear to have thought rather than as expressions of any universal
Catholic anthropology. They may, however, have been to some
extent part of that rather nebulous concept of the consensus of
the faithful, a possible factor in the formulation and formalization
of official teaching which may conceivably influence it, even if it
does not necessarily become a declared part of it. Conversely, they
sometimes led to a total or partial rejection of that teaching, as
happened with Charles Davis, or provoke a certain unease in the
official Church, as was the case with Teilhard de Chardin. In both
the theologians, philosophers and moralists and the imaginative
writers one can assume an intelligent awareness of the Catholic
view of man as accumulated, developed and transmitted over the
centuries, for the fundamental elements of the concept are the
common intellectual and imaginative property of literate
Catholics everywhere.

By the middle of the twentieth century, both Catholic thinkers
and Catholic novelists appeared to stress the opacity of the
human person. Both were faced with the difficulty of trying to
assert or suggest truths about him and at the same time letting
him be himself. For both groups too, this difficulty was linked to

the perception that one of the major characteristics of human beings is growth and development, that the major dimensions of human nature are both stasis and potentiality, and that inner orientations lie deeper than outward actions or apparent motives might suggest.

The difficulty of making statements about human beings engendered on the part of the theologians and philosophers a critical attitude towards traditional formulations of Catholic ideas about man, which were seen as inadequate and stultifying. Philosophy is, however, concerned with making statements about the matter in hand which are as far as possible universally valid and susceptible to discussion in language of a generalized and abstract nature. Literature deals with the complex, concrete, detailed and infinitely varied realities of specific human situations, for which formulas, abstractions and purely intellectually analytical language are not appropriate, or are only appropriate in a limited way and for certain specific purposes, such as providing a linguistic vehicle for authorial asides or general comment. The task of philosophy or theology is to make certain *statements* or to propose certain *hypotheses* about the general nature of the human person as lucidly and truthfully as possible, whereas that of imaginative literature is to *provide a picture of it in specific circumstances.* Those Catholic philosophers who found traditional Catholic formulas arid and inhibiting rejected them, saying in effect that it is not possible to talk about human nature and that it can only be experienced. Their particular gifts and training did not often allow them to formulate that experience in words. Those of the imaginative writer do allow them to do precisely that, and it would seem that once human nature has been depicted in this way, it is possible to talk about it and reflect on it meaningfully in terms approaching a level of philosophical generality. This is clearly what the three novelists we have looked at have done on occasion, and it is arguable that this dual approach is more fruitful than the more restricted methods of purely philosophical enquiry. The reality of personhood and of human relationships with other selves and God cannot be described in terms of philosophy. In the language and procedures of that mode of thinking, they can only be suggested. What the Catholic thinkers did not perhaps realize is that, to some degree, all kinds of thinking and imagining can be mutually enriching, and that an understanding of scholastic philosophy or of new formulations of theological ideas requires of the reader an effort of sympathetic creativity which alone can give it full meaning and significance.

Without wishing to create an artificial or even necessarily a critical distinction between Catholic fictional and Catholic theological man, one can maintain that the former may, and in the fiction we have looked at does, subsume and amplify the latter. The function of certain kinds of fiction, which we might call the reflective novel, and in this specific context the Catholic reflective novel, can perhaps be seen as primarily that of providing interlinked depiction and explanation of human nature and human situations. Its advantage is that it can both allow man to be man and encourage reflection on the modes of being, thinking and feeling proper to human persons. It seems that the subtle and imaginative depiction of real or apparently real human situations by writers like those considered here is not on occasion incompatible with traditional abstract formulations. In that sense, they go back to them or, more accurately, never abandon them. There is a dimension of their writing which attempts to portray, so to speak, the complex truth, and one which sees no real objection to suggesting it in the set phrases of a traditionally elliptical kind of language. These latter suggestions would be insufficient in themselves, perhaps, but as summaries or epitomes, they are not meaningless. Such formulations should never have been taken as exhaustive, but simply as indicative.

Greene's priests have been criticized for being mouthpieces and for presenting 'formulas which the complexity of life denies'. To think this is to misunderstand the function of a formula or an abstract statement, which is not to evoke the rich and concrete quiddity of a specific situation, but to isolate those elements common to all situations of that kind. It is, in other words, to suggest a general principle rather than to depict an individual case, to illustrate a universal truth rather than to provide a precise intelligence of particular circumstances. It would perhaps be truer to say that, like Fr Rank in *The Heart of the Matter*, they utter them knowing how difficult it is to present abstract statements to human beings caught up in existential situations, but believing that experience will, in one way or another, teach the truth of such observations. Such men could more properly be criticized for an inability to provide immediate and convincing examples rather than for their untruthfulness. The perception of notions of this kind seems to lie behind the thinking of Maritain and Mounier, and behind the criticisms of Hibbert and Davis it is possible to sense a wrong equation of terse and spare language with impoverished content.

Those Catholic philosophers and theologians mentioned here are important because their writings suggest that humanity is not exhaustively described in traditional formulations and may indeed be hidden rather than revealed by them. The novelists are important because ideas which may seem restrictive and straitened assume a new richness when filtered through an individual literary sensibility. The blood and guts of Greene's wartime Saigon, the sexual turmoil of the early sections of Undset's *Kristin Lavransdatter* and the spiritual anguish of Bernanos's country priest may well have a greater immediacy and impact than theological treatises on wisdom, prudence or chastity or the nature of religious experience. Both modes of experience, however, suggest the existence of a Catholic humanism in European culture worth a great deal more than the passing and condescending nod which was all that Sartre's Roquentin was prepared to give it in *Nausea*:

> The Catholic humanist, the late-comer, the Benjamin, speaks of men with a marvellous air. What a beautiful fairy-tale, says he, is the humble life of a London dockhand, the girl in the shoe factory! He has chosen the humanism of the angels. He writes for their edification, long, sad and beautiful novels which frequently win the Prix Femina (Sartre, 1962, 158)

But it was, after all, a little too early for him to have read or reflected on *Mouchette* or *The Power and the Glory*.

The novelists we have looked at represent the maturity of one kind of intelligent and thoughtful Catholic understanding of man, that of a creature in a one-to-one relationship with his Creator and bound in charity to his fellow human beings in the same situation. Since then, however, things have moved on, as we have seen. That kind of Catholic humanism is now old-fashioned and barely mentioned. In its place we have a model of a benevolent, sane, decent, unremarkable and non-mysterious social unit which is certainly not hung up on doctrine or eschatology. This reconstructed Catholicism has successfully brushed off all that old Catholic guilt, and engages in allegedly meaningful dialogue with the world. Perhaps today's Catholic has heard of great-uncle Pinkie, grandfather Scobie and even those funny old foreign relations in France and Norway and one or two other places, but if he met them in the street he probably would not recognize them, and even Roquentin's nod might be beyond him. What on earth can he tell his non-Catholic friends about them?

God as an idea in the human mind is now much less consciously and forcefully present than he used to be, even in the minds of characters created by Catholic authors, or those of the generalized human being in theological works. The idea that if the supernatural is abolished or denied, the natural disintegrates, which forms a powerful background to Bernanos's novels, is not new. Even if we take it as a purely psychological description, it is certainly not contrary to experience. Man as capable of God, as an image of God, as a creature able to accept or reject a certain kind of relationship with his creator and sustainer is one thing. Man as a social unit with no significant personhood, a conditioned operant existing in a horizontal continuum where all is relative, contingent and ultimately value-free is most definitely another.

The developed and expanded view of human beings detectable in certain kinds of imaginative literature and discussed here represents one end of the spectrum of possible ways of seeing and understanding ourselves. Somewhere alongside it, but rooted to a certain degree in a different area of the spectrum, is the socialized human being proposed by a spread of the contemporary Catholic writing of varying levels of orthodoxy, dissent or heresy. The older vertical view of man is not on the whole denied, but neither is it proposed as a valid, compelling or useful model. In its selective emphasis, which is no doubt felt to be necessary and relevant given the urgent problems of social, economic and political justice in the world of the late twentieth century, the newer model urges a narrower and narrowing view of human beings.

The central part of the range is occupied by three interesting groups, whose only common feature is the refusal of, or the inability to accept, or the reluctance to urge, the objective existence of God. The first is that of the Protestant death-of-God theologians, exemplified in John Robinson's *Honest to God* (1963) and Don Cupitt's *Taking Leave of God* (1980). For the latter at least, horizontalism is in a sense all, since in that 'modern and fully autonomous spirituality, which may claim to be the legitimate successor of earlier Christian spiritualism' God is a myth, a work of art, a necessary but not objectively true idea, a projection of the highest aspects of the purely human. Any verticality must therefore be purely metaphorical. The second comprises writers like Petru Dumitriu who, in *To the Unseen God* (1982) movingly describes his love for the God he cannot believes exists and for whom a desacralized and meaningless cosmos and human evil signifies our inability to achieve the action we need above all others: 'to love human beings, when they are as they are, and when there is no God?'. As Mircea Eliade had posed the problem twenty years earlier, in his *The Sacred and the Profane* (1959) in a desacralized cosmos, we cannot 'found the world', cannot acquire a true orientation, since 'properly speaking there is no longer any world, there are only fragments of a shattered universe'. The third contains the atheist existentialists who have so profoundly affected contemporary thinking (and in a sense provided a conceptual frame of reference for the writers mentioned above). What Camus called 'the absurd' and by which he meant essentially the desire for values, meaning and happiness in a universe indifferent to such needs has become the inescapable background against which we see and judge ourselves, our lives and our world to the point that religion or explanatory philosophies now seem to be the pure escapism he claimed they were. We feel compelled to imitate his Sisyphus, to achieve our 'difficult wisdom' in a stoical acceptance of our situation.

The other extreme is exemplified in the didactic and sometimes dogmatic literary theory and practice of the last thirty years or so. It is possible to argue that - chiefly and most remarkably in France - the novel as a genre has been recreated and rewritten to suit and express our new way of seeing ourselves. The depiction or analysis of character, the convention of the plot, the notion of a conscious, intelligent and knowledgeable narrator, the suggestion of purposeful and consistent thought and action on the part of the character and many of the other features of traditional fiction have been abolished in favour of the presentation of vague, shifting and semi-conscious psychological states akin to the tropisms characterizing the adaptation of an organism to tiny changes in its environment. The self-conscious protagonist is no more, since there is usually hardly a self to be conscious of. The new realism has its own new kerygma and hermeneutics in much contemporary phenomenological, structuralist and post-structuralist literary theory and criticism. Much has been said and written about this new reductionist writing, little about its opposite. My aim here has been to keep the latter visible.

Since neither of the two mutually exclusive views at either end of the spectrum is coercively verifiable or refutable, the honest mind must keep both, and the middle ground between them, in constant sight. The Catholic literary view of man is arguably the fullest picture of human beings in a Christian perspective available to us. It represents a developed and expanded version of a way of seeing human beings that over the centuries has by influence, antithesis or synthesis helped to shape the Western concept of human nature. Perhaps all human beings suffer from an inferiority complex and need to see themselves as persons. Certainly ideas of personal worth, uniqueness, autonomy, free will, responsibility, dignity and holiness (and also of a potentiality for negation, untruth, degradation and revolt) have all, whether we accept or reject them, played a part in creating or shaping our ways of picturing ourselves. In their turn, those ways affect our attitudes to each other and our behaviour.

In our contemporary intellectual world, where all has been deconstructed, the existence and status of the conscious, projective, teleologically-aware subject is at very least problematic. Human nature, objective reality and the notion of the self have all been called into question. That questioning is right and proper, and indeed the ability to engage in it can be seen as a specifically human attribute, but it is also permissible to find the conclusions it leads to implausible. The hypothesis that the external world is somehow dependent on our perception of it, or that our self is utlimately undistinguishable from other selves or its surroundings - in Ortega y Gassets's famous phrase, 'I am I and my circumstances', - is epistemologically no more convincing than assertions that man was born to know, love and serve God or is blighted by original sin, the victim of what Newman called the 'aboriginal calamity'. To see the dominant ideas of our own time as a coercive and established truth ultimately requires an act of the will. Whilst both perspectives may illuminate and in some ways 'explain' each other, they are mutually incompatible if we accept the principle of contradiction. Even a thorough-going relativist, for whom both might be *subjectively* (or if he is really modern, *sociologically*) valid, would find it extremely difficult to maintain that both are objectivly true. If that is the case, then we ought, in the absence of firm knowledge, to keep our options open.

At a time when all of us, and not only Catholics, are often called upon to think of human beings as primarily a nexus of social relationships rather than individual selves, one wonders to what extent those relationships will be impoverished by a weakening of the concept of the self. In Christian terms, Satan is the father of lies. If, through neglect, fashion, wrong thinking or pure relativism, we see ouselves not as individuals each in a unique relationship with God, not as primarily an image of God or capable of Him, we are perhaps, because we choose a reductionist picture of ourselves, fostering a lie and undermining a relationship with the divine. A Catholic shift from the vertical to the horizontal, from the primacy of the Four Last Things to a benevolent social concern, perhaps means a movement from eschatology to sociology and a view of human beings who can fulfil themselves and realize their potential in the here and now, where, we were once told, we have no lasting abode. St Paul said that of the great virtues of faith, hope and charity, the greatest is charity. To make it fully synonymous with social concern is to diminish it. If charity is simply the provision of decent and humane living and working conditions ('high wages and sanitation', to revert to Waugh) it is not enough. It must also show human beings that they are human, and that there is a dimension to their being which subsumes but goes beyond such concerns. The Catholic who is not satisfied with the primacy of the social risks abandoning his religion or at best espousing a new kind of dissidence. If he sees those wider implications, he has a hope of staying inside the Church as he understands it. That wider understanding is also what he has to offer the world. Whatever his own imperfection and limitations, whatever the failings of the *ecclesia semper reformanda*, human beings need to see themselves in a coherent and meaningful way, and both the individual and the institution have a duty to offer an alternative basis for understanding ourselves and living together.

Even if it is rejected, as will often be the case, it will help to keep alive the desire to be more fully ourselves that, in purely human terms, is our only hope. We cannot simply accept it because it is attractive, and says things we want to hear, or because it bolsters our waning faith in the freedom of existentialist choice or the greatness of the God that is part of ourselves. What we can do is to respect it for what it is: an expression of the enduring human desire to be human and to move towards ways of being more fully ourselves, and indeed of the other side of that desire, the proud and angry destruction of our own humanity or that of others. It is a particularly full and sophisticated version of that perpetual response to the existential world, and will mean or suggest different things to different people. For the Catholic concerned with the spirituality of his own religion, it offers imaginative and intellectual insights into the ways in which he can see himself, his neighbours and their relationshiop to God. For those who have 'taken leave of God' it represents a concrete and specific example of the only hope left to a metaphysics rejecting objective theism, the creation of a dignified moral and religious anthropology expressing in a vivid way the myth of an older Christianity. For the God-intoxicated who cannot believe, it can provide, because it is both realistic and not unhopeful, a possible consolation and a support in their struggle to see human life as human. For the atheist existentialist it offers the possibility of a leap that might just not be a consequence of bad faith, of a picture of human beings who believe in an order beyond their limited perceptions, which nevertheless in some sense shapes their lives and demands their assent, that could at rare moments seem credible. For those for whom tropisms and a fragmentary, elementary and solipsistic consciousness are the defining features of our humanity, it suggests that their paradigm is incomplete and exclusive, that in Dumitriu's words, 'being, the ensemble of known and unknown factors, is our homeland. God is our homeland. Or rather, that narrow and evershifting region between joy and desolation, that zone habitable by God, is our homeland' (Dumitriu, 1982, 74). For all, it is an illustration of Valéry's observation - in whatever sense we take it - that there is another world, but it is this one.

BIBLIOGRAPHY

GREENE

Fiction

There have been many editions of Greene's work. Only one is given here. A useful source of bibliographical information is Wobbe, R.A., Graham Greene: a bibliography and guide to research., New York, Garland, 1979.

The Man Within, London, Heinemann, 1964.

The Name of Action, London, Heinemann, 1930.

Rumour at Nightfall, London, Heinemann, 1931.

Stamboul Train, London, Heinemann, 1932.

It's a Battlefield, London, Heinemann, 1964.

The Bear Fell Free (limited edition), London, Grayson Books, 1935.

England Made Me, London, Heinemann, 1935.

The Basement Room and Other Stories, London, Cresset, 1935.

A Gun for Sale, London, Heinemann, 1936.

Brighton Rock, London, Bodley Head and Heinemann, 1970.

The Confidential Agent, London, Heinemann, 1939.

The Power and the Glory, London, Heinemann, 1959.

The Ministry of Fear, London, Heinemann, 1943.

Nineteen Stories, London, Heinemann, 1947.

The Heart of the Matter, London, Heinemann, 1951.

The Third Man and The Fallen Idol, London, Heinemann, 1950.

The End of the Affair, London, Heinemann, 1959.

Twenty-one Stories, London, Heinemann, 1954.

The Quiet American, London, Heinemann, 1956.

Loser Takes All, London, Heinemann, 1955.

Our Man in Havana, London, Heinemann, 1958.

A Burnt-out Case, London, Heinemann, 1961.

A Sense of Reality, London, Bodley Head, 1963.

The Comedians, London, Bodley Head, 1966.

May We Borrow Your Husband? and Other Comedies of the Sexual Life, London, Bodley Head, 1967.

Travels with my Aunt, London, Bodley Head, 1969.

The Honorary Consul, London, Bodley Head, 1973.

The Human Factor, London, Bodley Head, 1978.

Doctor Fischer of Geneva: or The Bomb Party, London, Bodley Head, 1980.

Monsignor Quixote, London, Bodley Head, 1982.

The Tenth Man, London, Bodley Head, 1985.

The Captain and the Enemy, London, Reinhardt, 1988.

Major Non-Fiction

Journey without Maps, London, Heinemann, 1936.

The Lawless Roads, London, Longmans, Green, 1939.

Why Do I Write: An exchange of views with Elizabeth Bowen and V. S. Pritchett, London, Marshall, 1948.

The Lost Childhood and Other Essays, London, Eyre and Spottiswoods, 1951.

Essais catholiques, Paris, Seuil, 1953.

In Search of a Character: Two African Journals, London, Bodley Head, 1961.

Collected Essays, London, Bodley Head, 1969.

A Sort of Life, London, Bodley Head, 1971.

Ways of Escape, London, Bodley Head, 1980.

UNDSET

Fiction

There have been many Norwegian, British and American editions of Undset's work. Only one, usually a British, edition is given here. The best bibliographical sources are Packness, Ida, Sigrid *Undset Bibilografi*, Oslo, Oslo University Press, 1963, and Krane, Borghild, *Sigrid Undset, liv og meninger*, Oslo, Gyldendal, 1970.

Gunnar's Daughter, (Fortelling om Vig-Ljot og Vigdis), translated by Arthur B. Chater, London, Cassell, 1936.

Jenny (Jenny), translated by W. Emmé, London, Cassell, 1921.

Images in a Mirror (Splinten av troldspeilet), translated by Arthur B. Chater, London, Cassell, 1938.

Kristin Lavransdatter (Kristin Lavransdatter), in one volume, translated by Charles Archer and J. S. Scott, London, Cassell, 1930.

The Master of Hestviken (Olav Audunsson i Hestviken and Olav Audunsson og ans born), in one volume, translated by Arthur G.Chater, London, Cassell, 1934.

The Wild Orchid (Gymnadenia), translated by Arthur G.Chater, London, Cassell, 1931.

The Burning Bush (Den braenende busk), translated by Arthur G.Chater, London, Cassell, 1932.

Ida Elisabeth (Ida Elisabeth), translated by Arthur G. Chater, London, Cassell, 1933.

The Faithful Wife (Den trofaste hustru), translated by Arthur G. Chater, London, Cassell, 1937.

Madame Dorothea (Madame Dorothea), translated by Arthur G. Chater, London, Cassell, 1941.

There has been one American, but no British, edition of Undset's *Four Stories* (*Selmer Broter, Miss Smith-Tellefsen* and *Simonsen* from *Fattige skjaebner, Thjodolf* from *De kloge Jomfruer*), New York, Knopf, 1959.

Maior Non-Fiction

Stages on the Road (Etapper Ny raekke), translated by Arthur G. Chater, New York, Knopf, 1934.

The Longest Years (Elleve Aar), translated by Arthur G. Chater, London, Cassell, 1935.

Saga of Saints (Norske helgener), translated by E. C. Ramsden, London, Sheed and Ward, 1934.

Men, Women and Places (Selvportretter og Landskapsbilleder), translated by Arthur G.Chater, London, Cassell, 1939.

Return to the Future (Tilbake til Fremtiden), translated by Henriette C.K.Naeseth, New York , Knopf, 1953.

Catherine of Siena (Caterina av Siena) translated by Kate Austen-Lund, London, Sheed and Ward, 1954.

It should be noted that two important works in this area exist only in German version. These are: *Begegnungen und Trennungen: Essays über Christentum und Germanentum* (Munich, Kosel und Pushet, 1931) and 'Fortschritt, Rasse und Religion' in *Die Gefahrdung des Christeutums durch Rassenwahn und Judenverfolg* (Lucerne, Vita Nova, 1935)

Two articles in English, so far uncollected and of some interest in connection with this study, are: 'Truth and Fiction', America, 67 (1942) p.270 and 'War and Literature', America, 68 (1942) p.242.

BERNANOS

Fiction

The standard French collected edition of Bernanos's fiction is *Oeuvres romanesques*, Paris, Gallimard, collection Bibliothèque de la Pléiade, 1963. The major translations of his works are listed below. The best English language biographical source is the MLA *Bibliography of Critical and Bibliographical References for the Study of Modern French Literature*, New York, Association of America, published annually.

The Star of Satan (Sous le Soleil de Satan), translated by Pamela Morris, London, John Lane, 1940. (A new translation by J.C. Whitehouse is in preparation for Bison Books, University of Nebraska Press, Lincoln, Nebraska)

The Impostor (L'Imposture), translated by J.C. Whitehouse (to be published by Bison Books, University of Nebraska Press, Lincoln, Nebraska, 1999)

Joy (La Joie), translated by Louise Varese, London, Bodley Head, 1948

The Crime (Un Crime), translated by Anne Green, London, Hale, 1936.

The Diary of a Country Priest (Journal d'un curé de campagne) translated by Pamela Morris, London, Bodley Head, 1937.

Mouchette (Nouvelle Histoire de Mouchette) translated by J.C.Whitehouse, London, Bodley Head, 1966.

The Open Mind (Monsieur Ouine), translated by Geoffrey Dunlop, London, Bodley Head, 1945.(A new translation by William Bush is in preparation, to be published by Bison Books, University of Nebraska Press, Lincoln, Nebraska)

Night is Darkest (Un Mauvais Rêve), translated by William J.Strachan, London, Bodley Head, 1953.

Non-Fiction

A Diary of My Times (Les Grands Cimetières sous la lune) translated by Pamela Morris, London, Bodley Head, 1938.

Plea for Liberty (Lettre aux Anglais), translated by H.L.Binsse and Ruth Bethell, New York, Pantheon Books, 1944.

Sanctity Will Out (Jeanne, Relapse et Sainte), translated by R.Batchelor, London, Sheed and Ward, 1947.

Tradition of Freedom (La France contre les Robots), translated by Helen Beau Clark, London, Dobson, 1950.

Important Untranslated Works

Le Crépuscule des vieux (essays), Paris, Gallimard, 1956.

La vocation spirituelle de la France (ed Jean-Loup Benanos) (posthumously published essays), Paris, Plon, 1956.

OTHER RELEVANT WORKS

Allers, Rudolf, 1931, *The Psychology of Character*, London, Sheed and Ward.

Atkins, John, 1957 (revised 1966), *Graham Greene*, London, Calder and Boyars.

Balthasar, Hans Urs von, 1956, *Le Chrétien Bernanos*, Paris, Seuil.

Bishops of the Netherlands, 1967, *A New Catechism*, London, Burns and Oates and Herder and Herder.

Böll, Heinrich, 1961, *Erzählungen, Hörspiele und Aufsätze* (Stories, Radio Plays and Essays), Cologne, Kiepenheuer und Witsch.

Corbett, Patrick, 1965, *Ideologies*, London, Hutchinson.

Cunningham, Adrian, 1968, *Adam*, London, Sheed and Ward.

Cupitt, Don, 1990, *Taking Leave of God*, London, SCM Press.

Davis, Charles, 1967, *A Question of Conscience*, London, Hodder and Stoughton, Deschamps, Nicole, 1966, *Sigrid Undset ou la morale de la passion*, Montreal, Montreal University Press.

Dumitriu, Petru, 1982, *To the Unknown God*, London, William Collins.

Eagleton, Terry, (Terence) 1966, *The New Left Church*, London, Sheed and Ward; 1970, *Exiles and Emigres: Studies in Modern Literature*, London, Chatto and Windus.

Eliade, Mircea, 1959, *The Sacred and the Profane*, London, Harper and Row.

Green, Martin, 1967, *Yeats's Blessings on von Hügel*, London, Longman's.

Griffiths, Richard, 1966, *The Reactionary Revolution: the Catholic Revival in French Literature*, London, Constable.

Gustafson, Alrik, 1968, *Six Scandinavian Novelists*, Minneapolis, American-Scandinavian Foundation.

Hart, Charles, 1916, many reprints, *The Student's Catholic Doctrine*, London, Burns Oates and Washbourne.

Hibbert, Giles, 1967, *Man, Culture and Christianity*, London, Sheed and Ward.

Hornsby-Smith, Michael P., 1987, *Roman Catholics in England: studies in social structure since the Second World War*, Cambridge, Cambridge University Press.

Kellogg, Gene, 1970, *The Vital Tradition: The Catholic Novel in a Period of Convergence*, Chicago, Loyola University Press.

Kloosterman, A.H.J., 1972, *Contemporary Catholicism: Thought since Vatican II*, London, Fontana.

Küng, Hans, 1977 , *On Being a Christian*, London, Collins Moëller, Charles, 1958, *Littérature du XXe siècle et christianisme, vol 1*, Tournai and Paris, Casterman.

Morris, Colin, 1972, *The Discovery of the Individual, 1050-1200*, London and Toronto, University of Toronto Press.

Murdoch, Iris, 1970, *The Sovereignty of Good*, London, Routledge and Kegan Paul.

Newman, John Henry, 1960, *The Idea of a University, with an introduction by Martin J.Svaglic*, New York, Holt, Rinehart and Winston.

O'Brien, Conor Cruise, 1952, *Maria Cross: imaginative patterns in a group of modern Catholic writers*, London, Chatto and Windus.

Pope John Paul II and the Episcopate of the Catholic Church, 1994, *The Catechism of the Catholic Church*, London, Geoffrey Chapman.

Pryce-Jones, David, 1963, *Graham Greene*, London, Edinburgh, Oliver and Boyd.

Robinson, John, 1963, *Honest to God*, London, SCM Press.

Sartre, Jean-Paul, 1948, *Existentialism and Humanism*, London, Methuen.

Sartre, Jean-Paul, 1962, *Nausea*, London, Hamish Hamilton.

Schillebeeckx, Edward, 1979, *God and Man*, London, Sheed and Ward, 1996, *New Elucidations*, San Francisco, Ignatius Press.

Sewell, Elizabeth, 1954, 'Graham Greene', in *Dublin Review*, 108 (1954).

Sonnenfeld, Albert, 1982, *Crossroads: Essays on the Catholic Novelists*, York, South Carolina, French Literature Publications Company.

Speaight, Robert, 1973, *Georges Bernanos: a study of the man and the writer*, London, Collins and Harvill Press.

Stratford, Philip, 1964, *Faith and Fiction: creative process in Greene and Mauriac*, Notre Dame University Press.

Strauss, E.B., 1953, *Reason and Unreason in Psychological Medicine*, London, H.K.Lewis and Son.

Thérèse of Lisieux, *History of a Soul* (many editions)

Vann, Gerald, 1963, *The Heart of Man*, London, Fontana, 1965, *Moral Dilemmas*, London, Collins Verity, Peter, 1987, 'The Church in the World', in *Priests and People*, 1,2 (1987).

Waugh, Evelyn, 1977, *A Little Order: a selection from his journalism edited by Donat Gallagher*, London, Eyre Methuen.

Weightman, John, 1973, *The Concept of the Avant-Garde*, London, Alcove Press.

White, Victor, 1960, *Soul and Psyche*, London, Collins and Harvill Press.

Wicker, Brian, 1966, *Culture and Theology*, London, Sheed and Ward.

Winsnes, A.H., 1953, *Sigrid Undset: a study in Christian realism*, London, Sheed and Ward.

INDEX

The Saint Austin Press' Titles

GENERAL SACRAMENTAL ABSOLUTION
Scott M. P. Reid
In this scholarly account, Reid argues that the use of General Absolution is not an appropriate response to the decline in confessions. A wide-ranging historical, canonical and pastoral perspective.

40 pages, paperback - stapled, £1.95 ISBN 1-901157-65-2

LIFE OF ST. EDWARD THE CONFESSOR
St. Aelred of Rievaulx
Translated into English for the first time by Fr Jerome Bertram, FSA. St. Edward built Westminster Abbey and was a great friend of the poor. An inspiring account of the life and miracles of England's Saintly King.

138 pages, paperback, £9.95,ISBN 1-901157-75-X

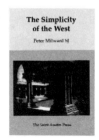

THE SIMPLICITY OF THE WEST
Peter Milward, S.J.
This work charts the idea of simplicity - as seen in the context of nature and tradition - through Socrates, St. Francis, St. Thomas Aquinas, to the present day. An exhilarating tour of Christian civilization with a profound message.

95 pages, paperback, £9.95, ISBN 1-901157-95-4

A BITTER TRIAL
Evelyn Waugh and John Carmel Cardinal Heenan on the Liturgical Changes *(Ed. Scott M. P. Reid)*
For the last decade of his life, Waugh experienced the changes being made to the Church's liturgy as "a bitter trial." In Heenan he found a sympathetic pastor and kindred spirit. This volume contains the previously unpublished correspondence between these prominent Catholics, revealing in both an incisive disquiet.
71 pages, paperback, £3.95, ISBN 1-901157-05-9

The Saint Austin Press' Titles

THE EARLY PAPACY
to the Council of Chalcedon in 451
Adrian Fortescue
A clear exposition and sound defence of the belief in the role of the Pope in the Church, drawing upon evidence from the Church Fathers up to 451 AD.

96 pages, paperback, £7.95, ISBN 1-901157-60-1

THE FACE OF THE NAZARENE
Noel Trimming
This dramatic and involving story is also a profound meditation on the Lord of the Millennia; Jesus Christ, the same yesterday, today and forever. It charts the impact of Christ on some of the people who knew him, in the hectic circumstances of their everyday lives.
157 pages, paperback, £9.95, ISBN 1-901157-90-3

NEWMAN'S MARIOLOGY
Michael Perrott
A study of the development of Newman's beliefs about Our Lady, from the staid "Anglican red-letter days" of his time in Littlemore to the intimate and inspiring poetry of "The Dream of Gerontius" and his "Meditations and Devotions." Scholary but immensely readable.
104 pages, paperback, £8.95, ISBN 1-901157-45-8

THE CATHOLICISM OF SHAKSPEARE'S PLAYS
Peter Milward, S.J.
The local tradition in Stratford is that Shakespeare "died a Papist." Professor Peter Milward, of Sophia University, Tokyo, argues that the whole of Shakespeare's work reveals a common thread of sympathy with the plight of persecuted Catholics under Queen Elizabeth and King James I.
144 pages, paperback, £7.95, ISBN 1-901157-10-5

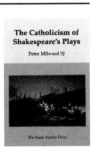

The Saint Austin Press' Titles

A VICTORIAN CONVERT QUINTET
Rev. Michael Clifton
In this fascinating study of the faith journeys of five converts to Catholicism from the Oxford Movement, Fr. Michael Clifton invites the reader to consider the lessons we might learn from this *Quintet* of learned men.
212 pages, paperback, £9.95, ISBN 1-901157-03-2

DARKNESS VISIBLE
A Christian Appraisal of Freemasonry
Rev. Walton Hannah
Addresses the question of whether involvement with Freemasonry is compatible with one's duty as a practising Christian. It includes the entire and authentic text of the Masonic ritual of the first three degrees and of the Royal Arch.
232 pages, paperback, £12.95, ISBN 1-901157-70-9

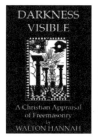

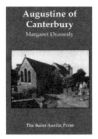

AUGUSTINE OF CANTERBURY
Margaret Deanesly
This study deals with St. Augustine's training, character and background; the origins of his mission; his work in Kent; the structure of the church he established; the nature of the ministry he founded for the continuance of his work.

175 pages, paperback, £12.95, ISBN 1-901157-25-3

CATENA AUREA
A Commentary on the Four Gospels
St. Thomas Aquinas
Drawing completely on the Church Fathers, St. Thomas provides an indispensable verse by verse commentary on the Gospels. Translated under Cardinal Newman, introduced by Aidan Nichols OP.
2,825 pages, hardback, 4-volume set, £85,
ISBN 1-901157-40-7